macromedia® coldfusion mx
training from the source

Kevin Schmidt

Nate Weiss

Macromedia ColdFusion MX: Training from the Source

 Published by Macromedia Press, in association with Peachpit Press, a division of Pearson Education.

Macromedia Press
1249 Eighth Street
Berkeley, CA 94710
510/524-2178
510/524-2221 (fax)
Find us on the World Wide Web at:
www.peachpit.com
www.macromedia.com

To report errors, please send a note to errata@peachpit.com.

Copyright © 2003 by Macromedia, Inc.

Notice of Rights
All rights reserved. No part of this book may be reproduced or transmitted in any form by any means, electronic, mechanical, photocopying, recording, or otherwise, without the prior written permission of the publisher. For information on getting permission for reprints and excerpts, contact permissions@peachpit.com.

Trademarks
ColdFusion, Flash, Macromedia, and the Macromedia logo are registered trademarks of Macromedia, Inc.

Throughout this book, trademarked names are used. Rather than put a trademark symbol in every occurrence of a trademarked name, we state that we are using the names in an editorial fashion only and to the benefit of the trademark owner with no intention of infringement of the trademark.

Notice of Liability
The information in this book is distributed on an "As Is" basis, without warranty. While every precaution has been taken in the preparation of the book, neither the author, Macromedia, Inc. nor the publisher, shall have any liability to any person or entity with respect to any loss or damage caused or alleged to be caused directly or indirectly by the instructions contained in this book or by the computer software and hardware products described in it.

Printed and bound in the United States of America

ISBN 0-321-16224-2

9 8 7 6 5 4 3 2 1

DEDICATIONS

To Andy
   —Kevin

For Jon. Wish you could see these things.
   —Nate

CREDITS

Authors
Kevin Schmidt
Nate Weiss

Macromedia Press Editor
Angela C. Kozlowski

Development Editor
Susan Hobbs

Technical Editor
Peter Reese

Production Coordinators
Connie Jeung-Mills
Myrna Vladic

Copy Editor
Wendy Katz

Indexer
Karin Arrigoni

Proofreader
Suki Gear

Cover Design
Steven Soshea, Macromedia, Inc.

Cover Production
George Mattingly, GMD

Compositors
Rick Gordon, Emerald Valley Graphics
Debbie Roberti, Espresso Graphics

BIOS

Kevin Schmidt is a Macromedia Certified ColdFusion Developer who has worked with ColdFusion for over 3 years. He is the manager of the Des Moines ColdFusion User Group as well as a member of Team Macromedia. He currently lives and works in Des Moines, Iowa.

Nate Weiss has been building web applications for many years, most of them with ColdFusion. Along the way, he became an active member of the ColdFusion developer community as a member of what is now the Team Macromedia peer-to-peer support program, and by contributing popular custom tags and other free, reusable code at his website, nateweiss.com. He has spoken on various topics at many of Macromedia's ColdFusion developer conferences, has written articles for the developer's section of the Macromedia website, and put together the WDDX SDK at openwddx.org. Nate can be reached at nate@nateweiss.com.

ACKNOWLEDGEMENTS

Thanks to my editors, Angela and Susan. Without them you wouldn't be reading this. Thanks to my extended family for encouraging me to continue writing. Yes Grandpa you are in there too! A special thanks to my wife Malia and son Andrew, who sacrificed spending time with me while I wrote. I enjoyed writing this book and I hope you, the reader, are able to enjoy it and learn from it.

—Kevin

As always, thanks to Angela Kozlowski at Macromedia Press for including me in this project, providing such excellent support, and generally making things happen. Thanks to Kevin Schmidt for the opportunity to work on this edition of the book, and thanks to Ben Forta, the ColdFusion uber-author, for providing wise counsel along the way. A special thank-you to Wendy Katz for dotting my tees and crossing my eyes [sic!], and to Wendy Sharp for helping us with the elements of style. Finally, a general shout out to my friends and family for their outstretched arms over the past couple of months.

—Nate

table of contents

INTRODUCTION   1

LESSON 1 INSTALLING COLDFUSION MX   4

Understanding ColdFusion
Installing ColdFusion Server
Logging In to the ColdFusion Administrator

LESSON 2 INTRODUCING DREAMWEAVER MX   20

Installing Dreamweaver MX
Starting Dreamweaver MX
A Quick Tour of Dreamweaver MX
Defining a Site
Creating Your First ColdFusion Page
Changing the Preview in Browser Settings

LESSON 3 VARIABLES AND FUNCTIONS   46

Using Variables
Using Functions
Using Several Functions Together
Using Variables and Functions in Separate Files
Including Code Automatically with Application.cfm
Understanding ColdFusion's Variable Scopes

LESSON 4 RETRIEVING DATA FROM DATABASES   66

Understanding Databases
Creating a Data Source
Exploring a Database in Dreamweaver
Getting Information from a Database
Outputting Information from a Query
Experimenting with How Data is Displayed
Formatting Data Using HTML Tables
Changing the Order of the Records
Creating Links to Detail Pages
Creating Detail Pages
Running Dynamic Queries

LESSON 5 CREATING SEARCH FORMS   104

Creating a Basic HTML Form
Creating an Action Page
Matching on More than One Field
Displaying a No Records Found Message
Experimenting with Comparison Operators
Combining the Form and Action Pages
Auto-Focusing the Search Field
Creating an Advanced Search Page

LESSON 6 BUILDING DATA ENTRY PAGES   128

Creating a Product Menu for Updating
Creating the Product Edit Form
Performing the Update
Deleting Records from a Database
Inserting Information into a Database
Adding Validation Rules
Optional: Using SQL's UPDATE and INSERT Statements

LESSON 7 CREATING SECURED PAGES   154

Introducing the <cflogin> Framework
Creating the Login Form
Presenting and Processing the Login Form
Adding Password Protection to Individual Pages
Providing a Way to Log Out
Implementing Per-User Privileges with Roles

LESSON 8 USING SESSION VARIABLES   180

Getting Started with Session Variables
Using a Session Variable to Remember Search Keywords
Adjusting When Session Variables are Discarded
Using Arrays to Remember Multiple Searches
Making the Search History More Intelligent
Allowing the User to Clear the Search History
Just for Fun: Switching to Application Variables

LESSON 9 SENDING EMAIL   208

Creating a Mailing List
Sending Bulk Email Messages
Telling ColdFusion Which Mail Server to Use
Allowing Users to Unsubscribe
Sending Database Information to Individual People

LESSON 10 CREATING FUNCTIONS AND TAGS   238

Creating Your First Function
Using Your New Function
Creating Specialized Functions
Creating Your Own Tags
"Installing" Tags in the Magic CustomTags Folder

INDEX   263

introduction

Macromedia ColdFusion MX is the latest version of Macromedia's powerful yet easy to use Web application server. It enables you to create dynamic Web sites quickly and easily with little or no programming experience. ColdFusion provides a variety of tools that give you the ability to query a database, output the results, and work with other information. You can use it to transform your Web site from a bland, static site into a powerful, dynamic destination on the Web.

With the MX release of ColdFusion, many new enhancements have been added that enable you to accomplish tasks that were not possible in previous versions. With all of its new capabilities, ColdFusion still offers its powerful and easy to use syntax, making it simple for a novice to learn as well as keeping experienced programmers on their toes.

NOTE *As you may have heard, the guts of the ColdFusion Server have been totally rewritten with Java for this version of the product. This, in turn, exposes the whole Java world to advanced ColdFusion programmers. Don't worry; you don't need to know Java to learn ColdFusion!*

This Macromedia Training from the Source book introduces you to ColdFusion and guides you step-by-step through some of the key features. Throughout this book, you work on projects with a single theme: creating and maintaining customer information for an online company. The 10-part curriculum includes these lessons:

Lesson 1: Installing ColdFusion MX
Lesson 2: Introducing Dreamweaver MX
Lesson 3: Variables and Functions
Lesson 4: Retrieving Data from Databases
Lesson 5: Creating Search Forms

Lesson 6: Building Data Entry Pages
Lesson 7: Creating Secured Pages
Lesson 8: Using Session Variables
Lesson 9: Sending Email
Lesson 10: Creating Functions and Tags

Each lesson begins with an overview of the lesson's content and learning objectives, and each lesson is divided into short tasks that break the skills into bite-size units.

Each lesson also includes notes that provide extra insights, keyboard shortcuts, and related techniques for those who are ready to absorb additional information.

As you complete these lessons, you learn how ColdFusion works, what it can do, and how you can use it to make your Web site better. When you finish these lessons, you should be able to create simple yet powerful ColdFusion applications.

All the files you need for the lessons are included in the Lessons folder on the enclosed CD. Files for each lesson appear in their own folders, titled with the lesson number.

Each lesson folder contains two subfolders: Start and Complete. As you work through each lesson, you will be adding code to the files in the Start folder. When you're done with each lesson, the files will be identical to the ones in the Complete folder. So, if you get confused at all while working through a lesson, you can "cheat" by looking at the finished version of the file in the Complete folder. Not every lesson requires starting or complete files, so in these cases the folders are empty.

The files you need for each lesson are identified at the beginning of that lesson.

WHO THIS BOOK IS DESIGNED FOR

Each book in the Macromedia Training from the Source series is based upon curriculum originally developed for use by Macromedia's authorized trainers. The lesson plans were developed by some of Macromedia's most successful trainers, and refined through timely experience to meet students' needs. We believe that Macromedia Training from the Source courses offer the best available training for Macromedia programs.

This book is intended for readers who are interested in taking their Web sites to the next level. We only ask that you understand HTML, and are able to write basic HTML pages without the help of a WYSIWYG editor. We'll take care of the rest. As you will see, you don't have to be a programmer to understand ColdFusion!

NOTE *You don't have to have Dreamweaver MX or ColdFusion Server already installed on your computer to use this book. There are 30-day trial versions of each included on the CD. The Dreamweaver trial will stop working after 30 days, but you can keep using the ColdFusion Server on your own computer for as long as you like.*

WHAT YOU WILL LEARN

By the end of this course, you will be able to:

- Understand what ColdFusion is and how it works
- Create and modify ColdFusion templates in Dreamweaver MX
- Create and display variables
- Pass URL variables between templates
- Work with functions
- Use functions to modify variables and format dates and times
- Work with conditional processing to control page flow
- Work with forms and send email
- Query a database to retrieve information
- Display information from a database
- Update information in a database
- Understand session management
- Write new functions and tags for your own use

MINIMUM SYSTEM REQUIREMENTS

- Pentium-compatible processor (Pentium II or higher recommended)
- Windows 95/98/ME or Windows NT 4.0/2000/XP
- Internet Explorer 4.5 or higher
- 128 MB RAM
- 200 MB hard disk space
- 256-color monitor capable of 800 × 600 screen resolution

installing ColdFusion MX

LESSON 1

Macromedia ColdFusion MX is a Web-application server that can be used to complete tasks as simple as creating a guest book for your Web site, or as complex as creating a full-featured online retail store. No matter what you want your Web site to do, chances are that ColdFusion can help you reach your goals.

Here's the basic idea: ColdFusion takes templates—pages that are a meld of HTML and ColdFusion code—and processes them in a special way before passing them on to a user's Web browser. Think of these templates as normal Web pages that have certain "blanks" or "placeholders" left in them. These placeholders contain ColdFusion code which fills in the blanks with whatever is appropriate whenever someone visits the page. Of course, what actually gets placed in the blanks is up to you. Perhaps one blank is filled in with the current date, and another is filled in with the current user's name, giving the page a personalized touch. Perhaps a third, larger placeholder area is filled in with the user's account information or purchase history, retrieved from your company's database.

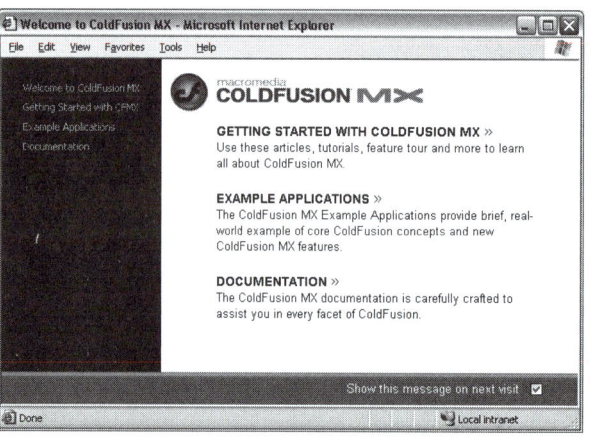

This lesson introduces you to ColdFusion MX, and walks you through the short process of installing it on your computer.

NOTE *If you're at all familiar with the mail merge feature in Microsoft Word or some other word-processing program, you can think of ColdFusion templates as being conceptually similar. Both can be thought of as easy but powerful systems for inserting names or other information into specific areas of a document on demand. ColdFusion is far more powerful, and the analogy breaks down when scrutinized closely, but the comparison is still helpful.*

All of its features aside, ColdFusion's real power lies in its simplicity and ease of use. Like HTML, ColdFusion's scripting language is based on tags, so the syntax will look familiar and accommodating right from the start. The names and attributes for the various ColdFusion tags are straightforward, which makes it easy to write new code (or to understand someone else's). This simplicity and ease of use leads us to another of ColdFusion's strengths: the speed with which you can build applications with it. Developers can put together applications in ColdFusion in a fraction of the time they might take using other languages.

In this lesson, you'll learn the limitations of ordinary HTML pages, and how ColdFusion helps to overcome them. You will examine a ColdFusion page in a browser, and view the source code. Finally, you'll install ColdFusion MX in preparation for later lessons.

WHAT YOU WILL LEARN

In this lesson, you will:

- Learn what ColdFusion is (and isn't)
- Understand how ColdFusion works
- Examine the source code of a ColdFusion-powered page
- Install ColdFusion Server
- Log in to the ColdFusion Administrator

APPROXIMATE TIME

This lesson takes approximately one hour and 15 minutes to complete.

LESSON FILES

Starting Files:

ColdFusionMX Tryouts/coldfusion-60-win-en.exe

Completed Project:

None

UNDERSTANDING COLDFUSION

You will use two different tools to create ColdFusion pages: the ColdFusion Server, and a text editor such as Macromedia Dreamweaver MX. You use the text editor to write the code for your ColdFusion pages. You then test and work with your pages by interacting with the server, just as your users will.

The special scripting language used in ColdFusion pages is called CFML, which stands for ColdFusion Markup Language. CFML differs from HTML, though the languages share a number of characteristics. Both are tag-based languages, and both are used to display pages in a Web browser. But HTML, used alone, can display only static data—information that doesn't change. ColdFusion can display dynamic information—data that changes in response to an event or user interaction. For example, dynamic content allows you to create pages that display information based on users' requests. With ColdFusion, you can run an online store, process orders, interact with users, and customize information to meet their changing needs.

NOTE *Dynamic content keeps users coming back to your site. Users aren't likely to keep returning to a site that never seems to change; if there's nothing new, what's the point of going back? If you keep the content fresh, however, and give people a reason to come back, they will be more likely to point their browser to your site again and again.*

NOTE *Think of the sites that you visit regularly. Why do you go there? You probably visit these sites for some kind of up-to-date information, opinions, or articles. For instance, news and financial sites that offer stock quotes are some of the most heavily trafficked sites on the Web because they offer current, frequently changing content. Keeping your site's content fresh is easy with ColdFusion.*

How does ColdFusion achieve this level of interactivity? When a user requests a page, the Web server passes the request to the ColdFusion Server. The ColdFusion Server fills in the various "blanks" in the template by querying databases, performing calculations, using conditional processing, or doing whatever else is specified. The ColdFusion Server then hands the completed HTML back to the Web server, which in turn sends the page back to the client for display. With this one added step and a bit of extra code, you've turned your site into something more than just words and pictures. It can be an up-to-the-minute catalog of products, or a forum where customers can interact.

Want to see a ColdFusion page in action? That shouldn't be hard to do; they are found all over the Web. One live page that's easy to find is Macromedia's home page (www.macromedia.com). Not surprisingly, Macromedia used a combination of ColdFusion and Flash, another of their products, to create this site.

NOTE *When you access this home page, you are actually accessing a page called www.macromedia.com/index.cfm. The .cfm extension means it's a ColdFusion page. The next time you're surfing the Web, look around and see how many of these you can find.*

While you're at the Macromedia home page, take a look at the source code for that page. (In Internet Explorer, choose View > Source; in Netscape Navigator, choose View > Page Source.) Hmm, it looks just like an HTML document! If you were to look at this page without knowing that it was written with ColdFusion, you might assume that the corresponding page on the Web server was an ordinary HTML page. What you can't tell by looking at the source code is that any number of ColdFusion's various features may have been used to construct the page the instant after you requested it. Any number of database queries, variables, and functions may have worked together to produce the HTML source code the browser receives.

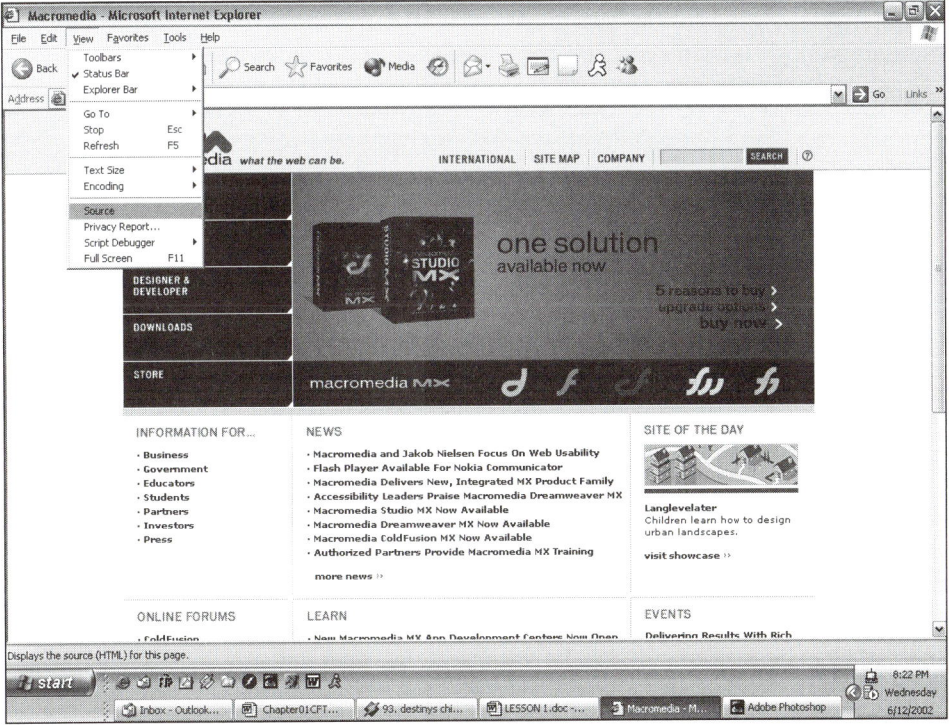

The point is that while a ColdFusion template may contain special CFML code for getting information from databases, performing calculations, and the like, the browser ends up getting plain old HTML code, with the various "blanks" filled in. Because the work of filling in the blanks is performed on the server side (in this case, on Macromedia's network), the browser doesn't know or care that ColdFusion was involved in the request. All it knows is that it asked for a page and received it.

Now let's get started. Before we dive in, we need to install ColdFusion MX on your computer.

INSTALLING COLDFUSION SERVER

Before you can work with ColdFusion templates, you first need to install the server.

1) Double-click the file *coldfusion-60-win-us.exe* in the ColdFusion MX Tryout folder on the CD.

This starts the installation of the ColdFusion Server. The installation will progress through its preparatory stages and stop on the welcome screen of the Install Wizard for ColdFusion MX.

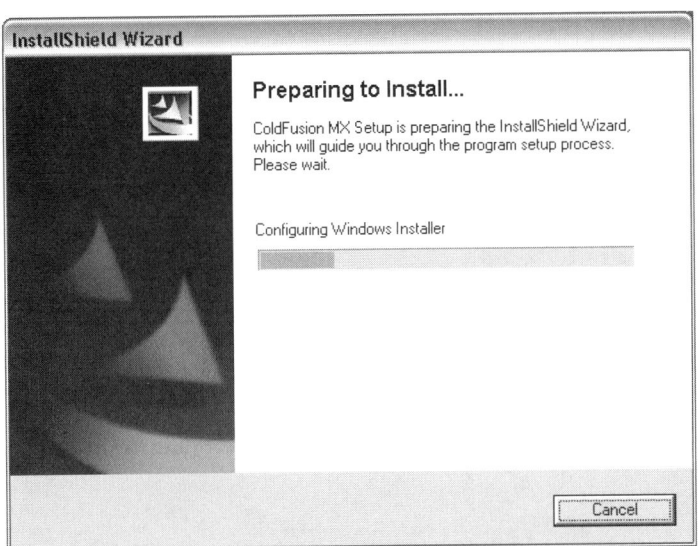

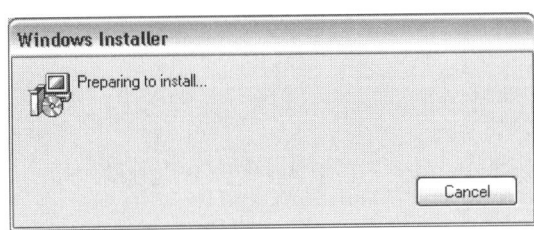

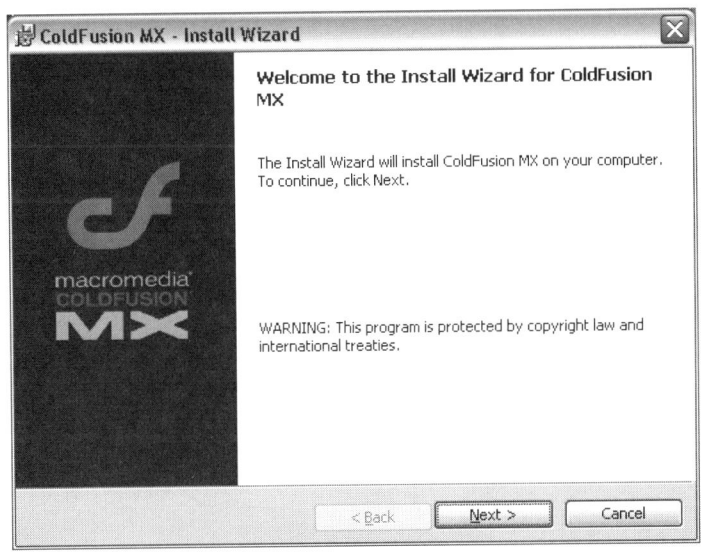

INSTALLING COLDFUSION MX

2) Click Next to continue with the installation.

You will be prompted to accept the terms of the license agreement.

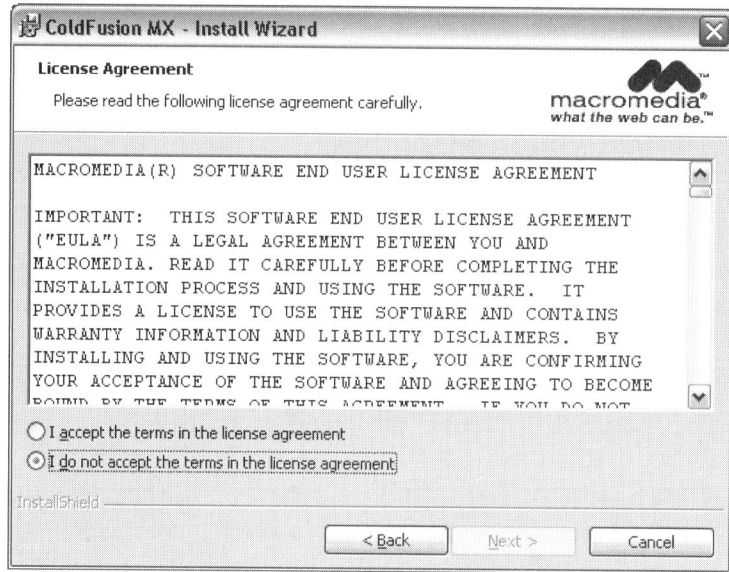

3) Select the radio button that says "I accept the terms of the license agreement" and then click Next.

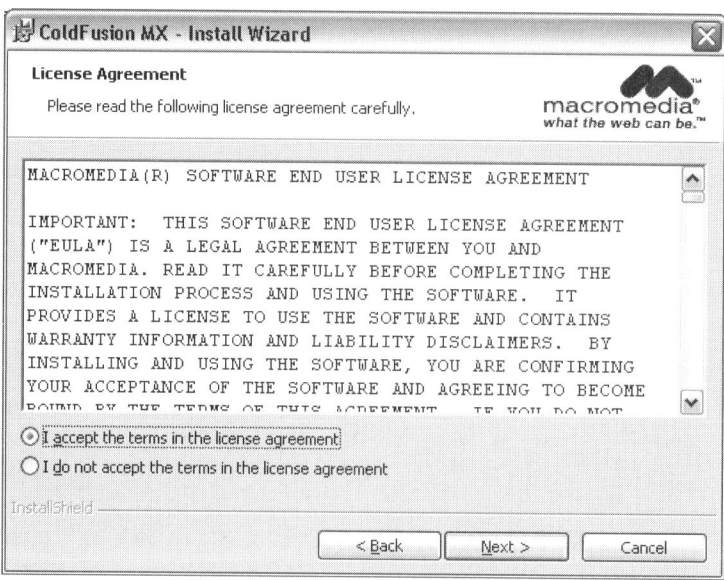

You will not be able to continue with the installation unless you accept the terms of the license agreement.

4) Enter your information on the Customer Information form and then click Next.

You don't need to enter any serial numbers. ColdFusion MX will be automatically installed as a 30-day, full-featured trial version. Even after the 30 days, you will be able to continue using the server for development and learning purposes.

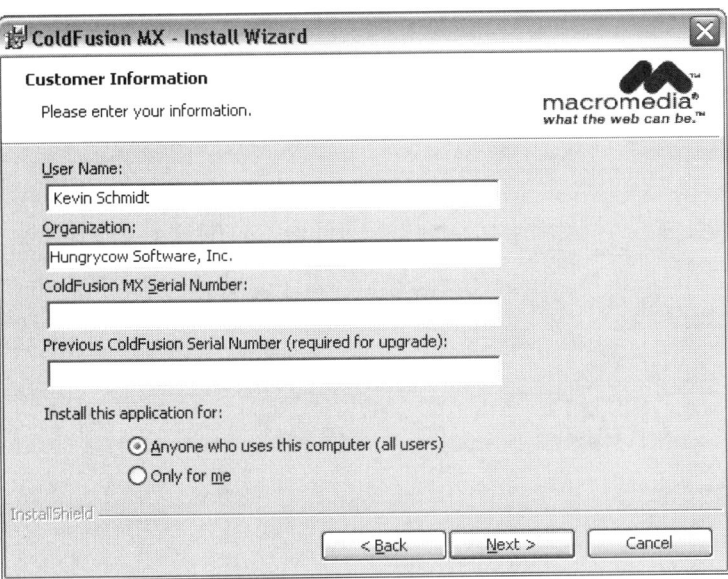

5) Select Standalone (Web Server port 8500) as the server with which you want to use ColdFusion, and click Next.

One of the new features of ColdFusion MX is that it comes with it own stand-alone Web server. While this Web server is not recommended for production-level servers, it is more than adequate for learning, development, and testing.

NOTE *Depending on the other software installed on your computer, you may see some other entries listed at this point in the process (other than the Standalone and Apache entries shown above). For instance, there might be an entry for Microsoft Internet Information Services (IIS). Just choose the Standalone option unless you have a specific need otherwise. The instructions and graphics in the rest of this book assume that you have chosen the Standalone option.*

6) Select the folder into which you want to install the ColdFusion files, and click Next.

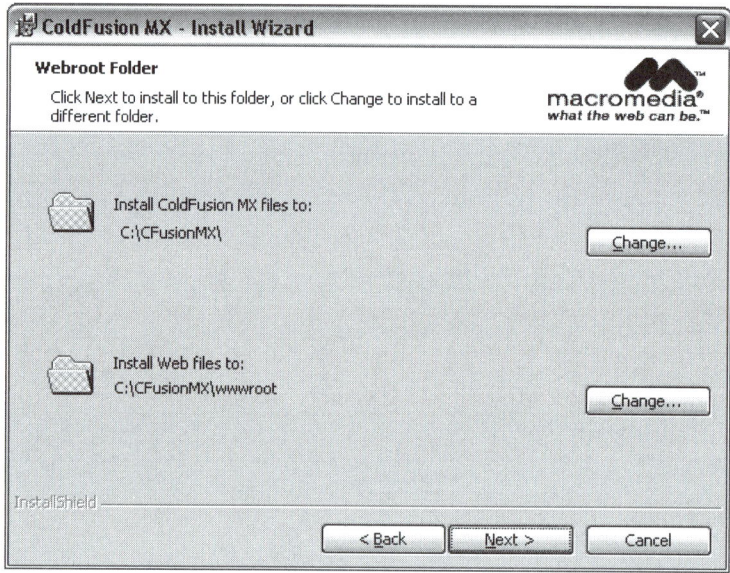

Although you can change the installation path for ColdFusion, it is not recommended for the purposes of this book, because the names of the default folders are used throughout the lessons. Changing the folder names or locations could get confusing.

7) Select the features you want to install, and click Next.

The server, documentation, and sample applications will be installed by default.
It is recommended that you install the sample applications and documentation now; these are excellent resources for you as you learn more about ColdFusion. However, it is not recommended to install these features in a production environment.

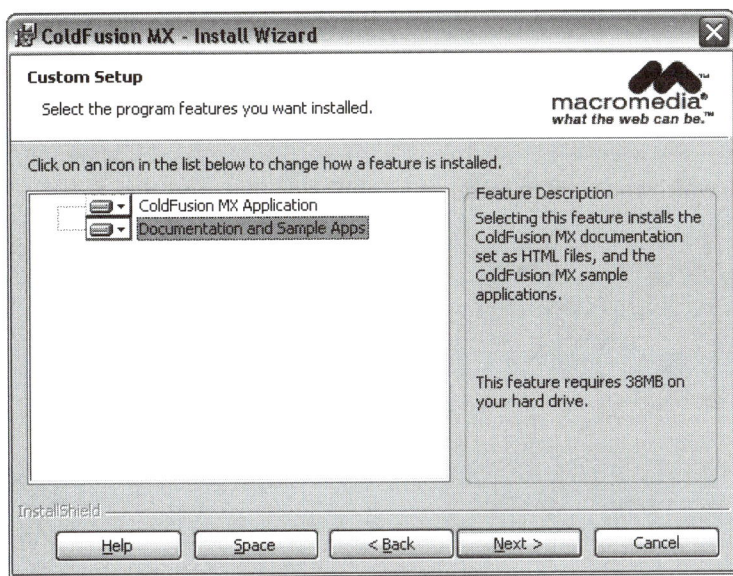

TIP *If you need to check how much hard drive space you have available, click the Space button to see the status of your hard drive.*

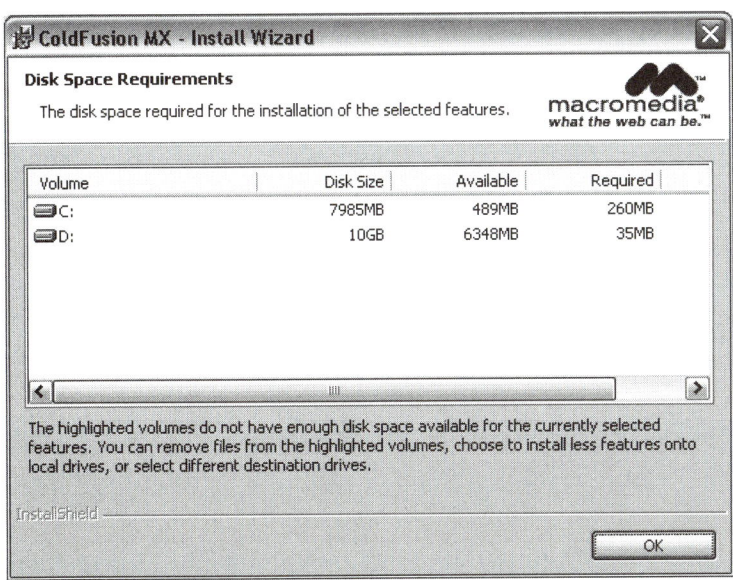

INSTALLING COLDFUSION MX

8) Choose a password to access the ColdFusion Administrator. Then click the check box for "Use the same password as above," and click Next.

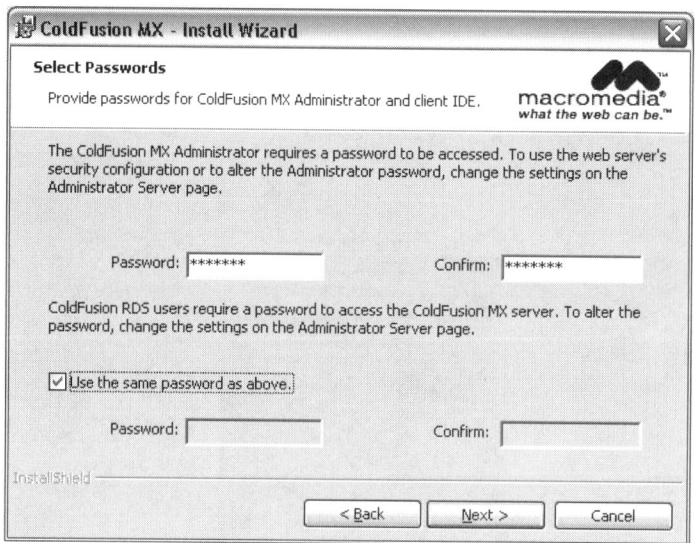

Make sure you write down your password, because there is no easy way to reset it or retrieve it. Always keep passwords in a safe and secure location.

9) Confirm your installation settings, and click Install.

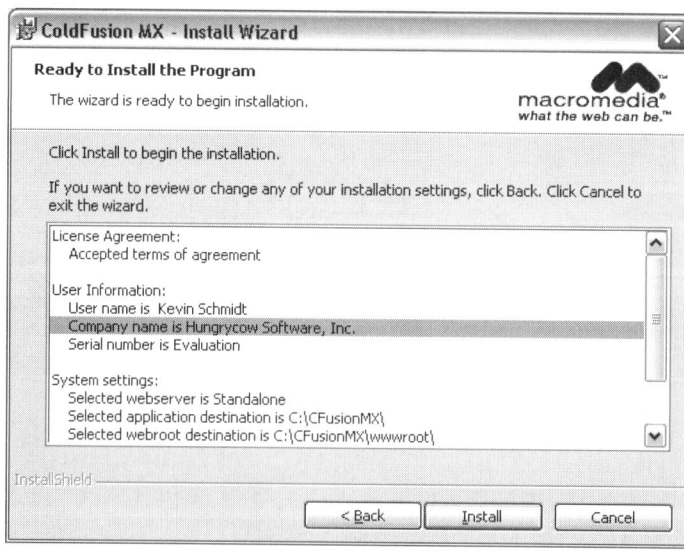

If you need to make any changes, you can click the Back button to return to the previous screen.

NOTE *If you are using a software-based firewall product such as Norton Internet Security or Personal Firewall, you should disable it temporarily before you click Install. You can re-enable it when the installation is complete. You may want to disconnect your computer from the Internet or other network while your firewall is disabled.*

10) Wait patiently.

The ColdFusion Server will take several minutes to install. Even if the status bar reaches the end, continue to wait.

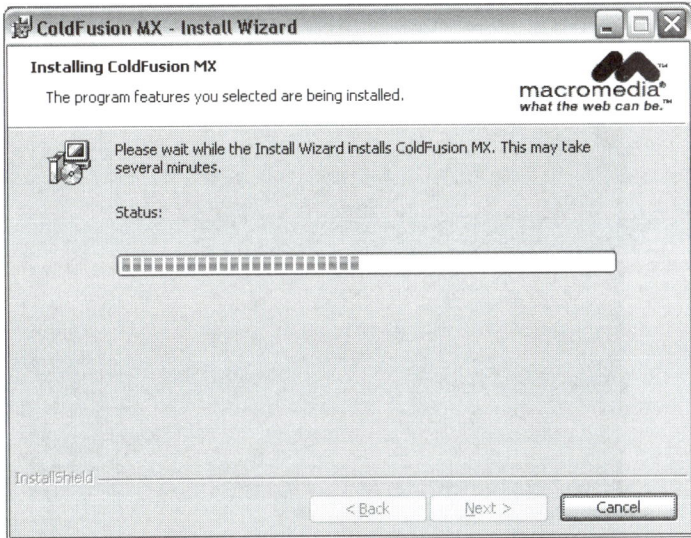

11) Click Finish to wrap up installing the ColdFusion Server.

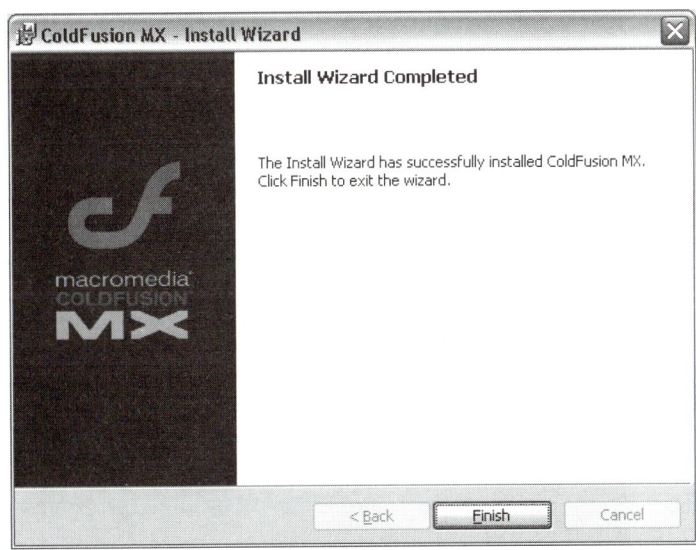

After a few moments, your browser will launch the ColdFusion Administrator. Additionally, a "Welcome to ColdFusion" window will appear.

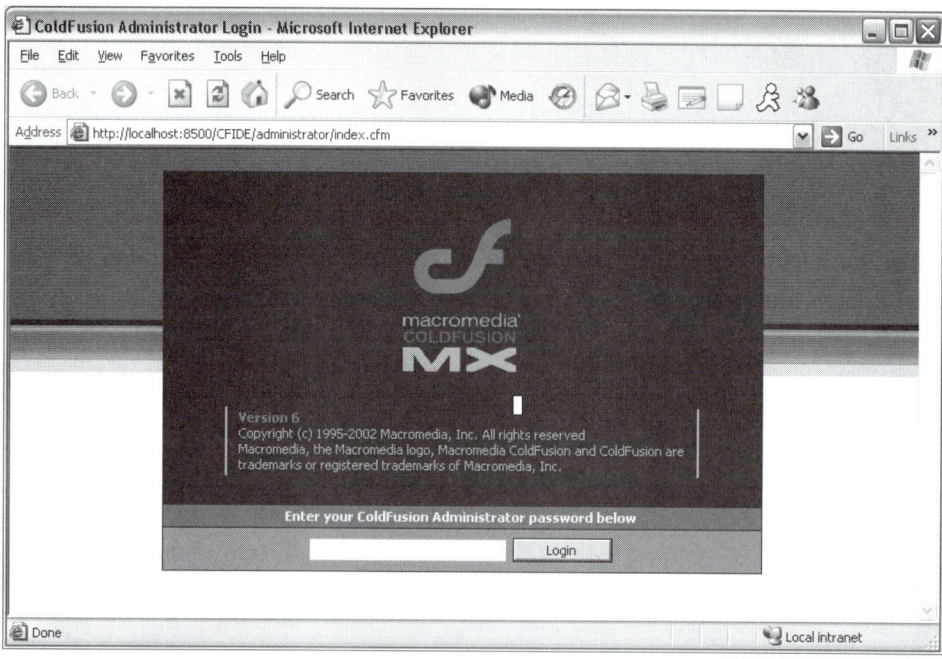

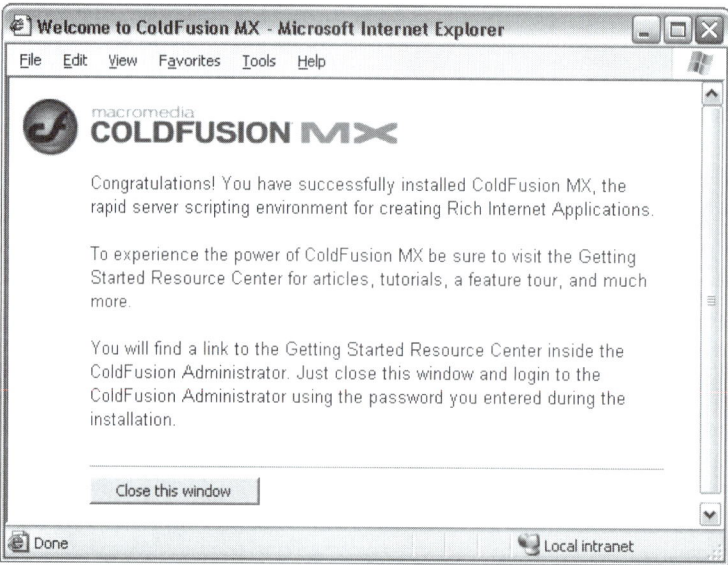

TIP *In the unlikely event that a problem occurs during installation, there is free installation support information available at http://www.macromedia.com/support/coldfusion.*

LOGGING IN TO THE COLDFUSION ADMINISTRATOR

At this point, the ColdFusion Server is installed. Now you will learn how to log in to the ColdFusion Administrator so that you can configure it as you move along in the lessons.

The ColdFusion Administrator provides the tools for controlling your ColdFusion Server. Using the Administrator, you can set up and maintain your data sources, manage log files, configure the email server, and control security. In other words, the Administrator is the hub for running your ColdFusion Server. The Administrator should have launched at the end of the installation procedure. Let's log in to see what it looks like.

NOTE *Think of the ColdFusion Administrator as being the equivalent of the Options or Preferences dialogs in the programs you use every day, such as Microsoft Word, Excel, or your Web browser.*

1) **Enter your password for the ColdFusion Administrator, and click Login.**

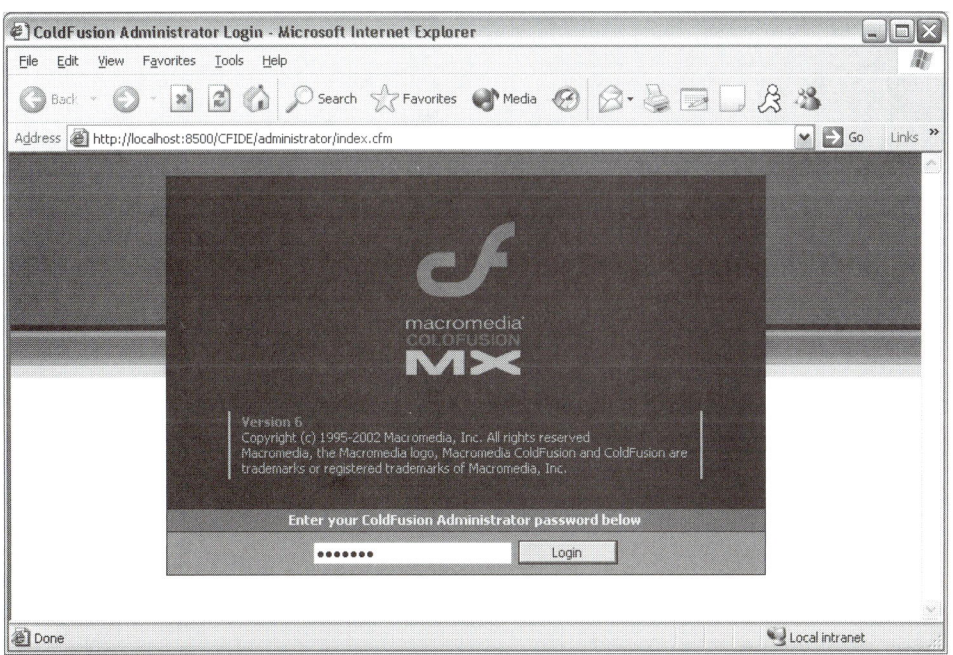

NOTE *When you need to access the Administrator in the future, you need only select the Macromedia ColdFusion MX > Administrator item from the Programs area of the Windows Start menu.*

By the way, you must have cookies turned on in your Web browser, or else you won't be able to use the Administrator. Cookies are generally enabled by default, so if you (or your network administrator) have not specifically turned them off, you're all set. If cookies have been disabled, however, you will need to bring them back. In Internet Explorer, go to Explorer Tools > Internet Options. Select the Security tab, and click the Custom Level button. Scroll down to Cookies and click the Enable radio button. In Netscape Navigator, choose Edit > Preferences, select the Advanced category, and click the desired radio button in the Cookie section.

TIP *Many browsers will allow you to enable cookies just for a particular site or particular zone of the Internet, so you should be able to easily tell your browser to accept cookies from the Administrator even if you don't want to enable them for the whole Internet. Consult your browser's Help or documentation for details.*

2) Take a quick look through the Administrator.

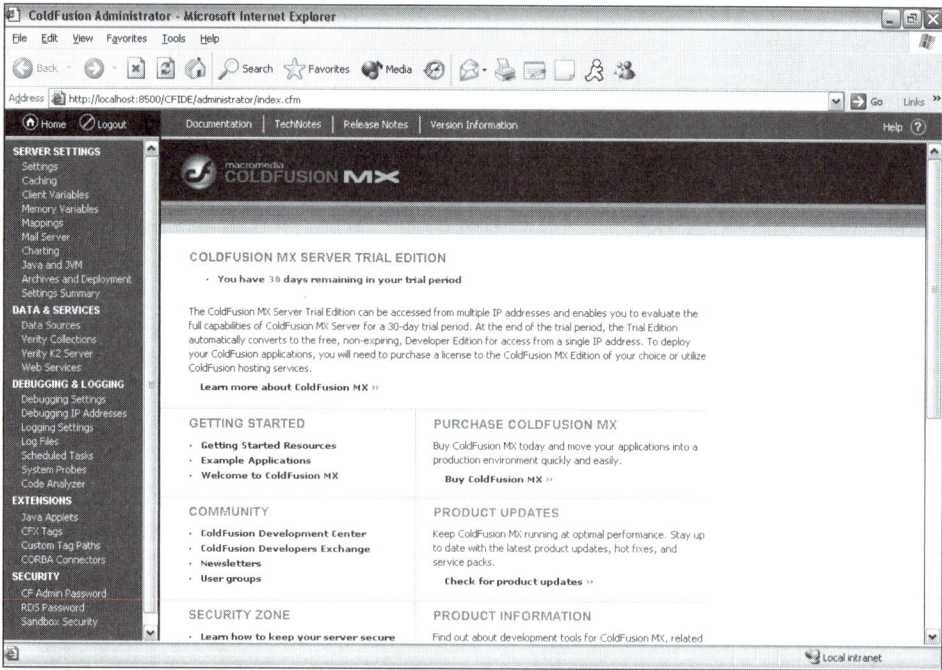

When you enter the correct password, the ColdFusion Server Administrator window opens. Feel free to take a look around, but do not make any changes yet. You will learn to work with the Administrator throughout this book.

NOTE *The first time you log in, the Welcome to ColdFusion MX window appears. It contains links to the documentation as well as sample applications. If you do not want this window to appear in the future, simply uncheck the box that says "Show this message on next visit," and close the window.*

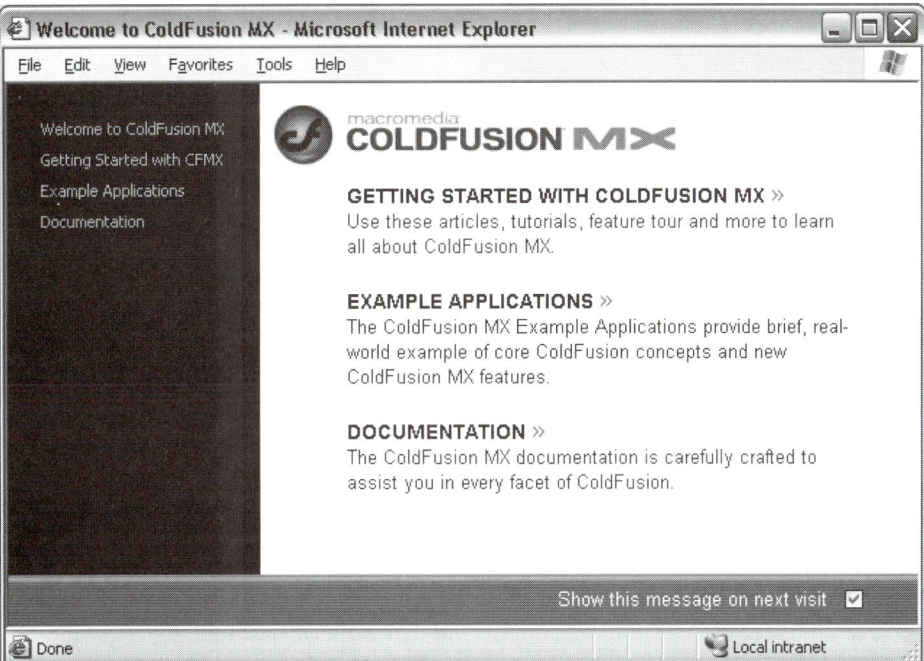

WHAT YOU HAVE LEARNED

In this lesson, you have:

- Learned the difference between a static HTML page and a dynamic ColdFusion page (pages 5–6)
- Examined the parts of a ColdFusion page in a browser (pages 7–8)
- Installed the ColdFusion Server (pages 8–16)
- Logged in to the ColdFusion Administrator (pages 17–19)

introducing Dreamweaver MX

LESSON 2

Dreamweaver MX is Macromedia's premier tool for designing and writing code for Web pages—whether they are written with ColdFusion, plain old HTML, or some other language. Dreamweaver can be described in many different ways, but for our ColdFusion-related purposes you should think of it as being a simple text editor (kind of like Windows Notepad), but with a whole lot of helpful bells and whistles added on.

You are not required to use Dreamweaver MX when you write your ColdFusion pages, but it does offer several advantages not available with competing tools. Because Dreamweaver MX is a Macromedia product, it is designed to integrate well with ColdFusion. It also offers tools to help with your HTML development, such as keyboard shortcuts for simple tasks, and wizards for more complex tasks.

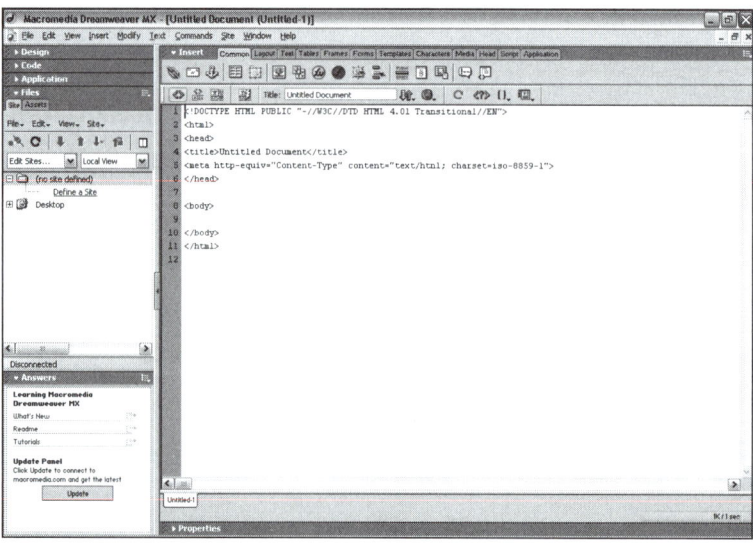

The MX version of Dreamweaver is the latest and greatest of this cornerstone in Web development software.

Many of the Dreamweaver tools enable you to streamline your coding and allow for quick development. These tools anticipate common programming needs and actions, and eliminate much of the need for repetitive typing. In this lesson, you will learn how to configure Dreamweaver MX for ColdFusion coding, and then you'll use Dreamweaver MX to create and edit a ColdFusion page.

NOTE *Along with ColdFusion, Dreamweaver provides support for Active Server Pages (ASP), Java Server Pages (JSP), PHP, and more. So, even if you choose to sometimes use another application server to create some of your pages, Dreamweaver can help you write your code quickly and easily.*

WHAT YOU WILL LEARN

In this lesson you will:

- Install and launch Dreamweaver MX
- Explore and become familiar with the Dreamweaver MX interface
- Create a site within Dreamweaver MX
- Create a ColdFusion page

APPROXIMATE TIME

This lesson takes approximately one hour to complete.

LESSON FILES

Starting Files:

ColdFusionMX Tryouts\dw_mx_trial_en.exe

Completed Project:

Lesson02\Complete\helloworld.cfm

INSTALLING DREAMWEAVER MX

You will be installing a 30-day evaluation version of Dreamweaver MX. This version will no longer work when the 30-day evaluation period is over. If you want to continue using Dreamweaver MX after 30 days, you will need to purchase a license from Macromedia. You can decide to use a different text editor later (such as the Notepad accessory application that comes with Windows), but be aware that many coding tasks will take longer with simpler editors.

1) Click Start > Run and then type D:\ ColdFusionMX Tryouts\dw_mx_trial_en.exe.
In this command, the D represents the letter of your CD-ROM drive where the ColdFusion Training from the Source disc is located. This will launch the InstallShield Wizard for Dreamweaver MX.

TIP *You can also launch the installer by double-click on the dw_mx_trial_en.exe file within the Windows Explorer.*

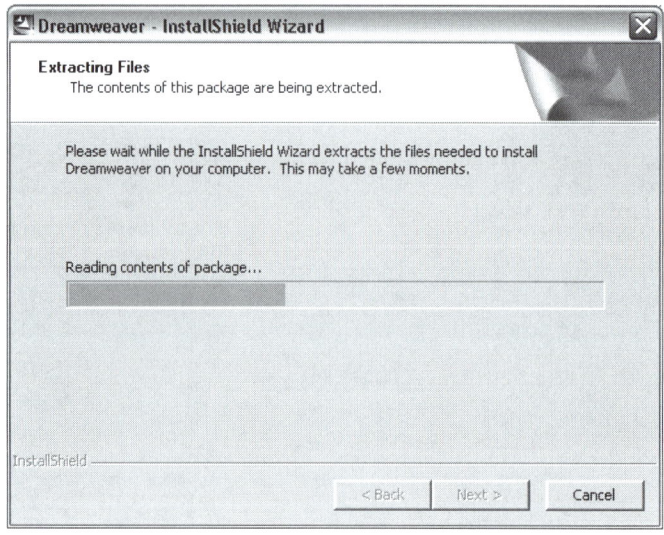

After the files have been extracted, you will briefly see two introductory screens, letting you know that the InstallShield Wizard is preparing to guide you through the rest of the installation.

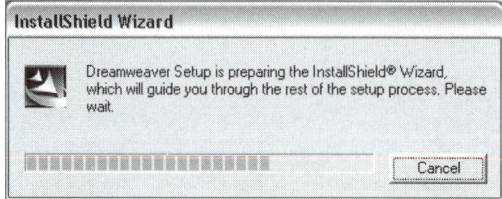

After the preparations are complete, you will see the Welcome screen for the InstallShield Wizard for Dreamweaver MX.

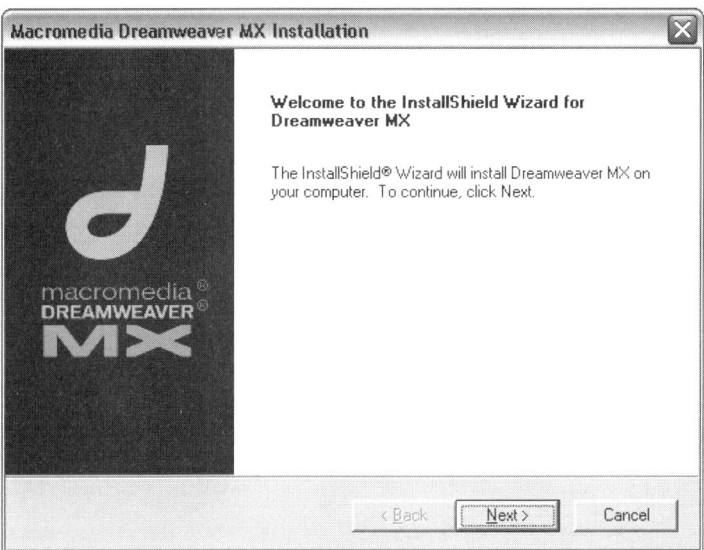

2) **Click Next.**

You will now be prompted to accept the license agreement for Dreamweaver MX. You must agree in order to continue with the installation.

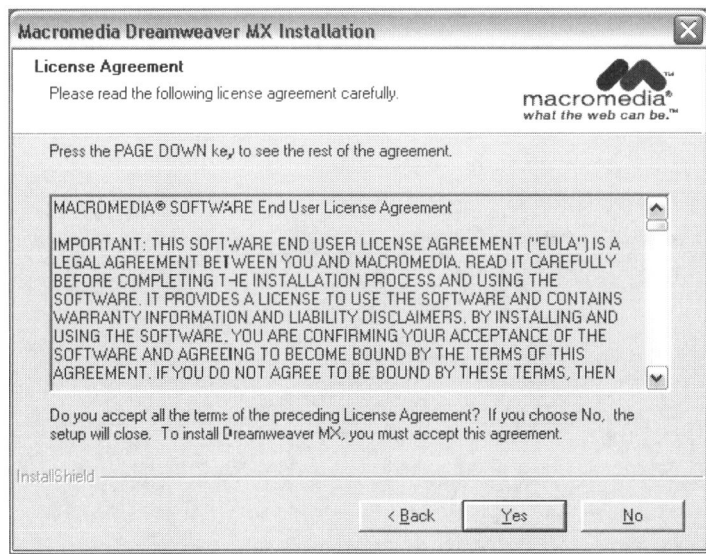

3) Click Yes.

Now you will need to choose a directory in which to install Dreamweaver MX. Unless you want to install Dreamweaver MX on another drive, leave the default directory. If you do want to install on another drive, click Browse, and choose or create a folder for the other drive.

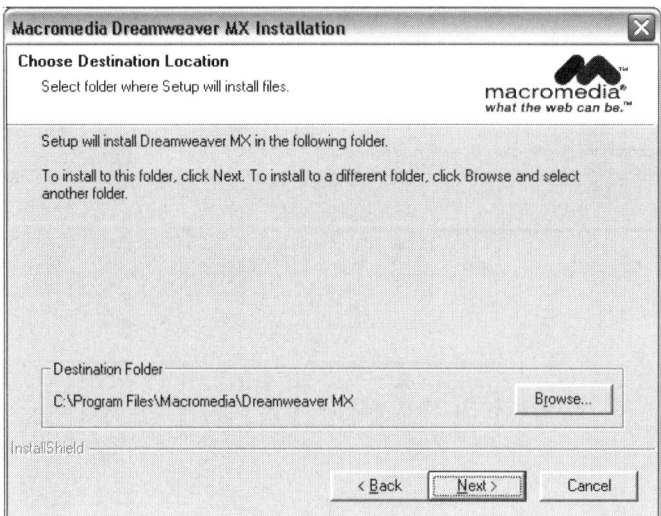

4) Click Next.

You will now be prompted to select the types of files for which Dreamweaver MX will be the default editor. After the installation is complete, any of the file types selected here will automatically open up in Dreamweaver when you double-click them from the Windows Explorer. Unless you have another program in which you want to work with these files, leave all of the boxes checked.

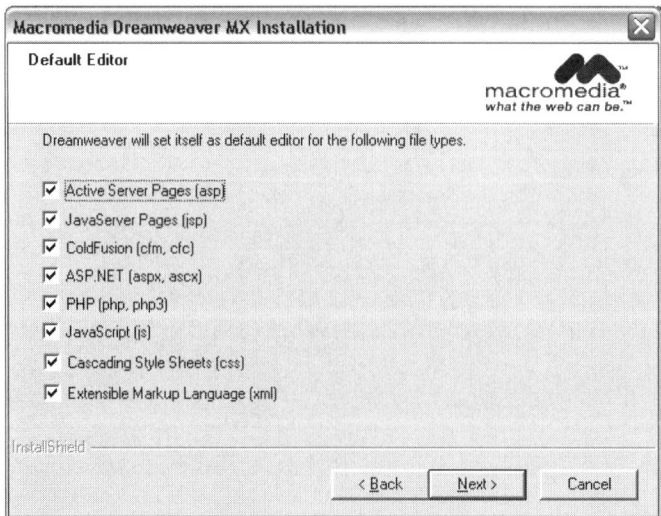

5) Click Next.

This step asks you to review and verify your installation selections. If you want to change a directory or any other options, now is the time to do so. Click the Back button until you reach the screen that contains the item you want to change, make your changes, and continue.

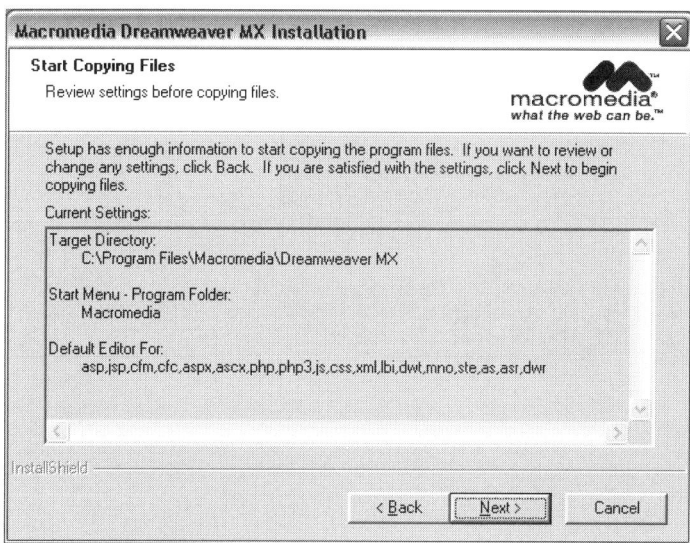

6) Click Next.

All the files necessary to run Dreamweaver MX will now be installed on your computer. This process will take a few minutes (depending on the speed of your computer), so wait patiently.

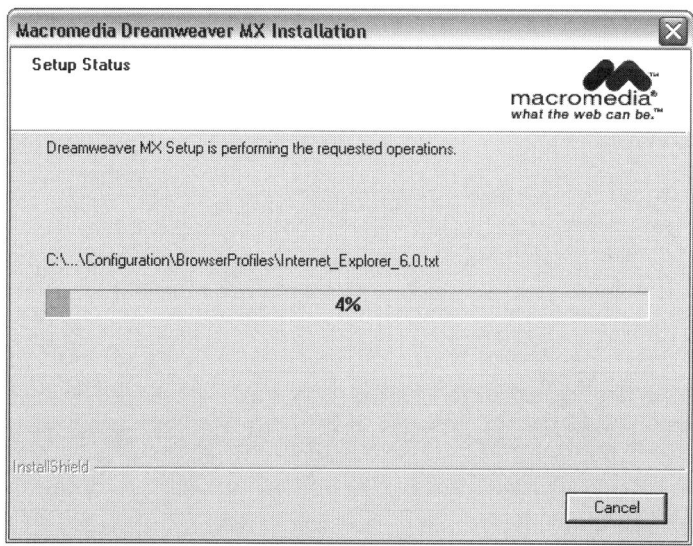

After this is finished, you will see the InstallShield Wizard completion screen.

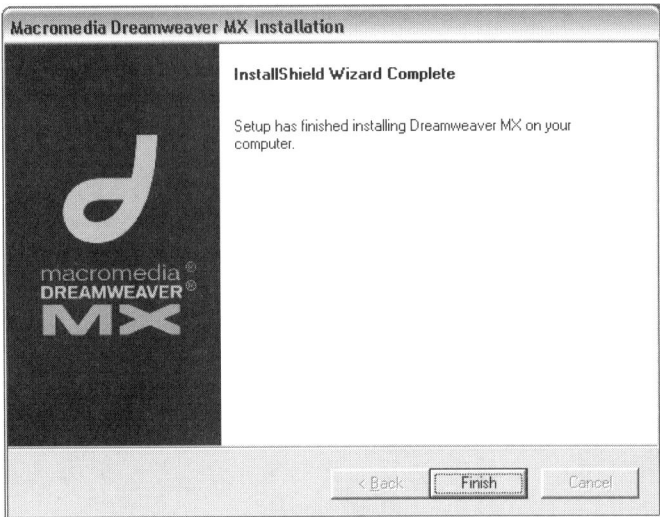

7) Click Finish.

You are now done installing Dreamweaver MX. A Web browser will now open and take you to the Readme file for Dreamweaver MX, which you can read at your leisure.

A file window will also open with a link to launch Dreamweaver MX.

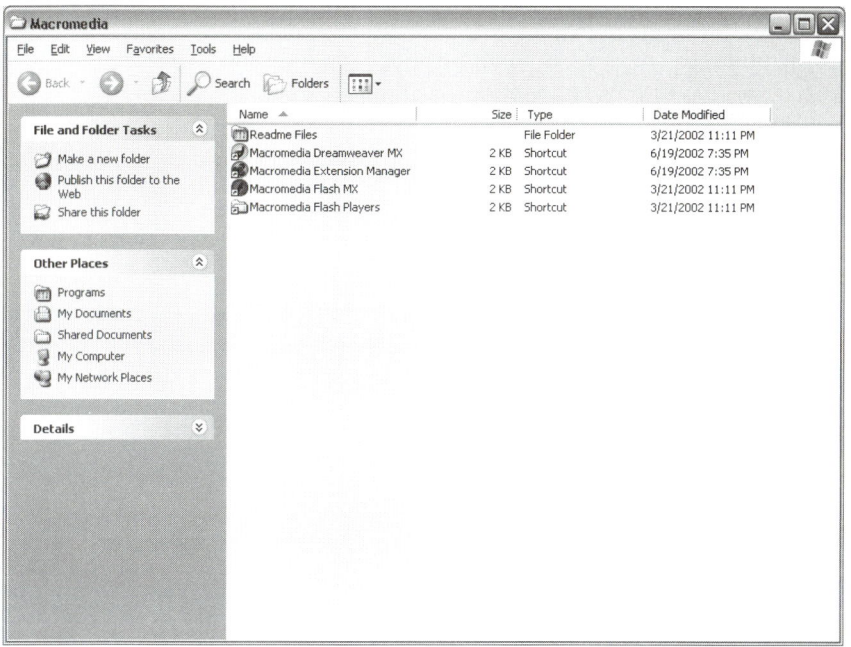

STARTING DREAMWEAVER MX

Now that Dreamweaver MX has been installed, you can now launch it and take a look around.

1) Double-click the Dreamweaver MX icon in the file window that opened in the previous task.

Of course, you can also use the Dreamweaver MX icon in the Windows Start menu (it will be located in the Programs group, filed under Macromedia). In either case, Dreamweaver MX will launch. You will be prompted with a screen that explains that this version is a 30-day trial. You can elect to try the trial, get more information, or quit.

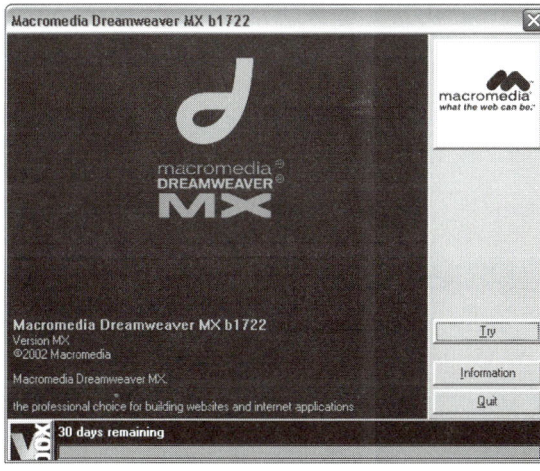

2) Click Try.

You will now be prompted as to what type of workspace you want. Make sure you select the Dreamweaver MX Workspace option, and check the HomeSite/Coder Style box.

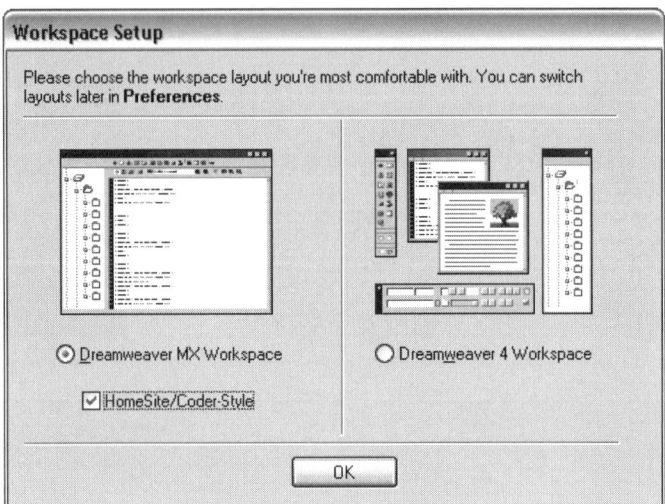

3) Click OK.

After the program starts, you will be prompted with a Welcome screen from which you can select different categories. The options available to you provide valuable information that is worth reading when you have time and want to learn more.

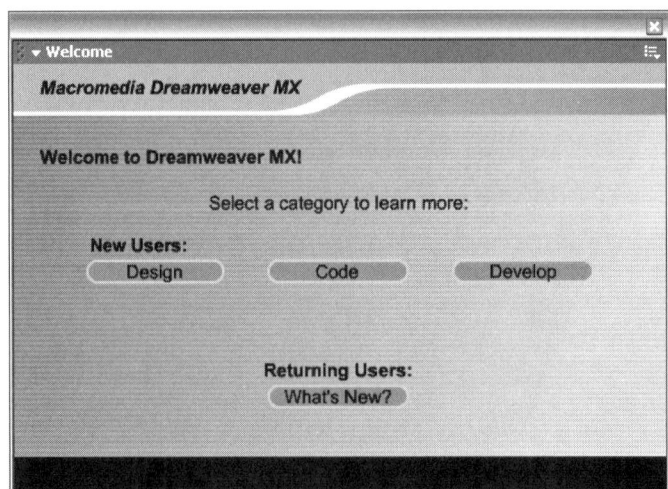

TIP *To look at the Welcome screen at some time in the future, just choose Help > Welcome from Dreamweaver's main menu bar.*

4) Close the Welcome window by clicking on the X in the upper-right corner.

You will now see and learn about the Dreamweaver environment in its default state.

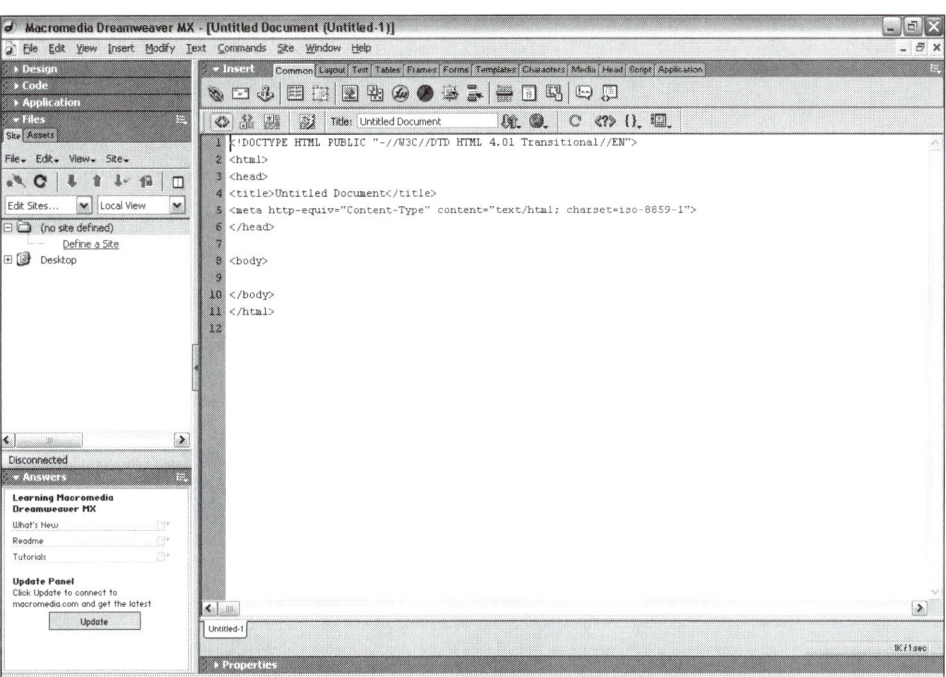

A QUICK TOUR OF DREAMWEAVER MX

Your first glance at the Dreamweaver interface may seem a bit overwhelming. The initial screen is split between several windows and toolbars. We'll walk through them to get an idea of their functions. In this task, you won't be producing anything—just getting familiar with the environment.

1) Look at the editor window at the right side of the screen.

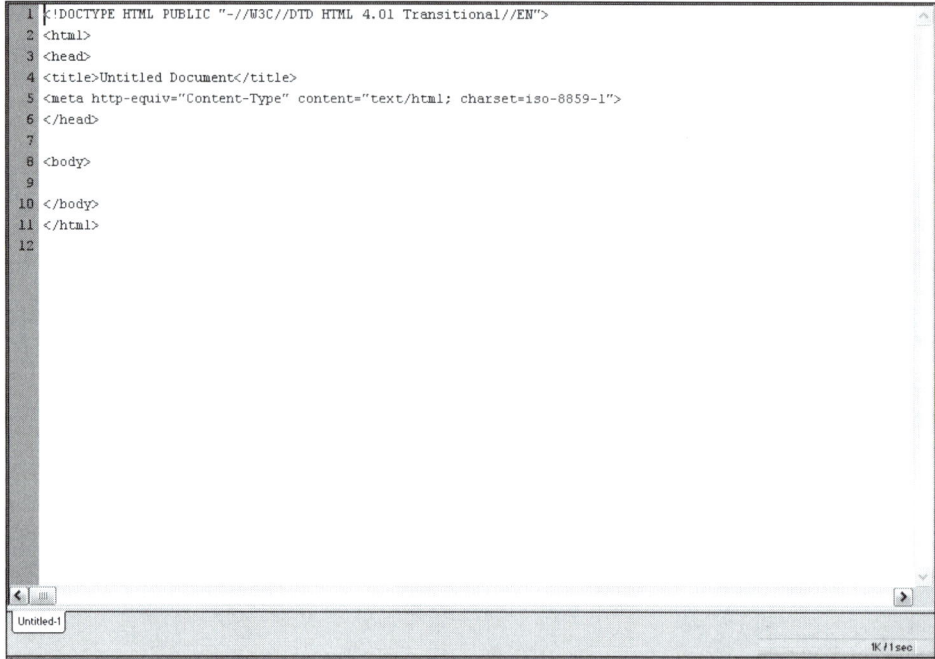

The editor window is the large panel on the right side of the Dreamweaver interface. All your coding will take place in this window.

2) Look at the Insert toolbar, located above the editor window.

The Insert toolbar contains all of the shortcut tools. The toolbar allows you quick access to some common HTML and ColdFusion tags. These tabs in the toolbar can help when you are just getting started (and even when you are an old pro) by inserting the correct code for a particular tag for you, without you having to do the actual typing. The tabs on the Insert toolbar provide buttons for creating tables, lists, and fonts, as well as some basic ColdFusion tags such as `<cfoutput>`, `<cfquery>`, and `<cfset>`. More advanced ColdFusion tags are also available, such as `<cfcookie>`, `<cfmail>`, and `<cfftp>`.

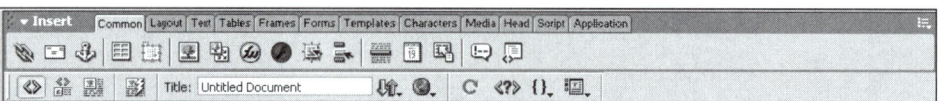

NOTE *Some of the tabs on the Insert toolbar vary based on the type of document you are developing. When you create a new ColdFusion document, the tabs for ColdFusion appear, as opposed to the ASP toolbars if you were creating an ASP document.*

3) Look to the left of the screen to see the central set of panels (Code, Files, and so on).

These panels give you access to the remainder of Dreamweaver's functionality. As you work through the lessons in this book, you will primarily be using the Files panel. There is a wealth of power in these toolbars. The rich feature set of Dreamweaver MX warrants an entire book of its own; this brief tour can't possibly do it justice.

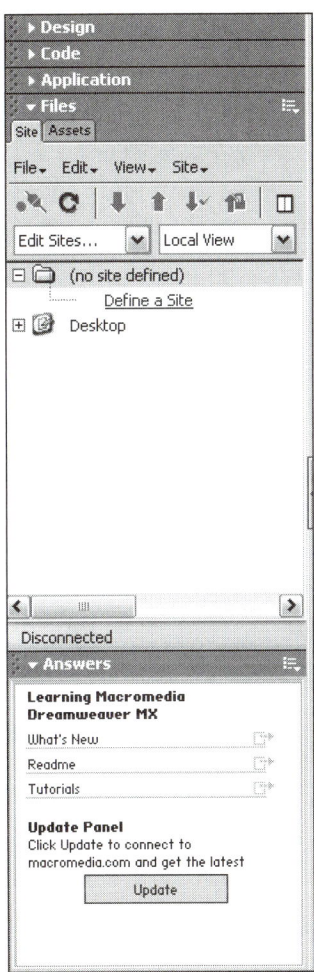

You now have a lay of the land, and are ready to take Dreamweaver MX out for a spin. Before you create your first ColdFusion page, you are going to set up Dreamweaver to work with the lesson files.

TIP *One tool that merits mentioning is the Reference tab on the Code panel. This tab contains references on Cascading Style Sheets, HTML, ColdFusion, JavaScript, ASP, JSP, and others. It is a great reference for the most seasoned programmer as well as a great tool to help beginners. You can get to it anytime by choosing Window > Reference.*

DEFINING A SITE

Dreamweaver uses sites as a way to make working on your files easier. A site is a collection of information pertaining to a particular Web site, including (but not limited to) the location of all the files used by the site. For now, all you need to be concerned with is the location of the files. So, by defining a site, you are telling Dreamweaver where all the files for a particular site are located. When you use sites, you don't have to browse to the files each time you access them; you just select a site from the Files panel.

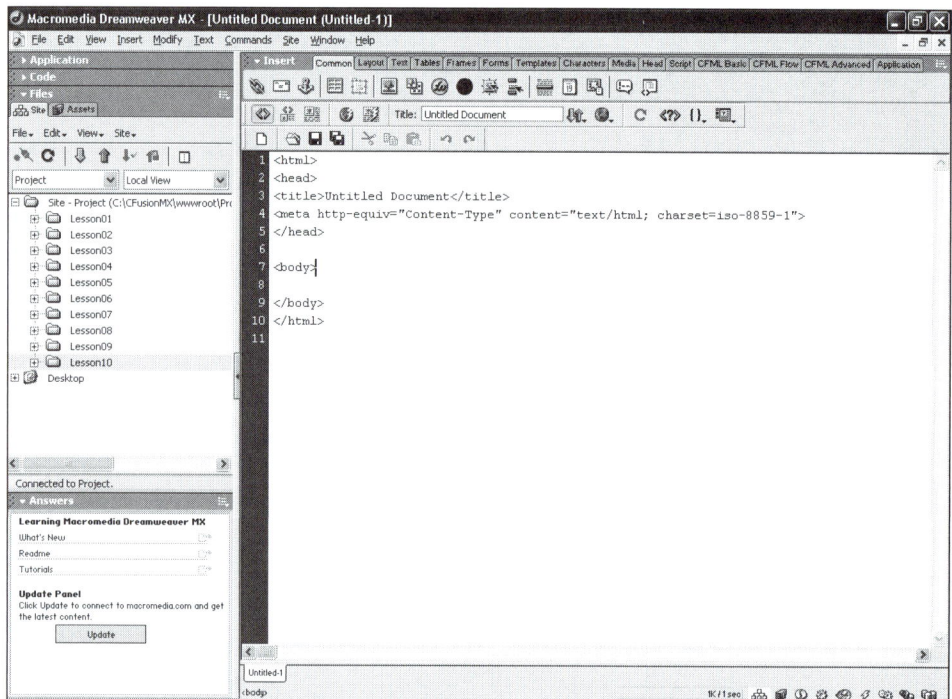

1) Create a folder called Project on your hard drive in the CFusionMX\wwwroot folder.

The wwwroot folder is where you put any files you want to work with when using ColdFusion MX. The default Web server that comes with ColdFusion MX is set up to serve documents located within this folder (often called the document root folder). Assuming that you accepted the default folder locations when you installed ColdFusion, your new folder should be located at C:\CFusionMX\wwwroot\Project.

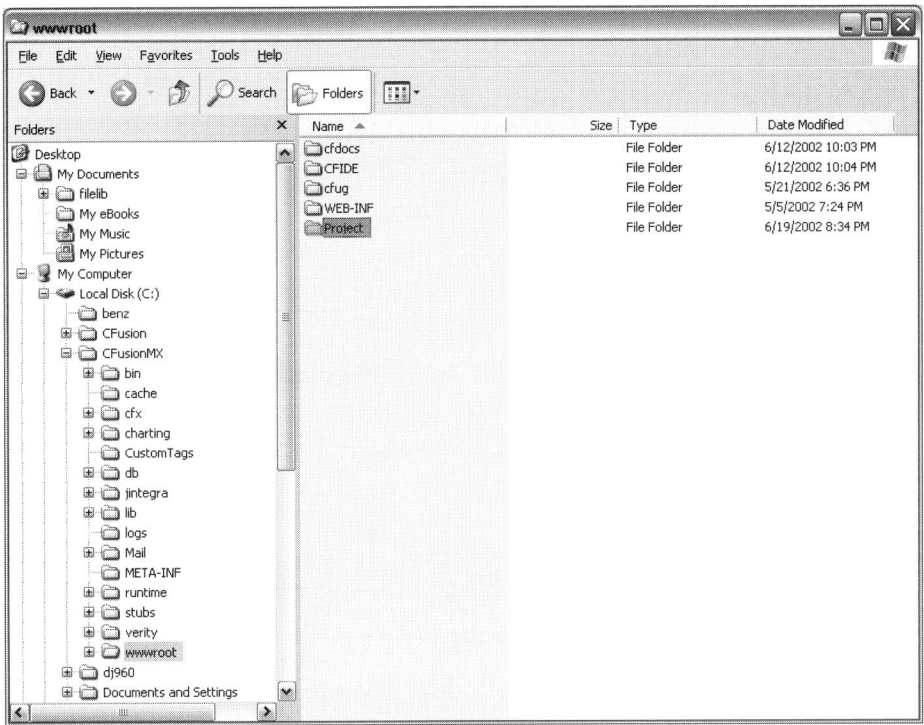

2) **Move all of the lesson folders from the CD (Lesson01, Lesson02, and so on) to the Project folder you just created.**

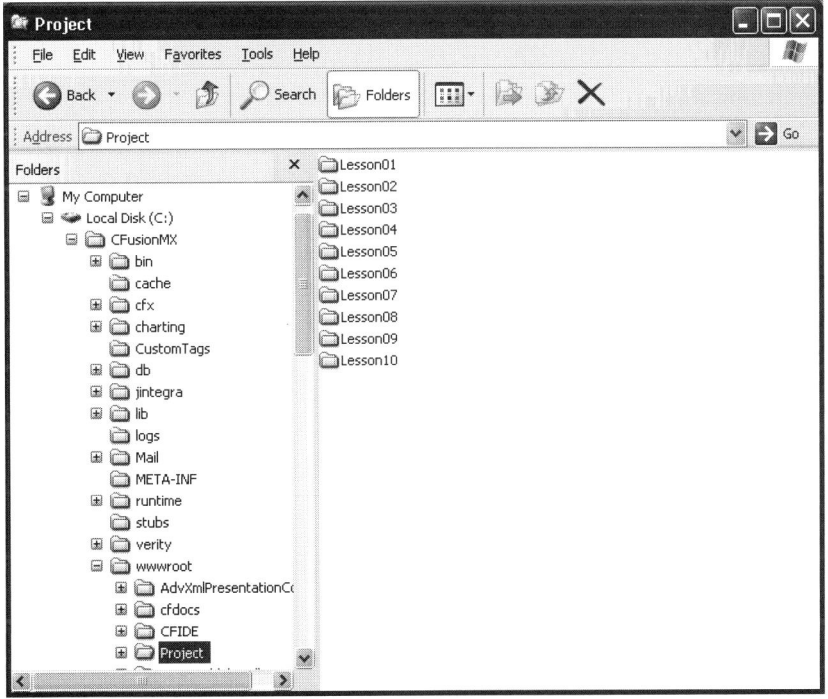

You now have all the project files needed for the book on your local hard drive.

3) Turn off the Read-only flag for the files you just moved.

Because the files you just copied came from a CD-ROM, the files in your Project folder will be set as Read-only files, which means that you won't be able to save any changes to them. The easiest way to make the files editable is to right-click on the Project folder in the Windows Explorer, choose Properties, uncheck the Read-only check box, and then click OK.

NOTE *Alternatively, you can leave the files in their Read-only state for now, and just turn the Read-only flag off for a particular folder or file when you start working on it.*

4) In Dreamweaver, choose Site > New Site from the main menu bar.

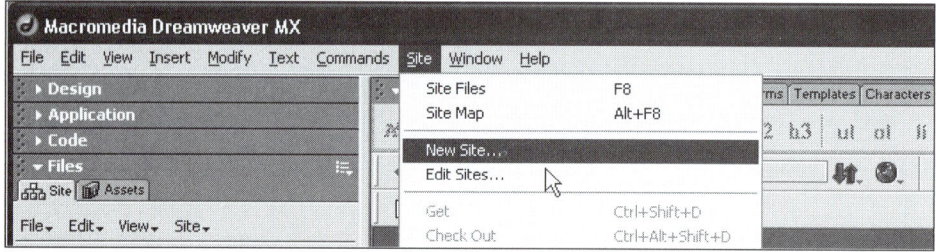

You will be presented with the Site Definition dialog. This is the first step to defining a site.

5) In the "What would you like to name your site?" text field, type *Project*.

TIP *You don't have to use the same name for the Site and the main folder that contains your site's files, but it's usually helpful to do so.*

6) Click Next.

You will be asked if you want to use a server technology with your site. ColdFusion is the default; however, if you look at your options in the drop-down menu, you will see that you are not limited to ColdFusion, but can also choose ASP, JSP, or PHP. Leave ColdFusion selected for now.

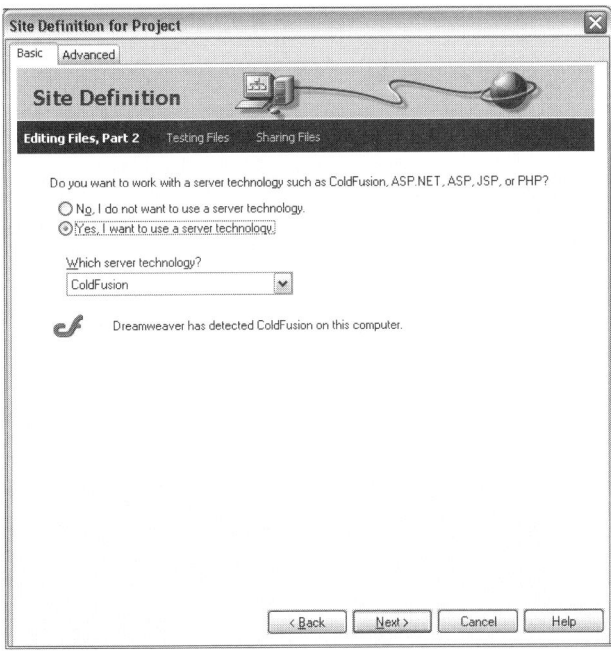

7) Click Next again.

You are now at the Editing Files, Part 3 window, and you need to tell Dreamweaver how you want to edit your files. In this case, you will be editing and testing your files locally, which is the default selection. The folder with which you are working should also appear in the file store box. Make sure it contains the path to the Project folder you created in Step 1 (assuming you chose the default locations when you installed ColdFusion, the correct path is C:\CFusionMX\ wwwroot\Project). You can use the folder icon to browse to that path if it is not already filled in for you.

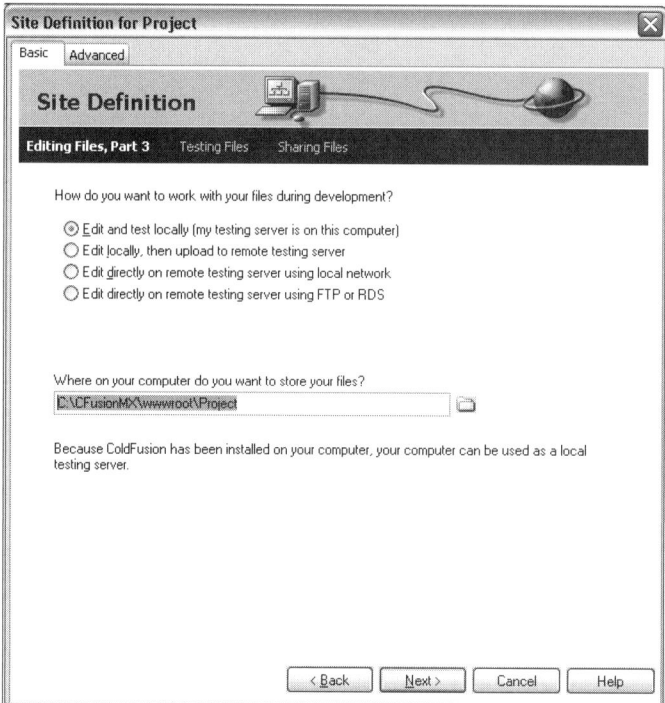

8) Click Next.

You now should define the URL for your site. This should already be entered for you; however, if it is not, enter the following URL: http://localhost:8500/project/.

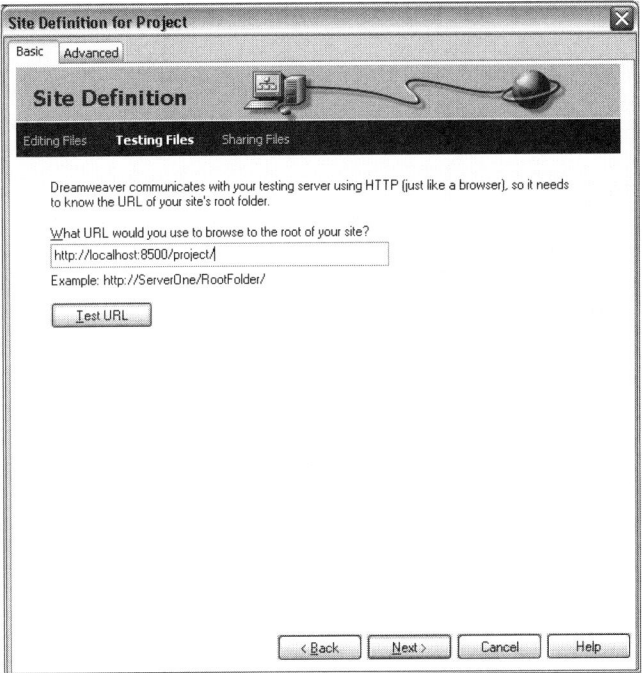

9) Click Next.

You need to tell Dreamweaver where to send the files when you are finished editing them. Because you are not copying these files to any other Web server, you can select No.

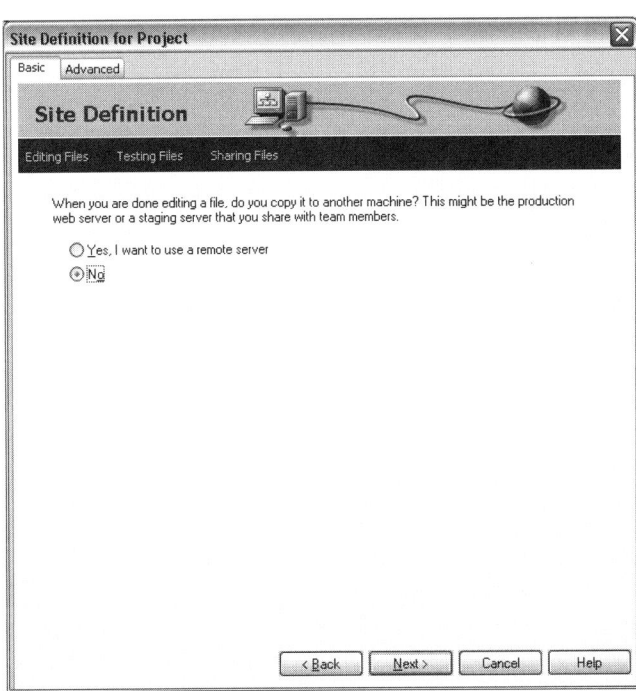

10) Click Next.

You are now prompted to confirm your settings. Look at the summary information and make certain it is correct. You can click Back to return to a previous page and make any changes necessary.

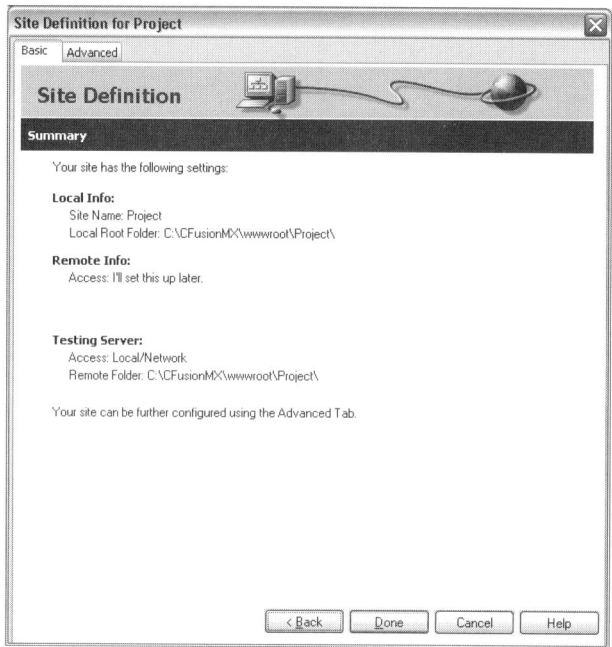

11) Click Done.

You have now created a site within Dreamweaver MX! Make sure that all the folders and files are now present in the Files toolbar, and that you are working with the Project site.

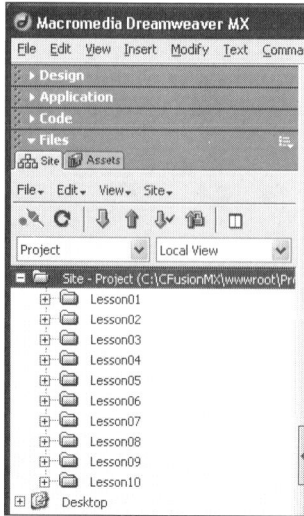

CREATING YOUR FIRST COLDFUSION PAGE

Now that you have gotten your feet wet, it's time to jump in and put that knowledge to use by creating your first ColdFusion page. You won't be doing anything fancy this time around, just creating a very basic page. It has become something of a tradition that when learning a new programming language, the first thing you do is to use the language to display a "Hello World!" message. It's a good way of getting started, and makes you a member of the programmers' club.

1) Still in Dreamweaver, choose File > New, and select Dynamic Page from the Category option and ColdFusion from the Dynamic Page option.

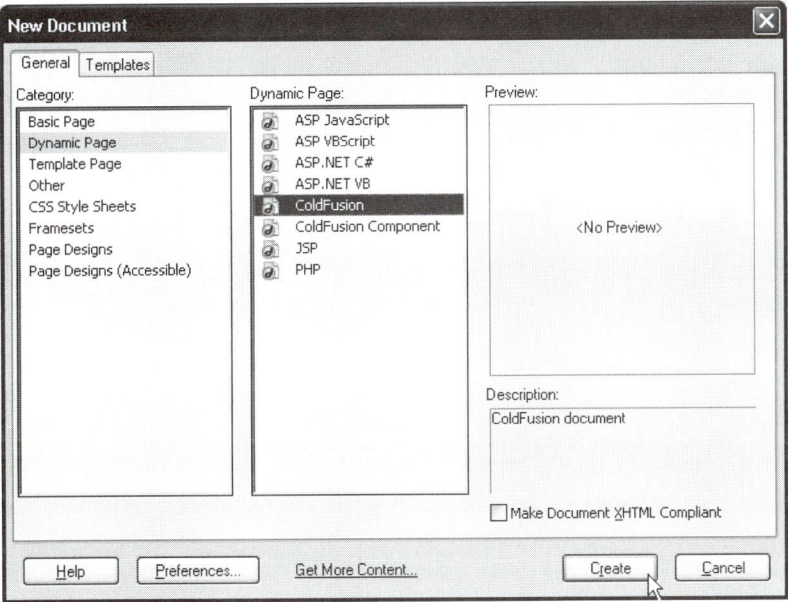

When you click Create, a new default template appears. This template already has the basic tags for an HTML document built into it, so you do not have to worry about adding them. You should also notice that the Insert toolbar now includes additional tabs specific to ColdFusion (CFML Basic, CFML Flow, and so on).

TIP *You can also create a default HTML document by pressing Ctrl+N.*

2) Position the cursor between the new document's <body> tags.

This puts you in the proper position for inserting the next few lines of code.

3) **Press the cfoutput button (marked "out"), located on the CFML Basic tab in the Insert toolbar.**

The dialog for the `<cfoutput>` tag appears. Sometimes you will fill in the fields in this dialog, but most of the time you can leave them all blank. Leave all the fields blank for now and click OK. At this point, you will notice that a pair of `<cfoutput>` tags have been added to the document.

TIP *Sometimes you will prefer to use the toolbar button as you just learned; at other times you may prefer to type the `<cfoutput>` tag yourself.*

NOTE *If you want, start over and try typing the `<cfoutput>` tag on your own. You'll notice that Dreamweaver anticipates what you're doing, allowing you to simply choose the tag from a drop-down list that appears while you're typing. The closing `</cfoutput>` tag also gets inserted for you automatically. These little timesavers really help you to write your code quickly and more efficiently.*

4) **Add some simple code between the `<cfoutput>` tags you just added, as in the following:**

```
<cfoutput>
  Hello, World!<br>
  The current time is: #TimeFormat(Now())#
</cfoutput>
```

```
 7  <body>
 8
 9  <cfoutput>
10    Hello, World!<br>
11    The current time is: #TimeFormat(Now())#
12  </cfoutput>
13
14  </body>
15  </html>
```

While it's easy to guess what this code is going to do, don't worry too much right now about totally understanding the syntax (like the funny-looking # signs). You'll learn about the details in the next lesson. For now, just trust us when we say that the `<cfoutput>` tag is one of ColdFusion's most important tools, and is probably the CFML tag that you will use most often. Anything that is put between a set of `<cfoutput>` tags will be interpreted dynamically by the ColdFusion Server. It doesn't matter what is between those tags—whether it be plain HTML text or a ColdFusion variable—the `<cfoutput>` tags tell ColdFusion that you want it to pay special attention to the block of code.

To put it another way, you generally place the `<cfoutput>` tag around any message or portion of a page that you want to be created on the fly each time the page is accessed. The `<cfoutput>` tag establishes the "blanks" that you would like ColdFusion to fill in as it prepares a page for delivery to the browser.

5) Click File > Save, and browse to C:\CFusionMX\wwwroot\Project\Lesson02\Start\.

The location of where you save your files is important. In order for you to be able to view your files in a browser you must save them in the CFusionMX\wwwroot folder, or a subfolder of the CFusionMX\wwwroot folder.

6) Type *helloworld.cfm* into the File name text box and then click Save.

You can also use Ctrl+S to save your files.

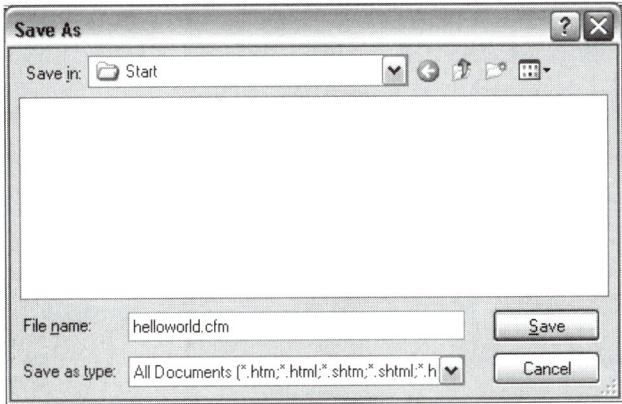

You have created and saved your first ColdFusion page. Now it's time to see what it does.

7) Open a browser, type http://localhost:8500/project/Lesson02/Start/ helloworld.cfm into the Address field, and press Enter.

You should see the Hello World! message displayed in the browser.

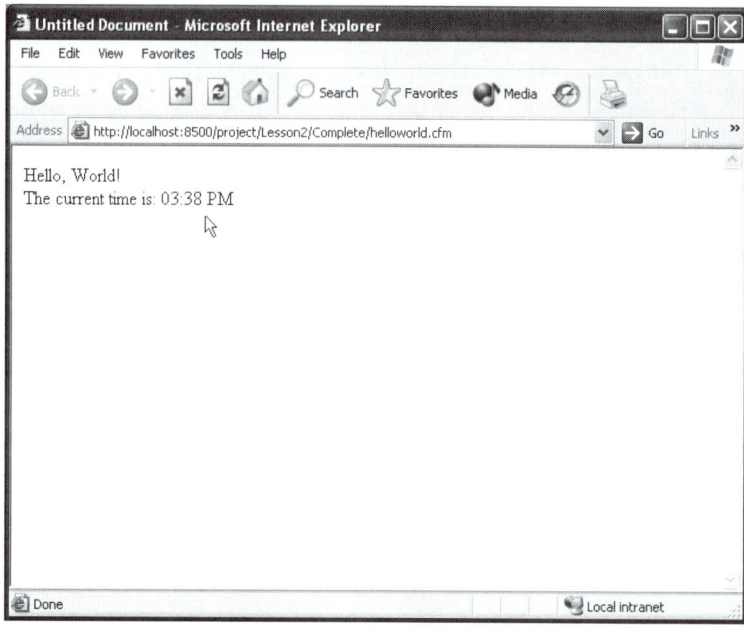

8) Click View > Source.

As you can see, the `<cfoutput>` tags are gone, and the strange-looking `#TimeFormat(Now())#` syntax has been replaced by the current time. ColdFusion has taken the information between the `<cfoutput>` tags, processed it, and returned the generated text in place of the `<cfoutput>` block.

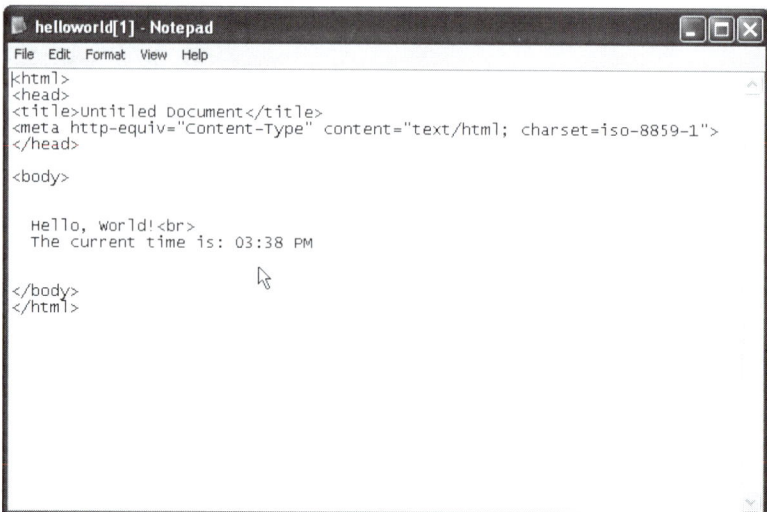

It wasn't hard at all to include dynamic, up-to-the-minute information (in this case, the current time) into an ordinary Web page. As you will learn in lessons to come, displaying information from databases is just as easy. That's when things start to get really interesting. In any case, congratulations! As a great master once said, you have taken your first step into a larger world.

You are now ready to move on to the bigger and better things that ColdFusion has to offer.

CHANGING THE PREVIEW IN BROWSER SETTINGS

Before you finish up with this lesson, let's make one small change to Dreamweaver's preferences. This change will make your ColdFusion development tasks even easier.

1) Still in Dreamweaver, choose Edit > Preferences.

The Preferences dialog appears.

2) Select the Preview in Browser category along the left side of the Preferences dialog.

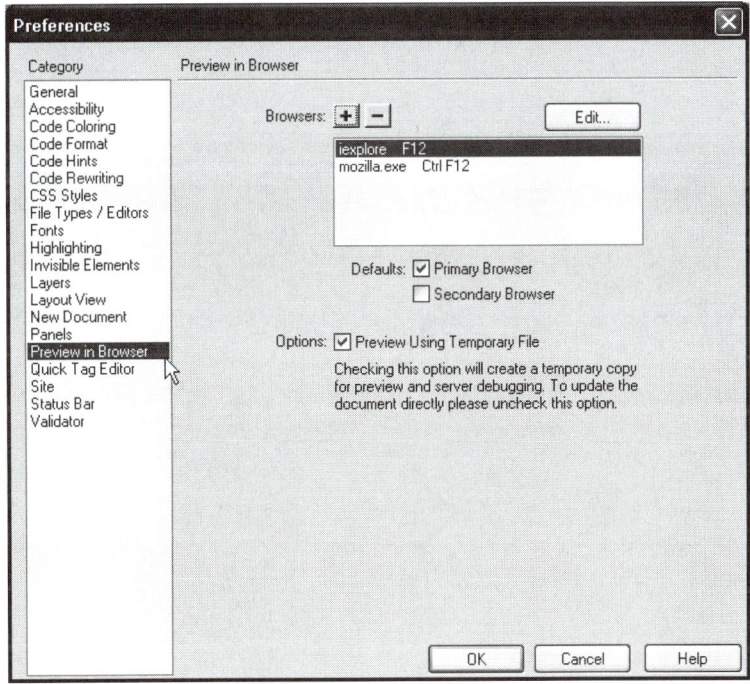

This portion of the Preferences dialog contains several settings for Dreamweaver's Preview in Browser feature. If you wish, you can also explore the other Preferences categories, to give you an idea of the types of things you can adjust later.

3) Uncheck the Preview Using Temporary File option.

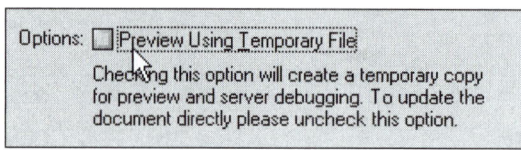

This option is helpful when working with static HTML files, but is less useful when working with dynamic documents that will be changing often. You can click the Help button if you want to find out more about how this option works. A good rule of thumb would be to uncheck this option if you will be working primarily with ColdFusion pages or other types of dynamic files, especially during development and testing.

4) Verify that your favorite browser is listed as the Primary Browser.

Dreamweaver will launch whatever browser is listed as the Primary Browser whenever you use the F12 keyboard shortcut in the future. If, for instance, you prefer Microsoft Internet Explorer, select its entry (it is usually listed as *iexplore*), then make sure the Primary Browser checkbox is checked. If you prefer Netscape Navigator or Mozilla, then select that entry and check Primary Browser.

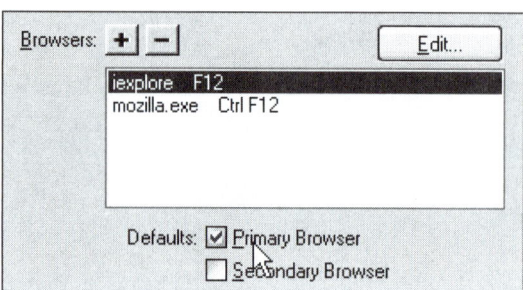

NOTE *If your favorite browser is not listed in the list of browsers in this Preferences dialog, you can click the Add Browser button (the plus sign near the top of the dialog), then fill in the Name and Application fields. The Application field should be the path to the browser's executable file (most likely an .exe file), which will be located in whatever folder you installed the browser software in.*

5) Click OK.

This saves your changes and closes the Preferences dialog.

6) Make sure the helloworld.cfm page is still open in Dreamweaver.

If it's not still open, go ahead and re-open it so that the code for the page is visible in the main editor portion of Dreamweaver's interface.

7) Press the F12 key.

Dreamweaver will launch your favorite browser, with the correct URL for the helloworld.cfm page already typed into the Address field for you. Your browser will display the page, without any need for you to type the URL for the page manually.

> **TIP** *If you prefer, you can also perform the same action using File > Preview in Browser.*

WHAT YOU HAVE LEARNED

In this lesson you have:

- Installed and configured Dreamweaver MX (pages 22–26)
- Explored Dreamweaver MX (pages 29–31)
- Set up project files on your local hard drive (pages 32–34)
- Created a site in Dreamweaver MX and installed the project files for this book within that site (pages 34–38)
- Output your first ColdFusion page (pages 39–43)
- Set up and used Dreamweaver's convenient Preview in Browser feature (pages 43–45)

variables and functions

L E S S O N 3

When you develop a Web site with ColdFusion, the two most important tools that you will use are variables and functions.

Variables are what you use when you want to store information to use later. Think of them as containers that hold pieces of information such as a name, a date, or a price. When you want to use a piece of information, you take it out of the container. The variable, or container, has a specific name; when you want to use the information in the variable, you reference it by that name.

You will use functions and variables in nearly every ColdFusion page you build. The ones you use in this lesson are the Now() and DateFormat() functions as well as a simple variable.

Functions offer a wide variety of built-in capabilities that can affect your templates in numerous ways. Each function performs a specific task, and has an expected result. The most commonly used functions are built right into the ColdFusion Server, although you can also create your own, or use functions that others have created.

In this lesson and the following lessons, we'll work on tasks related to the design, use, and maintenance of a Web site for a fictitious company called The Wireless Agent. Some of the activities will be related to the user experience, and some to the administrator; all involve using ColdFusion to handle different tasks.

WHAT YOU WILL LEARN

In this lesson you will:

- Learn what variables and functions are
- Create and display simple variables
- Create include files for sharing often-used variables
- Use Application.cfm to create simple global variables

APPROXIMATE TIME

This lesson takes approximately one hour to complete.

LESSON FILES

Starting Files:

Lesson03\Start\variables.cfm

Completed Project:

Lesson03\Complete\variables.cfm
Lesson03\Complete\CommonVariables.cfm
Lesson03\Complete\Application.cfm

USING VARIABLES

Variables are the bread and butter of ColdFusion development. You use them to store information such as names, products, values, details from a form, numbers, dates, times, and any other pieces of data that you will use later on. ColdFusion's variables are very flexible and easy to use: there's virtually no limit to what you can store in a variable, and you can name them just about any way you want.

Most of the time, you create a variable with the `<cfset>` tag, like so:

```
<cfset CompanyName = "The Wireless Agent">
```

As you can see, you provide two pieces of information to the `<cfset>` tag: the name of the variable that you want to create, and the information you want to store in the variable. The equals sign (=) is used to separate the two parts.

NOTE *ColdFusion variables are typeless, meaning that they do not have to be declared or created before you assign a value to them. Nor do they have to have a type specified. A ColdFusion variable can hold nearly any type of information.*

Once information has been stored in a variable, it's really easy to output or display the information in the variable later in your code. For instance, assuming that the `CompanyName` variable has been created near the top of a ColdFusion page (using the `<cfset>` tag just shown), you could output the company name later on in the same page as follows:

```
<cfoutput>Welcome to #CompanyName#.</cfoutput>
```

As you can see, in order to display the value of a variable, you use the `<cfoutput>` tag to tell ColdFusion to look for variables in that section of the page. Then, within the `<cfoutput>` block, you place # signs around the name of the variable. When a user visits the page, ColdFusion will replace the variable's name with its value before sending the page back to the browser.

NOTE *If you forget to include the* `<cfoutput>` *tags, then ColdFusion won't give special treatment to the # signs, which means that the variable names (including the # signs) will be displayed in the page.*

Let's take a look at how this works in an actual ColdFusion page. In this task, you will learn how to create and display variables, making it easier to keep your site fresh and up to date.

1) Open Dreamweaver MX, drill down in the folder structure to the Project site by selecting Project > Lesson03 > Start, and open the variables.cfm file.

The variables.cfm template will appear in the editor window.

NOTE *If you would like to look at the file on which you're about to work, open a Web browser, type http://localhost:8500/Project/Lesson03/Start/variables.cfm into the Address field, and press Enter. You should see the Wireless Agent Web page appear. You're about to add to this page, using some simple variables.*

2) At the very top of the page, type the following lines of code:

```
<cfset CompanyName = "The Wireless Agent">
<cfset CompanyPhone = "(800) 555-WIRE">
<cfset InBusinessSince = "3/18/1969">
```

Feel free to press the Enter key a few times after you enter these lines, to separate the code you just added from the regular HTML code in the page.

```
1  <cfset CompanyName = "The Wireless Agent">
2  <cfset CompanyPhone = "(800) 555-WIRE">
3  <cfset InBusinessSince = "3/18/1969")>
4
5
6
7  <!DOCTYPE HTML PUBLIC "-//W3C//DTD HTML 4.0 Transitional//EN">
8
9  <html>
10 <head>
11     <title>thewirelessagent.com</title>
```

3) **Scroll down to the main message area of the page, which is a `<td>` block near line 110, and insert the following code:**

```
<!---Insert message to user here --->
<cfoutput>
  <h3>Welcome to #CompanyName#</h3>
  <p>We've been serving the community since #InBusinessSince#.
  We hope you enjoy our site.</p>
  <p>You can also reach us by phone at #CompanyPhone#.</p>
</cfoutput>
```

```
109             <td width="10" bgcolor="99b5e2"></td>
110             <td width="522" height="300" bgcolor="99b5e2" valign="top" class="
111
112               <!--- Insert message to user here --->
113               <cfoutput>
114                 <h3>Welcome to #CompanyName#</h3>
115                 <p>We've been serving the community since #InBusinessSince#.
116                 We hope you enjoy our site.</p>
117                 <p>You can also reach us by phone at #CompanyPhone#.</p>
118               </cfoutput>
119
120             </td>
121             <td width="10" bgcolor="99b5e2"></td>
122           </tr>
```

NOTE *Note that these comments use three dashes at the beginning and end of the line, where ordinary HTML comments use only two. When you use three dashes, you create a CFML comment, which is extra-special because ColdFusion will remove it from the page before it sends the final HTML code back to the browser. In general, CFML comments are the best type of comments to use when creating a ColdFusion page. You'll be able to see them, but your users won't.*

4) **Save your work (File > Save).**

You can also use Ctrl+S as a shortcut for saving your work.

5) **View the page you just created with your browser.**

The easiest way to view the page is to simply press F12 in Dreamweaver. This will launch your Web browser with the current page already displayed. You can also view the page by opening your Web browser on your own, and then visiting the page you just edited by entering the following URL: *http://localhost:8500/Project/Lesson03/Start/variables.cfm*.

NOTE *Before you use the F12 key, make sure that you have disabled the Preview Using Temporary File option in Dreamweaver's preferences. Instructions for disabling this option are at the end of Lesson 2.*

In any case, you will see that ColdFusion has included the values of the variables you created in the message area of the page. Instead of hard-coding the company name, phone number, and other information in the body of the page, you were able to easily create variables for this information at the top of the page. This will make it easier to correct the page later if the company name, phone number, or other information were to change.

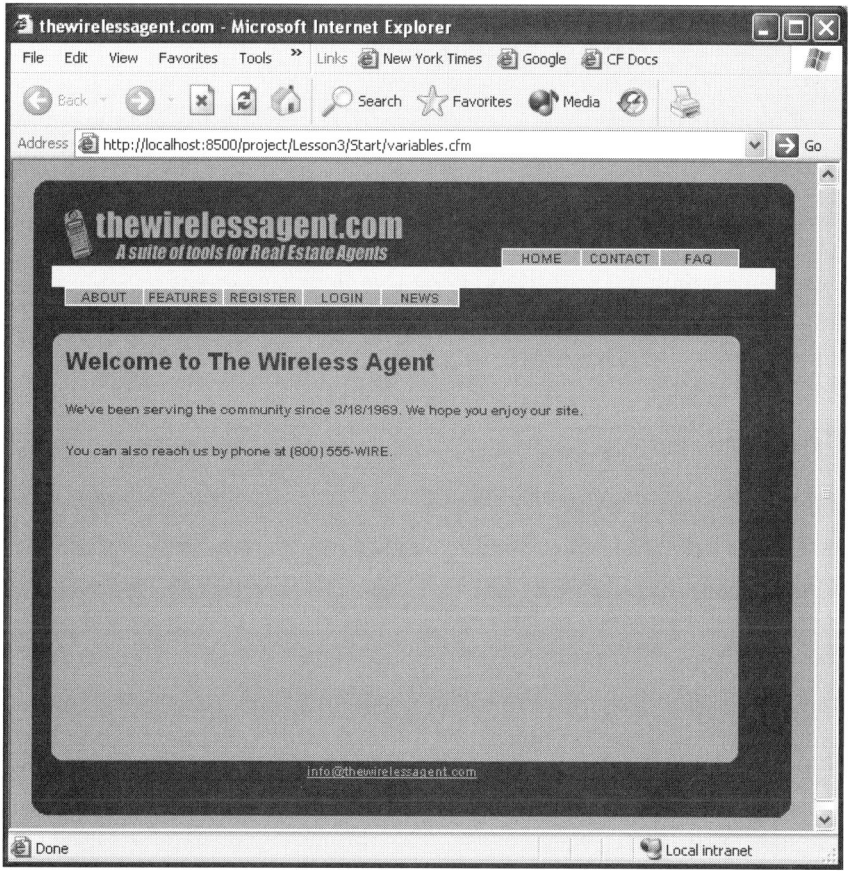

Clearly, this was a very simple example, but it already is exhibiting one of the advantages of using an application server product like ColdFusion to build your pages. By using variables, you were able to separate the information being displayed (in this case, the company information in the variables) from the visual presentation of the information. Whenever there is a relatively clean separation of information (or logic) and presentation, your application becomes easier to keep track of, edit, and maintain.

Don't close variables.cfm yet.

TIP *To make your life easier later, it is a wise idea to name your variables with clear, unambiguous names. With the variable* `CompanyName`, *for instance, there is little doubt as to what piece of information the variable holds. However, if you had simply named the variable* `Name`, *you might be confused later. In general, a good rule of thumb is to create your variable names out of at least two English words, using capital letters to make the variable names easier to read.*

NOTE *Variable names can contain numbers and letters but not spaces, and the first character needs to be a letter. Variable names can also include underscores; some people like to use underscores to separate the English words that make up a variable name. So, if you wish, feel free to use variable names such as* `company_name` *instead of* `CompanyName`.

There are a number of words that should not be used as variable names because they have special meaning to ColdFusion. For a complete list, see Chapter 1 of the CFML reference manual from Macromedia. You can view it online at http://livedocs.macromedia.com/cfmxdocs/CFML_Reference/Expressions.jsp.

USING FUNCTIONS

Functions are another important part of ColdFusion. They give you the ability to accomplish different types of tasks, such as changing text from uppercase to lowercase, displaying the current time, or performing mathematical operations. There are a lot of functions included with ColdFusion—far more than we will be able to discuss here. But once you learn how to use a few functions, you'll be well on your way to understanding how to use them all. You will find that ColdFusion's rich and flexible set of functions plays an important role in making your pages truly dynamic.

Every ColdFusion function performs some kind of processing, and makes the result of that processing available to you as its *result*. Of course, the type of information returned in the result varies depending on the nature of the function, but every ColdFusion function will return something. That's the whole reason why you call the function in the first place: to get the result of whatever processing the function knows how to provide.

For learning purposes, one of the most helpful functions to look at first is the `Now()` function. The `Now()` function is wonderfully simple. Whenever this function is called, it returns the current date and time (according to the server's internal clock). So, whenever you want to display the current date or time (or some related concept, like the current year or day of the week), the `Now()` function will nearly always be involved.

There are two principal ways to call a function. The first way to is to include it in a `<cfset>` tag when setting a variable; when the page is visited, the function's result is automatically stored in the variable. Just like the `<cfset>` tags you saw earlier, the name of the variable is specified first, followed by the = sign. Then type the name of the function you want to use, followed by a set of parentheses, like so:

```
<cfset CurrentMoment = Now()>
```

This will create a variable called `CurrentMoment`, which holds the current date and time (or, more precisely, the exact date and time at the moment the `Now()` function was called). You can then output the value of the variable in a `<cfoutput>` block in the basic same way that you worked with the `CompanyName` and other variables earlier in this lesson:

```
<cfoutput>The current date and time is: #CurrentMoment#</cfoutput>
```

The other principal way to call a function is to refer to it directly in a `<cfoutput>` block using # signs, just as with a variable:

```
<cfoutput>The current date and time is: #Now()#</cfoutput>
```

In either case, the end result of either of these `<cfoutput>` blocks will be to display the current date and time. Let's see how this works in an actual page, by adding the `Now()` function to the variables.cfm file you were working with a moment ago.

1) Add the following line to the top of variables.cfm, under the `<cfset>` tags you already placed there:

```
<cfset CurrentMoment = Now()>
```

```
1  <cfset CompanyName = "The Wireless Agent">
2  <cfset CompanyPhone = "(800) 555-WIRE">
3  <cfset InBusinessSince = "3/18/1969">
4  <cfset CurrentDate = Now()>
5
6
7
8  <!DOCTYPE HTML PUBLIC "-//W3C//DTD HTML 4.0 Trans:
```

2) Switch to Dreamweaver's Code and Design View by choosing View > Code and Design from the main menu.

While you will most frequently do your ColdFusion coding using the Code view alone, it is sometimes helpful to use Code and Design view to make it easier to locate the correct place to display variables in your pages. In this view, you can make changes to your page either by typing the HTML or CFML code in the Code portion of the screen, or by making the changes visually in the Design portion of the screen (which is a kind of editable preview area).

So, while this view doesn't really have anything to do with variables specifically, this is a good place to introduce the feature, because it will make the next change easier to complete.

3) In the Design portion of the view, click your mouse on the comment icon at the top right of the page (under the FAQ link).

This will cause the Code portion of the view to scroll down to the `<td>` block that corresponds to the blank area of the page (under the company logo) where the current date will be displayed. The Code view's cursor is now at the correct spot for adding text or variable output to the blank area of this page.

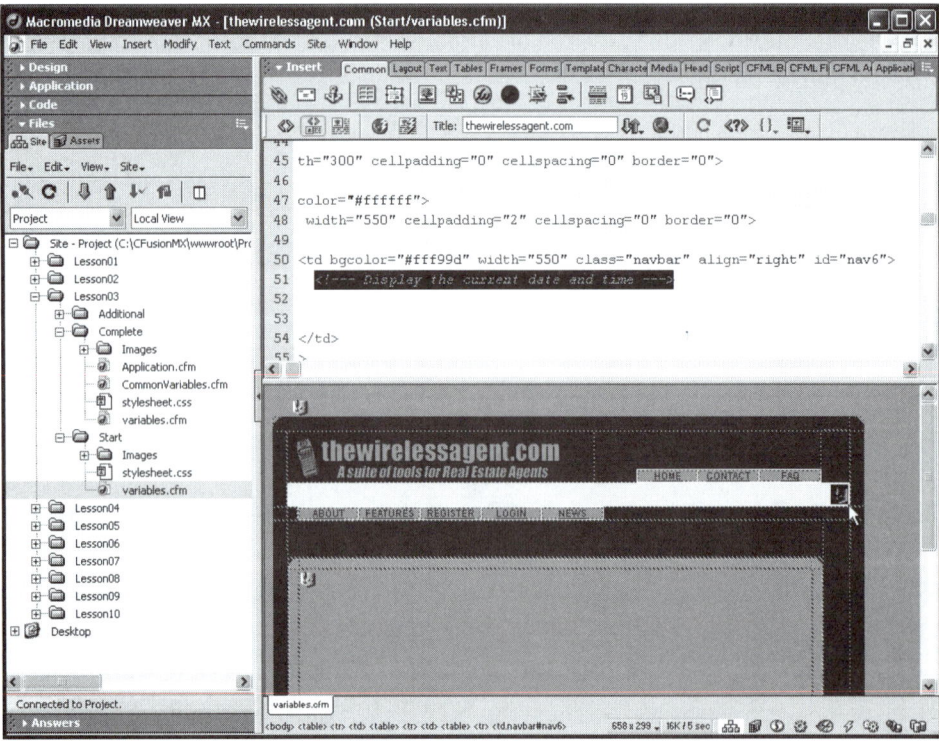

4) In the Code portion of the view, add the following code to the `<td>` that represents the blank area:

```
<!---Display the current date and time --->
<cfoutput>#CurrentMoment#</cfoutput>
```

5) Save your work and view the results in your browser as you did at the end of the last task.

TIP *If the previous version of the variables.cfm page is still open in your browser, you can simply use your browser's Refresh or Reload button to see your changes.*

The blank area at the top of the page will now contain the current date and time. It's in a slightly strange-looking format (which you will learn to fix in a moment) but the important thing to understand is that the page will now always include the exact date and time whenever the page is visited.

NOTE *If you want, you can go back and experiment with outputting the `Now()` function directly in the blank area of the page, rather than creating the `CurrentMoment` variable first and then outputting the variable's value. You can do it either way in your actual pages; except under the most extreme conditions, the code will perform just as efficiently either way.*

The value that `Now()` returns is what ColdFusion calls a *date/time value*. Simply put, a date/time value is a single value that represents a particular moment in history. To pinpoint a moment in history, you need two pieces of information: the date, and the exact time. So, date/time values (sometimes called date/time objects) always include both the date and the time. When you display a date/time value using `<cfoutput>`, it always appears in the following form (with different numbers depending on the actual date, of course):

```
{ts '2003-10-05 19:04:32'}
```

You'll learn how to make this look more appealing to human eyes in the next exercise, so don't close variables.cfm yet.

NOTE *If you're interested, the format used for this default date/time display is the same as that used by the JDBC and ODBC specifications. That makes sense, considering that one of ColdFusion's most important duties is to talk to databases.*

Hey, before you move on, think about what happened in this exercise. This is the first time you've seen a page that changes on its own from day to day (and minute to minute, and second to second). It's a humble beginning, but kind of cool nonetheless!

USING SEVERAL FUNCTIONS TOGETHER

You just learned how to use the `Now()` function to get the current date and time, as reported by the built-in clock on the server machine. It was easy enough to display the result, but the way the date and time are formatted isn't very user-friendly. In this exercise, you'll learn how to use the `Now()` function together with two other functions called `DateFormat()` and `TimeFormat()`. These will allow you to present the current date and time in a way that's more familiar and pleasing to the eye.

If you look in the CFML Reference section of the ColdFusion documentation, you will find the syntax for these two functions listed as follows:

```
DateFormat(date [, mask])
```

and

```
TimeFormat(date [, mask])
```

Unlike the `Now()` function, these two functions accept arguments. Arguments are pieces of information that you pass to a function. The function then performs some kind of operation on the information and returns the result. In the case of `DateFormat()` and `TimeFormat()`, each of these functions requires that you pass a date/time value as the first argument. The functions quickly format the date/time value into a nice-looking representation of the date (or time), returning the formatted version as the result.

As you can see, each of these functions also accepts a second argument called `mask`. The `mask` argument allows you to specify exactly how the date should be formatted. You use special characters in the mask to indicate whether you want the month to appear before the day or vice versa, whether you want the day of the week to be included, and so on.

> **NOTE** *Note the square brackets in the documented syntax for the functions; these brackets indicate that the mask argument is optional. All this means is that ColdFusion will format the date (or time) according to the mask if you provide one. If you don't, a default format will be used.*

This isn't the time or the place to get into all the special characters that you can use a date mask, but the basic idea is that you come up with something like `m/d/yyyy`, where the `m` represents the month (that is, a number from 1 to 12), the `d` represents the day of the month, and the `yyyy` represents the year (as a four-digit number). You can also use `mmmm` if you would prefer that the month be spelled out as a word, or `dddd` if you want to see the day of the week spelled out as a word. There are similar special characters for use in time masks: `h` for the hour, `mm` for the minute, `ss` for the second, and `tt` for AM or PM.

Consider the following examples, which assume that it's quarter past noon on October 5 in the year 2003, and assuming that a variable called `CurrentMoment` has been created using the `Now()` function as demonstrated in the last exercise:

`DateFormat(CurrentMoment, "m/d/yyyy")` displays the date formatted as **10/5/2003**.

`DateFormat(CurrentMoment, "dddd, mmmm d, yyyy")` results in **Saturday, October 5, 2003**.

`TimeFormat(CurrentMoment, "h:mm tt")` results in **12:15 PM**

`TimeFormat(CurrentMoment, "h:mm:ss tt")` results in **12:15:53 PM**

Okay, let's see how this works in practice. In this exercise, you'll add the `DateFormat()` and `TimeFormat()` functions to the variables.cfm page you worked on in the last exercise.

1) Make sure variables.cfm is still open.

We're just going to add the `DateFormat()` and `TimeFormat()` functions to the code we already placed in this document.

2) **In the code for the blank area of the page, edit the code you placed there earlier so that it looks like the following:**

```
<!---Display the current date and time --->
<cfoutput>
  #DateFormat(CurrentMoment, "mmmm d, yyyy")#
  #TimeFormat(CurrentMoment, "h:mm tt")#
</cfoutput>
```

```
<td bgcolor="#fff99d" width="550" class="navbar" align="right">

  <!--- Display the current date and time --->
  <cfoutput>
    #DateFormat(CurrentMoment, "mmmm d, yyyy")#
    #TimeFormat(CurrentMoment, "h:mm tt")#
  </cfoutput>

</td>
```

3) **Save your work and view the updated page by pressing F12 or reloading the page in your browser.**

Great! The current date and time are now displayed at the top of the page, formatted in the user-friendly fashion that most users would expect.

By the way, when providing an argument to a function, you are free to either provide a variable as you have already learned, or to provide another function directly. You have already seen it done this way:

```
<cfset CurrentMoment = Now()>
<cfoutput>#DateFormat(CurrentMoment, "dddd, mmmm d, yyyy")#</cfoutput>
```

You could also do it this way, creating a second variable called `CurrentDate` which contains the formatted date, so that the `<cfoutput>` block doesn't need to refer to the `DateFormat()` function:

```
<cfset CurrentMoment = Now()>
<cfset CurrentDate = DateFormat(CurrentMoment, "dddd, mmmm d, yyyy")>
<cfoutput>#CurrentDate#</cfoutput>
```

This would achieve the same thing, except without creating the intermediary `CurrentMoment` variable:

```
<cfset CurrentDate = DateFormat(Now(), "dddd, mmmm d, yyyy")>
<cfoutput>#CurrentDate#</cfoutput>
```

You could also do everything in place, without creating any variables at all:

```
<cfoutput>#DateFormat(Now(), "dddd, mmmm d, yyyy")#</cfoutput>
```

In other words, all that really matters is that the `Now()` function gets called, that the `DateFormat()` function gets called on its result, and that the final result gets outputted in a `<cfoutput>` block. Whether you do that in one, two, or three steps is up to you.

NOTE *As a very general rule, ColdFusion can output the value of a variable a bit faster than it can execute a function. So, if you plan on using the result of a function many times in the same page, there may be a tiny performance gain if you create a variable for the result once near the top of the page and then refer to the variable throughout the rest of your code, rather than calling the function repeatedly throughout the page. That said, ColdFusion's functions are generally extremely quick and efficient, so you shouldn't worry about this too much.*

USING VARIABLES AND FUNCTIONS IN SEPARATE FILES

This lesson has shown you how to create simple variables in the top portion of a ColdFusion file and then display the variables in the remainder of the page. There are many advantages to using variables in this way. For instance, the `CompanyName` and `CompanyPhone` variables can ease maintenance by keeping all information about the company at the top of the page. If the company's name or phone number changes (not so infrequent or improbable in today's day and age), the information can just be changed at the top of the page without anyone having to wade through all the HTML code.

Okay, so that's a help, but what if the company name appears on 10 pages, or 100? Wouldn't it be nice to be able to create the variables in just one file, and have any changes automatically reflected throughout all pages in your application?

Well, I have some good news for you. It turns out that it's really easy to set up such a situation. First, you place all the `<cfset>` tags in a separate file, all by themselves. Let's say you name the file CommonVariables.cfm. You can then have all your other pages *include* the code in that file, using a ColdFusion tag that you haven't seen yet: `<cfinclude>`. This tag is extremely easy to use, and opens up a whole new set of possibilities for making your code more organized and easier to maintain.

The `<cfinclude>` tag takes one attribute called `template`, which is the name of the file that you want to include. When ColdFusion encounters the `<cfinclude>` tag, it automatically processes all the code in the included file, just as if all the code were in one file. So, all you have to do is to use `<cfinclude>` near the top of each page to include the CommonVariables.cfm file; you can then refer to the variables from the included file in the remainder of the page. This is a really simple but powerful way to create "global" variables that are shared by an entire application.

NOTE *Actually, the included file can contain any ColdFusion code that you want, not just `<cfset>` tags. No matter what ColdFusion syntax is contained within the file, it will be executed whenever a `<cfinclude>` tag includes it.*

Let's see how this works in practice. In this exercise, you will move your `<cfset>` tags to a separate file. You will then include the code in the new file with the `<cfinclude>` tag.

1) Make sure the variables.cfm file is still open; re-open it if not. Use File > New to create a new ColdFusion document.

These will be "source" and "destination" documents, respectively.

2) Delete everything in the new document so that it is completely empty.

Because this new document is only going to contain `<cfset>` tags (rather than any HTML code that should be sent to the browser), you want to start with a blank file that doesn't contain the usual `<html>`, `<body>`, and related tags.

3) Copy the `<cfset>` lines from the top of variables.cfm and paste them into the new document.

The idea here is to isolate the `<cfset>` lines within their own document, where they can be easily reused by other ColdFusion pages.

4) **Save the new document as CommonVariables.cfm, in the same folder as variables.cfm.**

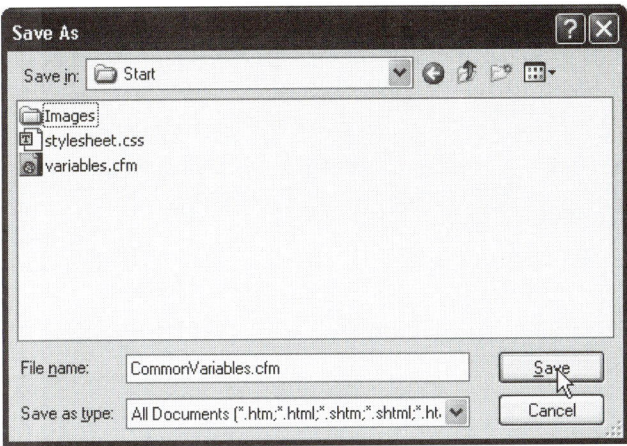

5) **Go back to variables.cfm and replace the `<cfset>` lines with the following line:**

   ```
   <!---Include commonly-used variables --->
   <cfinclude template="CommonVariables.cfm">
   ```

6) **Save your work and view the updated version of variables.cfm with your browser.**
You should see the exact same result that you did before. Even though the `CompanyName`, `CompanyPhone`, and other variables are being created in the CommonVariables.cfm file, you can refer to them directly in variables.cfm. If you had 10 pages that displayed the company name and other information, you would just need to place the `<cfinclude>` line at the top of each page; you could then refer to the variables anywhere after the `<cfinclude>` tag. If the company name or phone number changes, you need only make the change in CommonVariables.cfm; the new values will be reflected by all the other pages the next time they are visited.

Congratulations—you're on your way to writing easier to maintain code!

INCLUDING CODE AUTOMATICALLY WITH APPLICATION.CFM

Hey, we've come this far—let's go even one step more toward making it even easier to share those variables amongst all your pages. Let's say you have 100 pages in your application. You've just learned that you can make your most commonly used variables available to each of the pages by putting the `<cfinclude>` tag at the top of each file. But what if you don't even want to do that much work? Isn't there some way to tell ColdFusion to include the CommonVariables.cfm automatically, without having to add that `<cfinclude>` tag to every single page?

The answer is to create a special file called Application.cfm. If a file is named Application.cfm, ColdFusion gives it special treatment; it automatically executes all the code in the file whenever any of the other pages in your application are visited.

Here's how it works. Whenever you visit a ColdFusion page (for instance, the variables.cfm page that you created in this lesson), ColdFusion checks to see if there is a file called Application.cfm in the same folder. If so, the code in Application.cfm is automatically executed before the requested page is executed (just as if there were a `<cfinclude>` tag at the top of the requested page).

NOTE *In more sophisticated applications, the Application.cfm file often contains a `<cfapplication>` tag to ColdFusion's Session, Client, or Application variable features. You will learn about these features in Lesson 8.*

It's easy to see this in action. In this exercise, you will create an Application.cfm file that creates the `CompanyName`, `CompanyPhone`, and other variables. You will be able to refer to these variables anywhere in your other files, without needing to include the file with the `<cfinclude>` tag.

1) If it's not open already, open the CommonVariables.cfm file that you created in the previous exercise.

This is the file that contains the `<cfset>` lines that create our helpful variables.

2) Save the file as Application.cfm, in the same folder as variables.cfm.

Use File > Save As to do this.

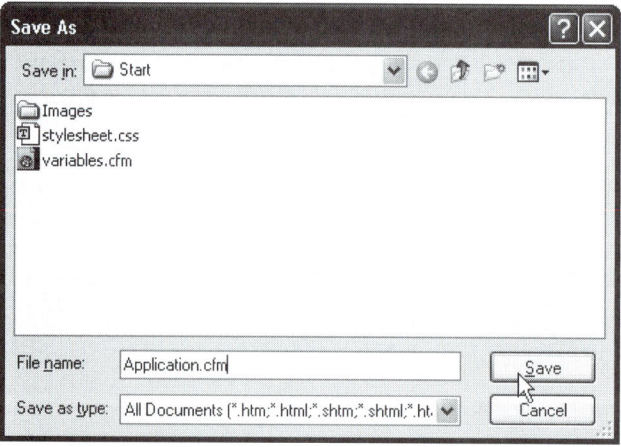

NOTE *Make sure to name of the Application.cfm file exactly as shown, with a capital A. If ColdFusion is running on a non-Windows machine, the case of the filename is important, so you should get in the habit of paying attention to the case of your filenames. That way, you won't run into any problems if you move your application files to a UNIX or Linux server later.*

3) Remove the `<cfinclude>` tag from the variables.cfm file.

ColdFusion is going to automatically include all the code in the Application.cfm file on its own, so it's important to remove this `<cfinclude>` tag now. Otherwise, the code in Application.cfm file will be included twice—once automatically, and once by `<cfinclude>`.

NOTE *It's important to keep in mind that every line of code in Application.cfm will be executed every single time anyone visits any of your pages. That's generally fine if Application.cfm just includes simple `<cfset>` tags (even if there are quite a few of them), because ColdFusion compiles your files into efficient Java files behind the scenes. In general, you should just make sure that isn't any complex code in your Application.cfm file. You'll learn more about all this in Lesson 8.*

4) Save your work and visit variables.cfm again with your browser.

The page should still behave just as it did before. The variables in Application.cfm can be used in any other page in the same folder. As you start to build more sophisticated pages, you will rely on Application.cfm to handle any type of processing that should be applied to all the pages of a particular project.

NOTE *If ColdFusion doesn't find an Application.cfm file in the current folder, it also looks in the parent of the current folder. If no Application.cfm file is found there, it looks in that folder's parent, and so on until an Application.cfm file is found, or until there aren't any more parent folders to look in. This allows you to organize all of the files for an application using any number of folders and subfolders, as long as they are all contained within a single top-level folder. All you have to do is place a single Application.cfm file in the top-level folder; it will be automatically included in every page request. And don't worry, ColdFusion is able to do all this without slowing things down!*

NOTE *At this point, the CommonVariables.cfm file is no longer being used, so you can delete it if you want. Another option would be to leave the file intact and put a `<cfinclude>` tag in Application.cfm that includes CommonVariables.cfm, instead of putting the series of `<cfset>` tags in Application.cfm itself. ColdFusion doesn't care one way or another; just do what makes sense for you and your application.*

UNDERSTANDING COLDFUSION'S VARIABLE SCOPES

Whew! You learned a lot about using variables in this lesson. There's one more idea I'd like to discuss while we're on the subject, to get you ready for the next few lessons.

ColdFusion provides a number of different *scopes* for creating variables. These scopes can be thought of as different storage areas within ColdFusion's memory. There are approximately seven variable scopes that you are likely to use in your ColdFusion applications, each behaving in a slightly different way.

In general, the main reason why you choose to store a variable in one scope rather than another is to control how long the variable remains stored in ColdFusion's memory. The seven variable scopes listed below can be broken into two general groups. The scopes in the first group are **short-term** variable scopes; variables stored in these scopes are available only while ColdFusion is processing the current page. The scopes in the second group are **longer-term** variable scopes; variables stored in these scopes continue to live (or "persist") in ColdFusion's memory between page requests, allowing you to create applications that keep track of what users are doing as they move around in your applications.

Short-term variable scopes:

- **Ordinary variables**, which are usually created using the `<cfset>` tag. This is the most common type of variable. You saw this type of variable used throughout this lesson.

- **URL variables**, which are automatically set when special information is included in the URL for a page. You will learn about these variables in Lesson 4.

- **Form variables**, which are set by the browser when a user submits a form. You will learn about these variables in Lesson 5.

Longer-term variable scopes:

- **Session variables**, which are shared by all pages in an application, but are kept separately for each user. These variables are good for storing information about the current user's visit, like the contents of a shopping cart, or remembering information about their most recent search. You will learn about these variables in Lesson 8.

- **Application variables**, which are shared by all pages in an application and are good for maintaining things like counters or other application-wide statistics. You will get a very brief introduction to these variables in Lesson 8.

- **Client variables**, which are similar to session variables except they are stored more permanently on the server. These variables are good for remembering a user's preferences or ID number. These variables aren't discussed specifically in this book, but you use them in much the same way as you use Session variables.
- **Cookie variables**, which are similar to client and session variables, except the information is stored on the browser machine, rather than being under ColdFusion's direct control. Again, you won't use these variables in this book's examples, but you use them in the same basic way you use Session or Client variables.

NOTE *There are some other variable scopes that aren't discussed in this book. These additional variable scopes include the Server scope, the Request scope, the CGI scope, and the This scope. Generally speaking, these variable scopes are for specialized or advanced tasks. Depending on the types of pages you are building, you may not ever have cause to use them. In any case, if you are curious about these additional scopes, you can find more information about them in the ColdFusion documentation.*

WHAT YOU HAVE LEARNED

In this lesson, you have:

- Learned the uses of variables and functions (pages 46–48)
- Used simple variables to hold and display commonly used information (pages 49–51)
- Used `Now()`, `DateFormat()`, and `TimeFormat()` to display the current date (pages 52–59)
- Learned to create variables in separate files to ease maintenance (pages 59–61)
- Created an Application.cfm file to make variables available to all other pages (pages 61–63)

retrieving data from databases

LESSON 4

Most sophisticated Web applications store or access some type of information in a database. Depending on the application, a database might be used to store information about products for sale, news headlines, customer profiles, or membership information. No matter what type of information you are working with, ColdFusion makes it easy to retrieve, display, and update the information in nearly any way you wish.

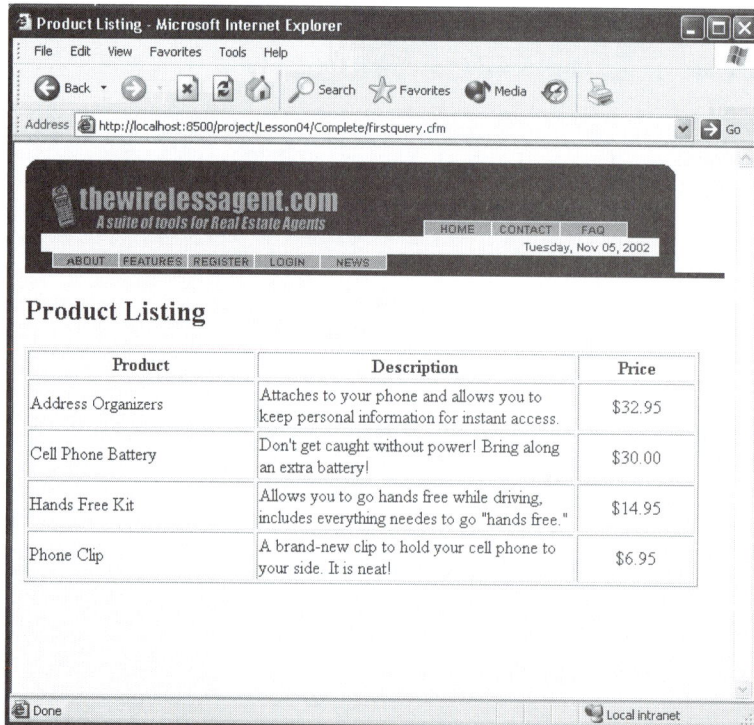

ColdFusion makes it easy to retrieve and display information stored in a database.

In this lesson, you work with a Microsoft Access database (although ColdFusion works equally well with enterprise-level products such as Microsoft SQL Server and Oracle databases). The database holds information about products for sale at the Wireless Agent site. You use ColdFusion to retrieve and display information about these products, effectively publishing the database on the Web.

WHAT YOU WILL LEARN

In this lesson, you will:

- Learn what databases are and some common uses for them
- Create a ColdFusion data source
- Use SQL to return information from a database
- Output information returned from a database
- Create a set of product list and detail pages

APPROXIMATE TIME

This lesson takes approximately two hours to complete.

LESSON FILES

Media Files:
None

Starting Files:
Lesson04\Start\products.mdb
Lesson04\Start\header.cfm

Completed Project:
Lesson04\Complete\firstquery.cfm
Lesson04\Complete\header.cfm
Lesson04\Complete\productdetail.cfm
Lesson04\Complete\productlist.cfm

UNDERSTANDING DATABASES

A database is a must for nearly any site that serves up dynamic content. When you register for services at a site, your information is most likely stored in some type of database. Similarly, any time you search for a product on a Web site (powered by ColdFusion or not), you are probably accessing a database that tracks all of the company's products.

So, what's a database? In theory, it's just about anything that allows you to store and find pieces of information. A phone book can be thought of as a database of names and phone numbers; so could an old-fashioned Rolodex. In today's world, of course, people usually use the word *database* to refer to computer software specifically designed to store and retrieve data. There are many popular database products on the market today, including Microsoft's Access and SQL Server products, Oracle's line of database server products, and the open-source MySQL database server.

All of these products allow you to store just about any type of information that you wish, no matter what your needs. Pretend for a moment that you've chosen which database software you are planning to use for a project, and have just sat down with the other people working on the project to discuss what to do next. In broad strokes, a typical team's interaction with a database product can be divided into three phases:

- First, a database structure is designed, appropriate for holding whatever type of information you plan to store and collect. As a ColdFusion developer, you may be doing the database design as a part of the creation of your Web application. In other situations, the database design may already exist, created by someone else at some other time.

- Second, SQL code (which you'll learn about shortly) is written to interact with the database. This interaction usually includes retrieving information from the database, and may also include inserting new information into the database or modifying what's already there. Each of these interactions is usually called a *query*. It will come as no great surprise, then, to learn that most database interactions in ColdFusion are performed using the `<cfquery>` tag.

- Third, tuning and maintenance is performed on the database over time. Tuning generally means creating *indexes* to speed up the database's performance, or adjusting the database software's use of memory. Maintenance generally means performing backups and keeping the database software up to date.

This book doesn't attempt to cover all three of these phases. In general, ColdFusion is only used for the second phase (the actual retrieving and updating of information). For purposes of this book, we are going to use a pre-existing database design as if it had been created for us by someone on our team. The database design is included on the CD-ROM, and will be used for the first time shortly.

NOTE *To put it another way, you don't need to know how to design a database (the first phase) to work with ColdFusion, but you do need to know enough SQL to get information in and out of an existing database (the second phase). You will begin to learn the basics of SQL in this book.*

NOTE *If you have never worked with a database before, you may need to consult a different book to introduce yourself to the basics of the other phases. In particular, if you are starting a brand-new Web development project soon, you will need to understand something about the first phase. Most database software includes documentation that covers basic database design, so try looking there first.*

In any case, today's database products are all centered around the concepts of *tables*, *fields*, and *records*. Think of a table as being a lot like a spreadsheet in Excel (or some other spreadsheet application). As you know, spreadsheets are split up into columns and rows. Typically, you use the columns to track different types of information (descriptions, amounts, dates), and you use the rows to record specific occurrences of the information (the actual amounts and actual dates).

Database tables are not much different. They, too, are divided up into columns and rows; the columns are often called *fields*, and the rows are often called *records*. Each column (field) has a name that describes its purpose; perhaps `ProductName`, `UnitPrice`, and `Description` if the table is designed to store product information, or `FirstName`, `LastName`, and `PhoneNumber` if it's designed to store information about people. Each row (record) represents a specific occurrence of the information (a specific product, or a specific person).

A typical database design will contain at least a few different tables (perhaps 5, perhaps 50), each tracking a different type of information (products, people, shopping carts). Each table usually contains one column that holds a unique ID number for each record; these ID numbers are used to associate records in one table with certain records in the others (all the products purchased by a particular person, or sold by a particular company).

NOTE *There are also other types of database products, which don't necessarily use tables, columns, and rows as the main means of thinking about information. For instance, there have been a few different* object database *packages available over the years, and a number of native XML packages have been introduced lately. Some products combine all three concepts. That said, the venerable table/column/row model is still the predominant model (by an extremely long shot), and is the only one discussed in this book.*

CREATING A DATA SOURCE

Assuming that the database design is already in place (see phase one in the previous section), it's time to start using ColdFusion to retrieve and display information from the database. The first thing you need to do is to use the ColdFusion Administrator to create a *data source* that tells ColdFusion where to find your new database. Depending on the type of database software you are using, you might tell ColdFusion to find the database in a particular file (that's how it works with Microsoft Access). With higher-end database products, you provide ColdFusion with the name of a database server; the database server is responsible for dealing with your requests for data as efficiently as possible (that's how it works with Oracle, Sybase, and SQLServer).

In any case, the ColdFusion data source can be thought of as a way of giving your database a simple, universal name. In your ColdFusion pages, you will simply refer to the data source using this name; the ColdFusion server will take care of doing whatever is necessary to actually interact with the database.

Let's create a data source for the example database file included on the CD-ROM for this book.

1) **On your local c:\ drive, create a folder called *databases*.**

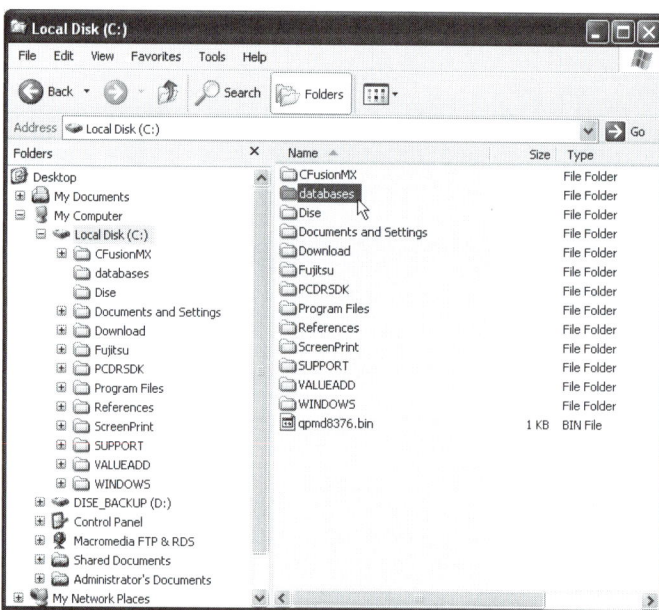

You will store this book's database file in this folder.

2) **Move the products.mdb file to the c:\databases folder you just created.**

The products.mdb file is located on your CD in the Lesson04\Start folder.

TIP *It's important to note that we're not putting the database file anywhere within the wwwroot folder. You don't want people to be able to access the file in its raw form, so it should always be kept out of the wwwroot folder to prevent people from downloading it directly.*

3) Make sure the products.mdb file is not marked as Read-only.

Because the database file you just copied came from a CD-ROM, Windows may be considering it to be a Read-only file, which would keep you from being able to make changes to the database later. The easiest way to solve this problem is to right-click on the products.mdb file in the Windows Explorer, choose Properties, uncheck the Read-only check box, and then click OK.

4) Open ColdFusion Administrator by clicking Start > Programs > Macromedia ColdFusion MX > ColdFusion Administrator.

You will use the ColdFusion Administrator each time you need to work with a new database.

5) Enter your password and then click Login.

You created your password when you installed ColdFusion Server.

6) Select Data Sources from the navigation panel under the Data & Services heading.

After you have selected Data Sources, the Data Sources page opens, and you'll see a summary of all the data sources that currently exist. Assuming that you installed the sample applications when you installed ColdFusion, the following data sources are probably listed: cfsnippets, CompanyInfo, and exampleapps.

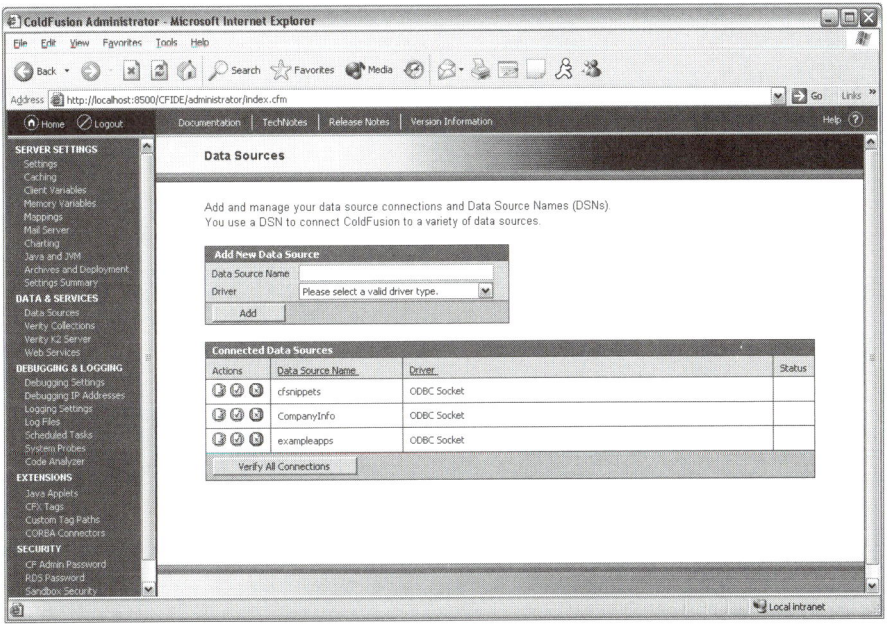

RETRIEVING DATA FROM DATABASES

TIP *The sample applications can be accessed on the home page of the ColdFusion Administrator, under Getting Started.*

7) Under Add New Data Source, type *products* into the Data Source Name field.

You can use just about any name that you wish when creating a data source, but it usually makes the most sense to give it the same name as the database for which you are creating the data source. In this case, we are using an Access database file called products.mdb, so it's sensible to use *products* for the data source name (that is, the database filename without the extension). If you were using an Oracle or SQL Server database called Celebrities, you might use *celebrities* as the data source name.

As you start to build more applications and additional data sources, meaningful and standardized names can help keep things straight. That way, six months from now, you won't find yourself scratching your head and wondering what a particular data source is for.

8) Select Microsoft Access from the Driver drop-down menu.

You must select the proper database so ColdFusion will know how to connect to your database. If you select something other than Microsoft Access, it will not work.

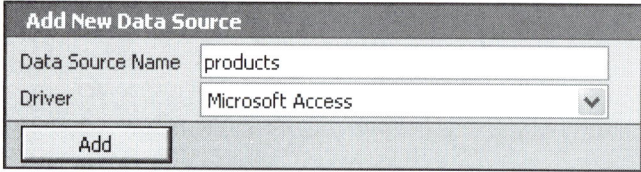

9) Click Add.

You will see a screen where you can enter additional information about the database, including the actual location of the database.

10) Click the Browse Server button next to the Database File field.

At this point, you may see a prompt asking you for permission to install some additional browser components. If so, just click the OK or Yes button so that ColdFusion can present you with a tree-based representation of your machine's drives.

TIP *If you prefer, you can just type the location of the database file (c:\databases\products.mdb) manually instead of clicking the Browse button. If you choose to do this, skip the next step.*

11) Find and select your products.mdb file, and then click Apply.

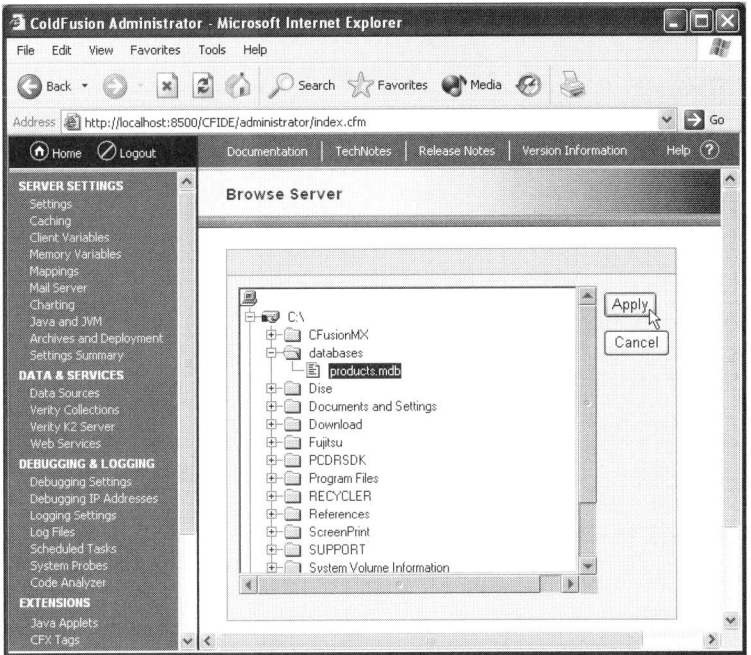

Your database should be in C:\databases. After you have found it and clicked Apply, you will return to the configuration page for the new data source, and the Database File field will be filled in with the location of your products.mdb file.

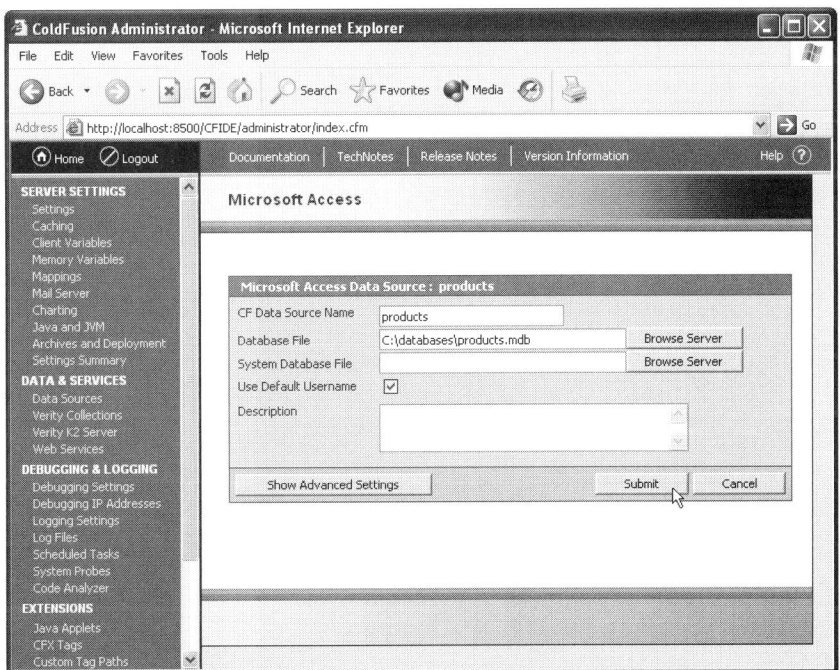

NOTE *The example database you're using for this book is very simple; it's not secured, and thus doesn't require a password. If you were using a database that did require a password or other security information, you would now click the Show Advanced Settings button, where you could enter whatever additional information was necessary.*

12) Click Submit.

This is the final step in creating your data source. After you have clicked Submit, you will be sent back to the initial Data Sources screen. If the data source is set up correctly, the status contains the value **ok** and you should see a message in green at the top that reads "datasource updated successfully."

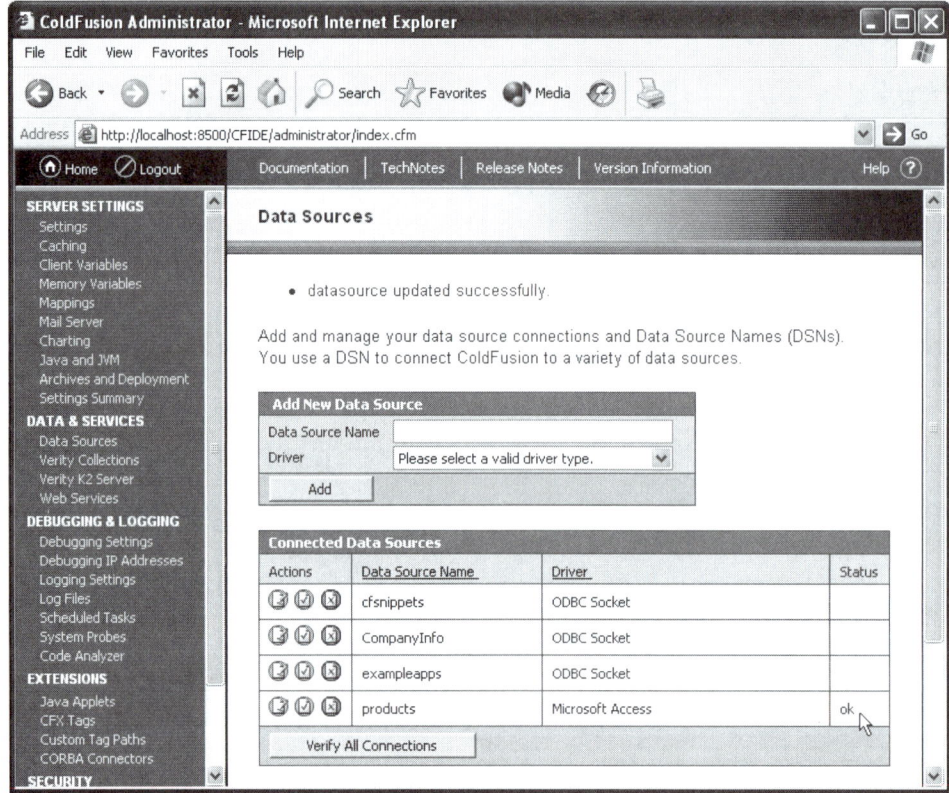

NOTE *If the data source was not set up properly, you will see the word "error" under the status field, and a long error message in red at the top. The error message will help you understand what the specific problem is. Common problems include specifying the incorrect location for the database, or forgetting to specify any location.*

You are now ready to use ColdFusion to access information from the database.

EXPLORING A DATABASE IN DREAMWEAVER

Now that a data source has been set up in the ColdFusion Administrator, you can use Dreamweaver MX to take a look at the tables and data stored in the database. In this exercise, you will learn how to use Dreamweaver's Databases panel to explore the example database for this book.

1) Open Dreamweaver MX and select the Project site in the Files panel.

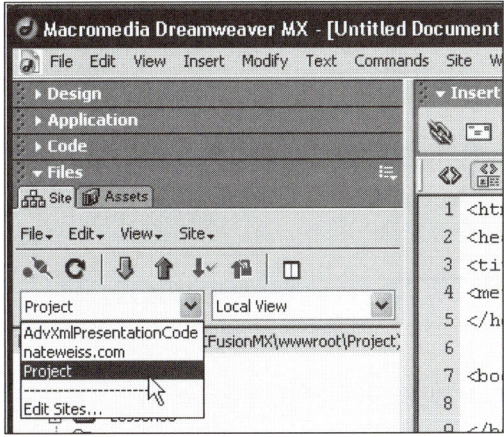

Dreamweaver needs to connect to the ColdFusion server to be able to display information about your database. Because Dreamweaver stores information about how to connect to the ColdFusion server along with each site definition, you need to have the Project site selected.

2) Open the header.cfm page from the Lesson04\Start folder in the Project site tree.

NOTE *It actually doesn't matter which file you open; any ColdFusion file will do. All that matters is that you open one of the ColdFusion (.cfm) files within the Project site.*

3) Show the Databases panel by choosing Window > Databases.

By default, the Databases panel appears as a tab within the Application panel group. When it first appears, it will probably show a checklist with five steps (three of which will be checked off already), as shown in the next step. Click the Refresh button (at the top right corner of the Databases panel) if you don't see the list.

TIP *You can also use the Ctrl+Shift+F10 keyboard shortcut to open the Databases panel.*

4) Click the "RDS Login" link within the checklist.

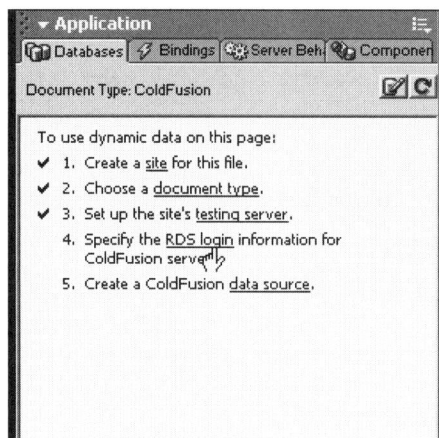

The Login to ColdFusion Remote Development Services (RDS) dialog appears. Dreamweaver needs to know the password to use when connecting to the ColdFusion server to get information about your databases.

5) Provide your ColdFusion RDS password and click OK.

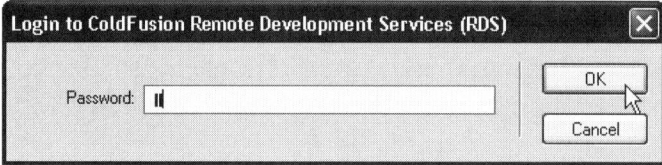

You chose the RDS password while you were installing ColdFusion MX. If you followed the instructions in Lesson 1, the RDS password is the same as the password you use for the ColdFusion Administrator. If you decided to create a different RDS password during installation, use that password now.

After you click OK, the checklist that appeared previously in the Databases panel should be replaced with a tree-like representation of each database that has been registered as a data source in the ColdFusion Administrator. One of the top-level items in the tree should be marked products, for the data source you created earlier in this lesson.

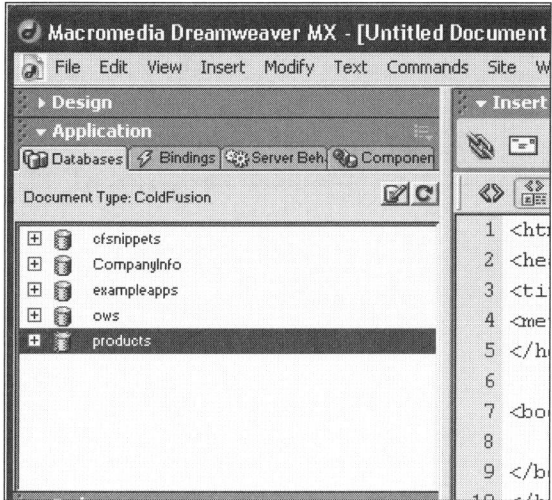

6) **Expand the "products" item in the tree.**

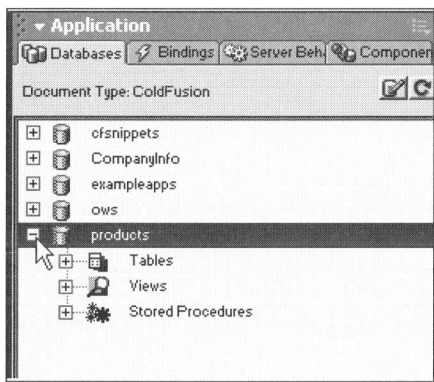

Three items appear within the "products" item: Tables, Views, and Stored Procedures. The Tables item is the most important one, and the only one you'll be exploring in this book.

7) **Expand the Tables item.**

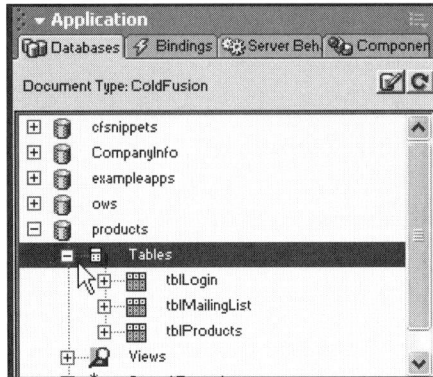

Three items appear within the Tables item: tblLogin, tblMailingList, and tblProducts. These tree items correspond to the three tables in this book's example database. Of the three, the tblProducts table is the most important and the one you will use most often. The other two tables will not be used until you get closer to the final few lessons.

8) **Expand the tblProducts item.**

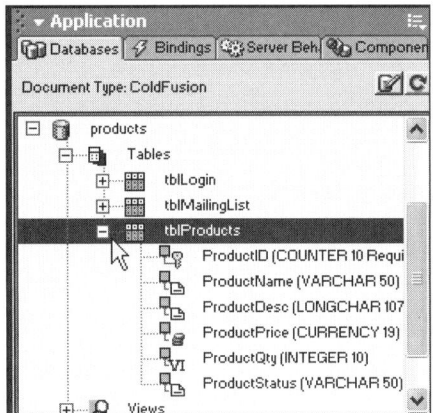

Six items appear within the tblProducts item, representing the six columns that make up the tblProducts table in the database. The columns in the tblProducts table are as follows:

- **ProductID**—this column contains a number for each row of data in the table. The database automatically takes care of creating a unique number for each row (in this case, for each product).

- **ProductName**—this column contains a short name for each product. Each product's name can be up to 50 characters long.

- **ProductDesc**—this column contains a description for each product. The descriptions can be of virtually any length.

- **ProductPrice**—this column contains the current price for each product. Each price can be any number; the database automatically takes care of making sure each price is stored with two digits after the decimal point.

- **ProductQty**—this column represents the current number of items in stock for each product.

- **ProductStatus**—this column contains a textual description of each product's status (such as in stock, back-ordered, and so on).

9) **Right-click on the tlbProducts item, then choose View Data.**

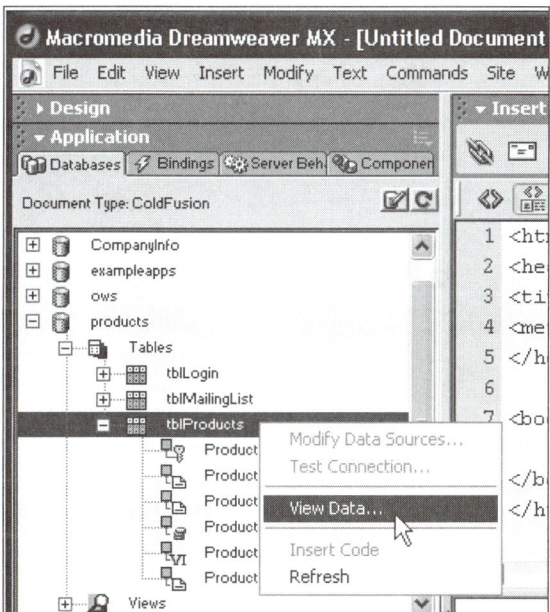

The View Data window will appear, which gives you a quick and convenient way to take a look at the data in a particular database table.

NOTE *You can't change the data from the View Data window, or add or remove columns. The View Data window is just a simple way to look at the information that's currently sitting in a table.*

10) **Look through the information in the tblProducts table.**

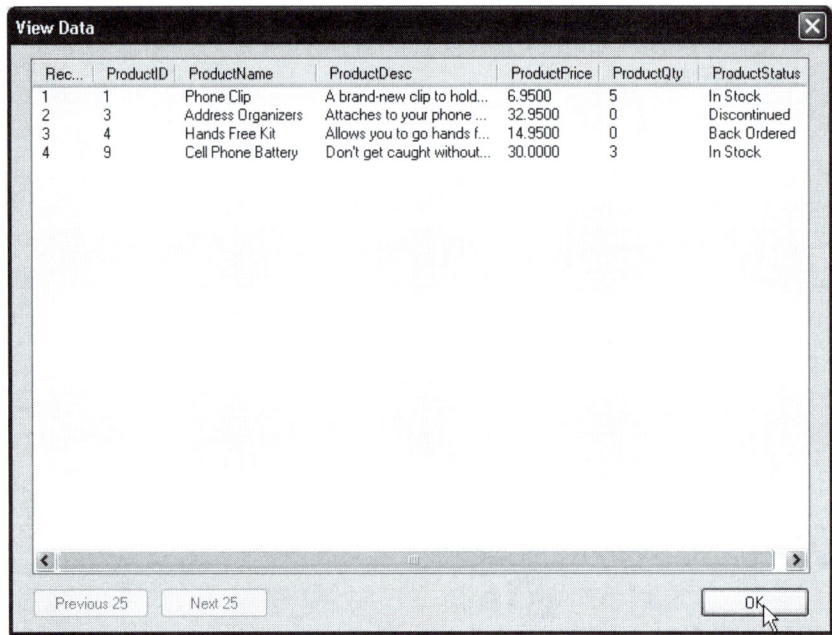

Just make yourself a bit familiar with the columns and rows of data, so that you'll know that things are working when you create ColdFusion pages that retrieve and display this data later. If you wish, you can also look through the information in the tblLogin and tblMailingList tables, even though they won't be used until the last few lessons in this book.

GETTING INFORMATION FROM A DATABASE

To get information out of your database, you will use simple syntax from two languages: ColdFusion and SQL. The ColdFusion part of the code is what establishes a connection to the database; the SQL code is the part that the database understands, so it knows what information you are looking for.

1) **Open Dreamweaver MX and select the Project site.**

If you haven't worked on any other sites in Dreamweaver MX since you last worked on the Project site, the site should still be open.

2) **Create a new ColdFusion page using the File > New menu command.**

In the New Document dialog box, make sure to select Dynamic Page > ColdFusion before clicking the Create button. That tells Dreamweaver that you plan to save the new file as a ColdFusion page (that is, with a .cfm extension).

3) **Type `Product Listing` in the Title field in the document toolbar.**

This simply places the words Product Listing between the HTML `<title>` tags at the top of the new document. You could have typed the words between the `<title>` tags on your own just as easily.

4) **Add the following code at the very top of the new file:**

```
<!---Retrieve product information from database --->
<cfquery name="ProductQuery" datasource="Products">
</cfquery>
```

You will use the `<cfquery>` in almost any situation where you want to retrieve information from a database. You will almost always need to specify the two attributes you just typed: `name` and `datasource`.

The `name` attribute establishes a name for referring to the retrieved data later on in your ColdFusion code. ColdFusion will contact the database, retrieve whatever information you are looking for, and make the information available to your code as a recordset with the name you specify here.

NOTE *The recordset will contain all the rows of relevant data that currently reside in the database. You'll see how to work with the recordset in a moment.*

The `datasource` attribute tells ColdFusion which database to access. The value you provide for `datasource` must match a named data source in the ColdFusion Administrator. Here you are specifying the `products` data source that you created in the last exercise.

5) **Between the `<cfquery>` tags, type the following SQL code:**

```
SELECT * FROM tblProducts
```

```
1  <!--- Retrieve product information from database --->
2  <cfquery name="ProductQuery" datasource="Products">
3  SELECT *
4  FROM tblProducts
5  </cfquery>
6
7  <html>
8  <head>
```

This `SELECT` code demonstrates the simplest possible SQL syntax for retrieving information from a table in a database. In this case, the idea is to retrieve information about products, which happens to be stored in a table called tblProducts. The `*` character used here is a wildcard that instructs the database to include data from all columns (fields) of a table. You can use this syntax whenever you intend to retrieve all the information in a particular database table.

> **NOTE** *In SQL there are four basic commands: `SELECT`, `INSERT`, `UPDATE`, and `DELETE`. They all do exactly what they sound like. `SELECT` is used to retrieve information. `UPDATE` is used to make changes to existing records (rows) in the database. `INSERT` is used to add new records, and `DELETE` is used to remove records. There are also many keywords that can be used to make your commands more specific. The `FROM` and `WHERE` clauses specify what table to select information from, and specific conditions that the information must meet.*

You have now completed your first query. It will retrieve all the records in the tblProducts table, making them available to your code as a ColdFusion recordset named `ProductQuery`.

6) Between the page's `<body>` tags, type the following code:

```
<!---Include logo and navigation header at top of page --->
<cfinclude template="header.cfm">
```

You first saw the `<cfinclude>` tag in Lesson 3, where it was used to include several `<cfset>` lines for commonly used variables. Here, `<cfinclude>` is being used to include a file called header.cfm, which contains a page header (company logo, links for navigation, and so on) for the fictitious Wireless Agent company.

This `<cfinclude>` step doesn't really have anything to do with retrieving information from a database, but it will help make the file you're working on look more official, like a real Web page.

> **NOTE** *What you're learning here is that `<cfinclude>` can be used to include any type of commonly used text, HTML code, or CFML code (or any combination thereof). ColdFusion will treat the contents of the included file just as if the code were typed in directly, right where the `<cfinclude>` tag appears. Use `<cfinclude>` whenever you think you might use a chunk of code in multiple places, or when it just seems convenient or sensible to keep something in a separate file.*

7) Under the `<cfinclude>` line you just added, type the following code:

```
<!---Title this section of the page --->
<h2>Product Listing</h2>
```

```
<body>

<!--- Include logo and navigation header at top of page --->
<cfinclude template="header.cfm">

<!--- Title this section of the page --->
<h2>Product Listing</h2>
```

This code just adds the words *Product Listing* to the page, in large type, under the page header.

8) Use File > Save to the page as *firstquery.cfm* in the Lesson04/Start folder, and then view the page with your browser.

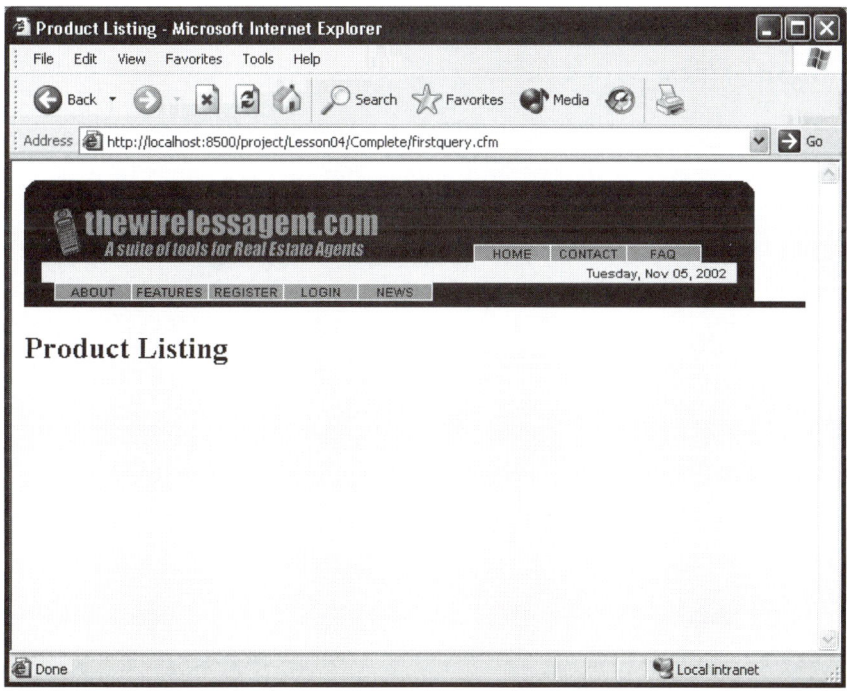

TIP *Remember, you can view the page quickly and easily by pressing F12, or by entering the URL for the page in your browser's address field. In this case, that URL would be http://localhost:8500/Project/Lesson4/Start/firstquery.cfm.*

Hmm. Where's the information from the database?

Okay, it's a trick question. The page won't show any information from the database just yet. In fact, the addition of the `<cfquery>` alone hasn't changed how the page looks at all. That's because the `<cfquery>` tag only *retrieves* information from a database; it doesn't display it. In the next exercise, you'll learn how to output the information returned by the query. Don't worry, that part's easy too!

So don't close this file yet. You will be adding a bit more code to it shortly so it actually displays information about the products in the tblProducts table.

OUTPUTTING INFORMATION FROM A QUERY

After you have retrieved information from a database, you will most likely want to display the information in some form. You can use whatever type of HTML formatting you like when outputting information from a database query. If you want it to be displayed as simple text, you can do that. If you want to use HTML tables to display the information in neat rows and columns, you can do that too. If you want to display images or icons next to each piece of information, you can dress up the display with HTML `<img>` tags. Naturally, you can include whatever formatting you wish, using the usual HTML techniques for controlling font size, color, bolding, italicizing, and so on.

In this exercise, you will learn how to display the information in a query recordset.

1) In firstquery.cfm, after the `<cfinclude>` line you added earlier, add the following code:

```
<!---Output information about each product --->
<cfoutput query="ProductQuery">
</cfoutput>
```

You've seen the `<cfoutput>` tag before, but this is the first time you're seeing it with a query attribute. Adding the `query` attribute doesn't change `<cfoutput>`'s basic job: to look for and evaluate variables, functions, and anything else surrounded by # signs.

So what does the `query` attribute do, exactly? It tells ColdFusion to "loop" over the data in the `query` recordset, executing the code between the `<cfoutput>` tags once for each row of data. Within the `<cfoutput>` block, you can output the value of a column by surrounding the column name with # signs, just like a normal variable. You'll see how this works in the next step.

2) **Between the `<cfoutput>` tags, add the following code:**

   `#ProductName#<br>`

   ```
   21  <!--- Output information about each product --->
   22  <cfoutput query="ProductQuery">
   23     #ProductName#<br>
   24  </cfoutput>
   ```

Because the `<cfquery>` tag at the top of the page uses the `*` wildcard to retrieve all columns from the tblProducts table, you can refer to any of its columns by name using # signs. It so happens that one of the columns in the tblProducts table is called ProductName. That's why `#ProductName#` has special meaning in this `<cfoutput>` block. When ColdFusion processes the `<cfoutput>` block, it will evaluate the `#ProductName#` part like a variable, replacing it with the actual product name stored in the database.

3) **Save your work and view the page with your Web browser.**
When you open the page, you should see a list of all the products in the database. Assuming that you haven't added more records on your own, you should see four products. Congratulations—you have now successfully completed your first data-aware page with ColdFusion.

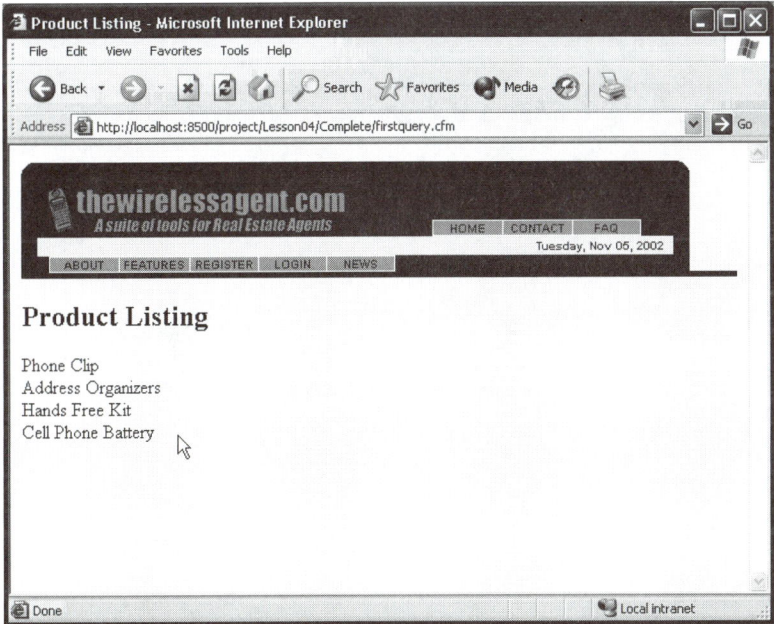

Don't close the file yet. You'll soon be editing the `<cfoutput>` block to make the display a bit more sophisticated.

EXPERIMENTING WITH HOW DATA IS DISPLAYED

The last exercise showed you how to query a database for information, and then display that information on a Web page. So far, the only information being displayed about each record is the product name, and the way the information is presented is pretty simplistic. You can, of course, include whatever details you wish about each record. This exercise will show you how the product information can be presented in a variety of ways.

Each of these steps is a series of experiments with the display and formatting of product information from the database. After each step, you'll be asked to save your work and view the changes in your browser.

1) Add a pair of `<ul>` tags around the `<cfoutput>` block you created earlier, and a pair of `<li>` tags around the `#ProductName#` expression, like so:

```
<!---Output information about each product --->
<ul>
  <cfoutput query="ProductQuery">
    <li>#ProductName#</li>
  </cfoutput>
</ul>
```

When you save your work and re-load this page in a browser, you'll see that the records from the database are now presented as a bulleted list.

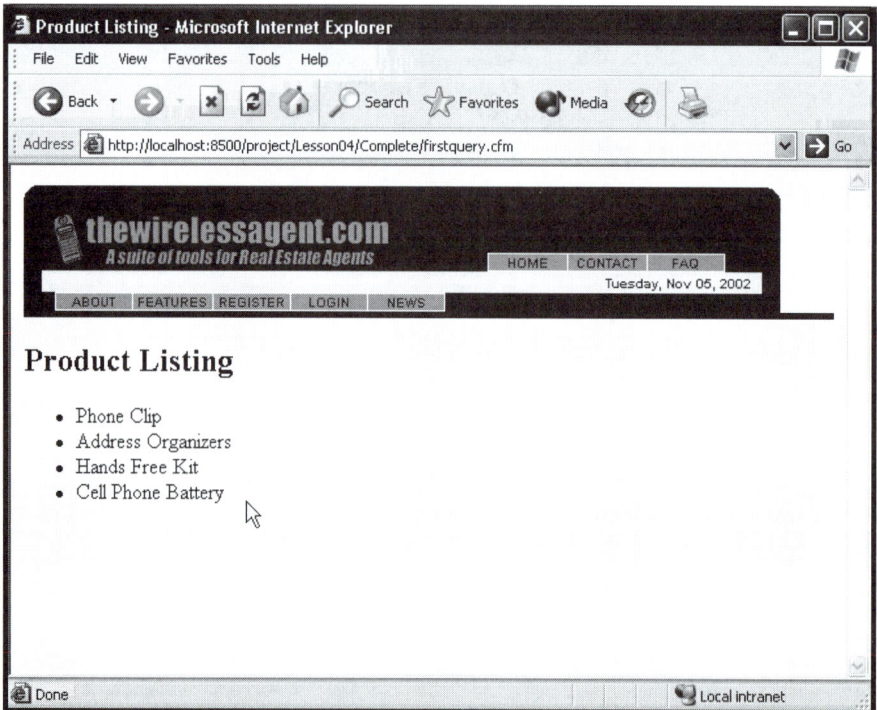

If you use your browser's View Source command to view the HTML source for the page, you will see that ColdFusion has interpreted the instructions in the `<cfoutput>` block by delivering the following block of HTML to the browser:

```
<ul>
    <li>Phone Clip</li>
    <li>Address Organizer</li>
    <li>Hands Free Kit</li>
    <li>Cell Phone Battery</li>
</ul>
```

NOTE *This is ordinary HTML syntax for a bulleted list. The `<ul>` tags indicate that the whole block should be presented using bullets, and the `<li>` tags are used to mark each bulleted item. Please refer to an HTML reference guide for details.*

2) Change the pair of `<ul>` tags to `<ol>` tags instead, then save your work and view the changes.

You'll see that the records are now presented in a numbered list, rather than a bulleted list.

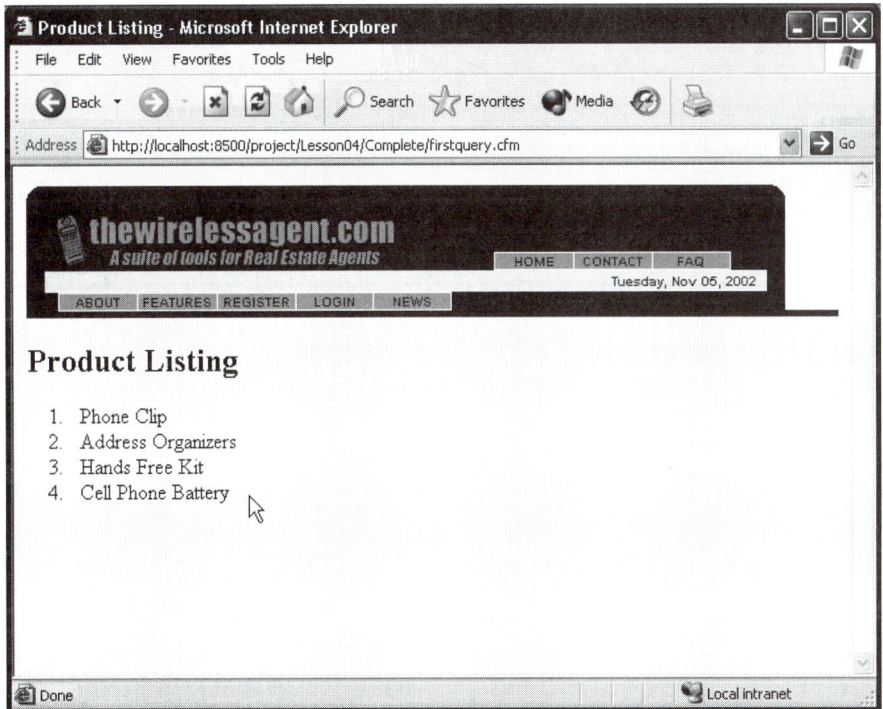

3) **Replace the whole `<cfoutput>` block (including the `<ol>` or `<ul>` tags) with the following:**

```
<!---Output information about each product --->
<select>
  <cfoutput query="ProductQuery">
    <option>#ProductName#</option>
  </cfoutput>
</select>
```

When you save and view this version of the page in your browser, you will see that the product names now appear in a drop-down list.

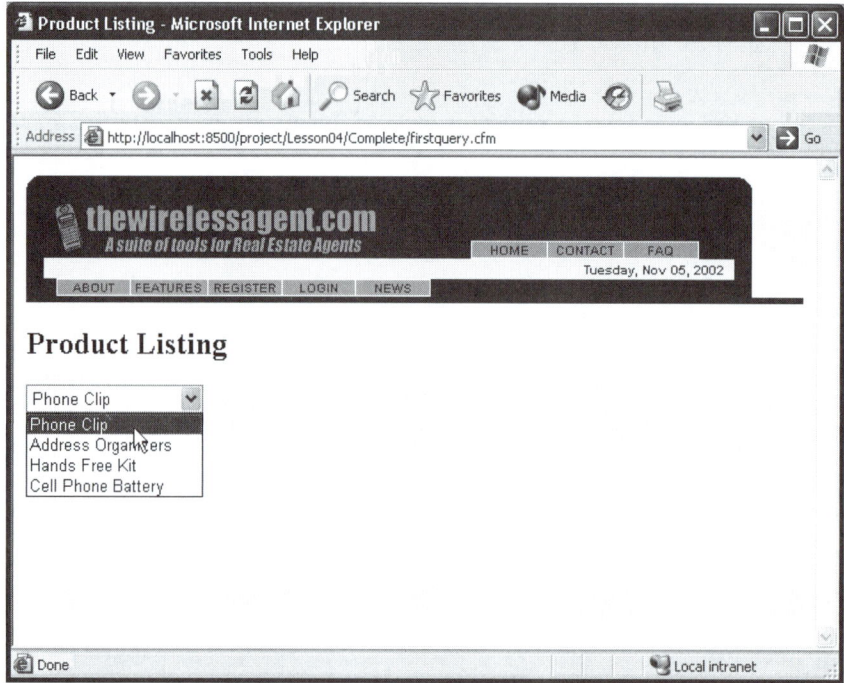

As you can see, the ColdFusion elements (the `<cfoutput>` tag and the # sign expression) haven't changed from the previous version. It's the HTML code inside and outside the `<cfoutput>` block that is different. By changing the HTML tags just before and after the dynamic portion of the page (that is, around the `<cfoutput>` tags) and the ones that surround each piece of information (inside the `<cfoutput>` tags), you can change the way information is presented on your site.

NOTE *Later in this book, you will learn how to create forms that contain checkboxes, text entry fields, and so on. You'll also learn how to use ColdFusion to create pages that will process information that users enter into forms on your pages.*

4) **Replace the whole `<cfoutput>` block (including the `<ol>` or `<ul>` tags) with the following:**

```
<!---Output information about each product --->
<cfoutput query="ProductQuery">
  <p>
    <strong>#ProductName#</strong><br>
    #ProductDesc#<br>
    <span style="color:blue">
      Price: #DollarFormat(ProductPrice)#
    </span>
  </p>
</cfoutput>
```

When you save this version of the file and view the results with your browser, you will see that the price and description for each product are listed along with the product name. In addition, the product name is in bold (thanks to HTML's `<strong>` tag), and the price is in blue (thanks to ordinary HTML and style syntax in the `<span>` tag). The price is also nicely formatted with two decimal points and a dollar sign, thanks to ColdFusion's built-in `DollarFormat()` function. The `DollarFormat()` function also takes care of adding commas in the appropriate positions if the amount exceeds 1,000.

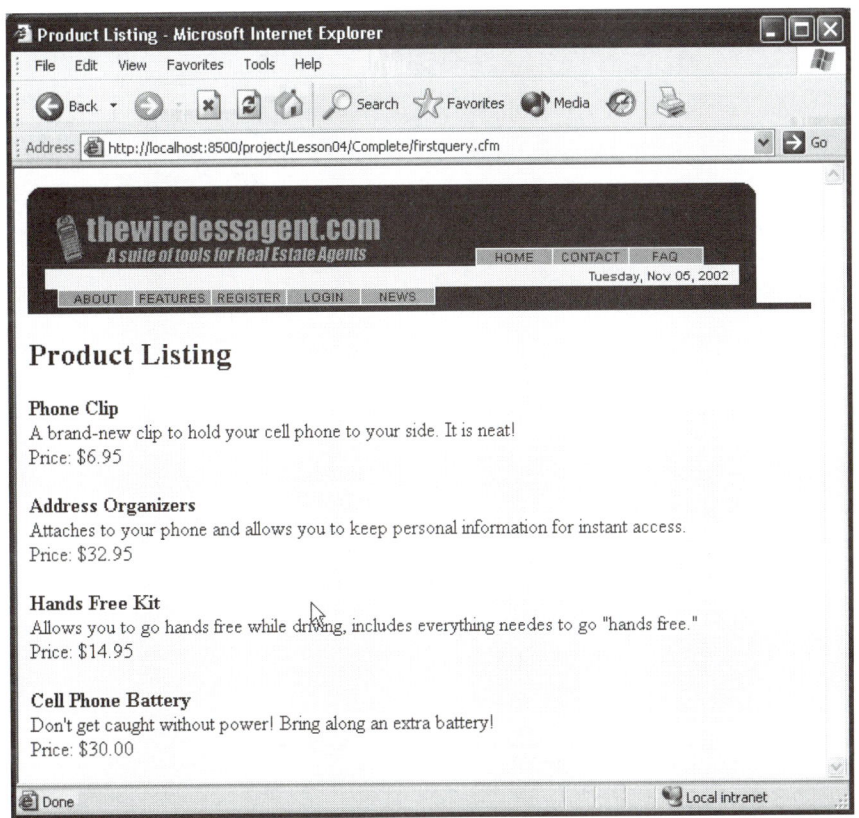

> **TIP** *If you want your application to work with currencies other than the dollar, use the* `LSCurrencyFormat()` *function instead of* `DollarFormat()`. *Details are provided in the ColdFusion documentation.*

Don't close the firstquery.cfm file yet. There are more formatting experiments on the way!

FORMATTING DATA USING HTML TABLES

In the last exercise, you saw how you could change the presentation of information from a database by adding various HTML tags outside and around the `<cfoutput>` block that loops over a query. You can use a similar technique to present the data in neat rows and columns on screen, using ordinary HTML table tags.

1) Still in firstquery.cfm, remove the existing `<cfoutput>` block and replace it with the following:

```
<table width="600" border="1">
  <tr>
    <th width="200">Product</th>
    <th width="300">Description</th>
    <th width="100">Price</th>
  </tr>
</table>
```

This is the beginnings of an HTML table with three columns (one for the product name, one for the description, and one for the price). You can view your changes to the page at this point if you wish, but it won't be terribly interesting because it doesn't yet display any information from the database.

2) Add the following code directly after the closing `</tr>` tag, but before the `</table>` tag:

```
<!---Output information about each product --->
<cfoutput query="ProductQuery">
<tr>
  <td>#ProductName#</td>
  <td>#ProductDesc#</td>
  <td align="center">#DollarFormat(ProductPrice)#</td>
</tr>
</cfoutput>
```

```
21  <table width="600" border="1">
22    <tr>
23      <th width="200">Product</th>
24      <th width="300">Description</th>
25      <th width="100">Price</th>
26    </tr>
27    <!--- Output information about each product --->
28    <cfoutput query="ProductQuery">
29    <tr>
30      <td>#ProductName#</td>
31      <td>#ProductDesc#</td>
32      <td align="center">#DollarFormat(ProductPrice)#</td>
33    </tr>
34    </cfoutput>
35  </table>
```

3) Save your work again, and view the changed version of the page with your browser.

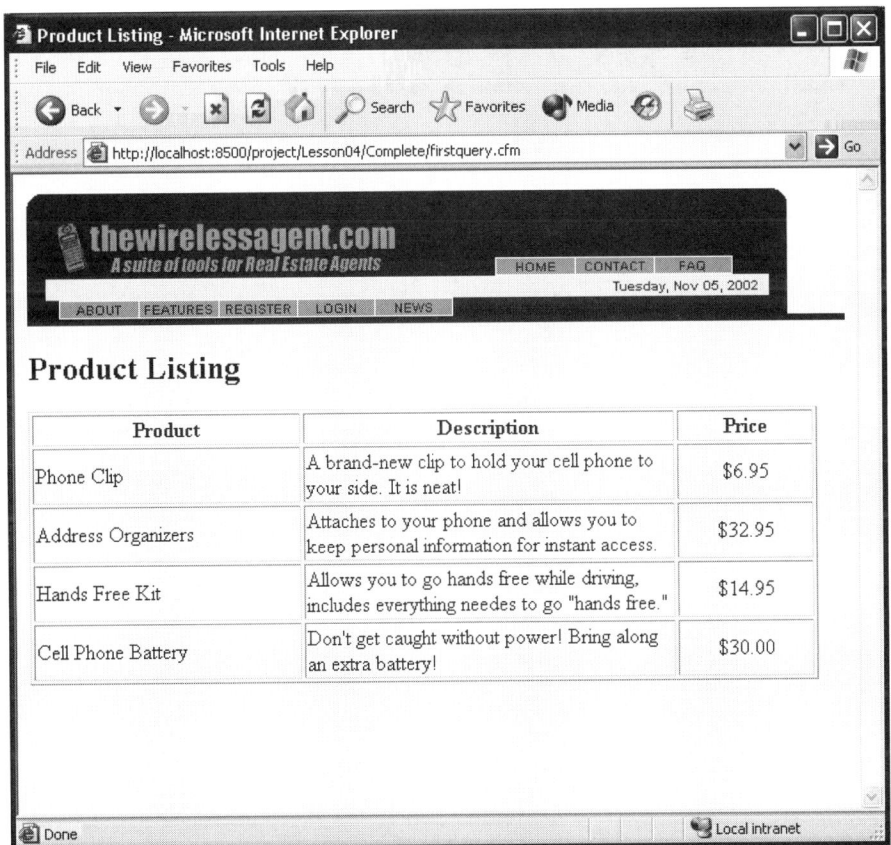

The product information is now being displayed in neat columns and rows, with a column heading (label) at the top. This required only a bit more work than the versions of the page you created in the previous lesson, and the ColdFusion-specific syntax you are using here still hasn't changed. The only additional knowledge needed for this is an understanding of basic HTML table tags.

This is one of the great things about ColdFusion. It makes it easy to add the power of a database to your existing knowledge of HTML. This, in turn, makes it easy to design and build data display pages that look exactly as you want them to. Just come up with the appropriate HTML for the page, and then add `<cfoutput>` tag and # sign expressions to insert the information from your database on the fly.

NOTE *One aspect of this exercise that can get a bit confusing is the use of the word* table. *As you know, the product information is being stored in a database table; that's what is being queried by the* `<cfquery>` *at the top of the firstquery.cfm page. This exercise has shown you how to display that data in a visual HTML table on screen. So, in this case, the database table and the HTML table are holding the same basic information (product names, prices, and so on). But they are separate concepts. The HTML* `<table>`, `<tr>`, *and related tags do not necessarily have anything to do with database tables (or vice versa).*

CHANGING THE ORDER OF THE RECORDS

If you visit the version of the firstquery.cfm page you have now, you'll notice that the records (that is, the products) don't appear to be in any meaningful order. Ordinarily, you would expect to see the records in alphabetical order or some other sensible order. In this exercise, you'll learn how to tell the database how you'd like the retrieved records to be ordered. You'll use the **ORDER BY** keywords from SQL to specify the desired order.

1) **Still in firstquery.cfm, add the following line to the end of the SQL statement:**

   ORDER BY ProductName

```
1  <!--- Retrieve product information from database --->
2  <cfquery name="ProductQuery" datasource="Products">
3    SELECT *
4    FROM tblProducts
5    ORDER BY ProductName
6  </cfquery>
```

As you can see, it's easy to add **ORDER BY** to a query. Simply type the words **ORDER BY**, then the name of the column that you would like the records to be sorted by. If the column contains textual or character-type information (like a product name or description), the records will be sorted in alphabetical order, from A to Z. If the column contains numeric information (like a price or ID number), the records will be sorted numerically, from lowest value to highest.

2) Save your work, then take a look at the revised version of the page in your browser.
You'll see that the products are now shown in alphabetical order.

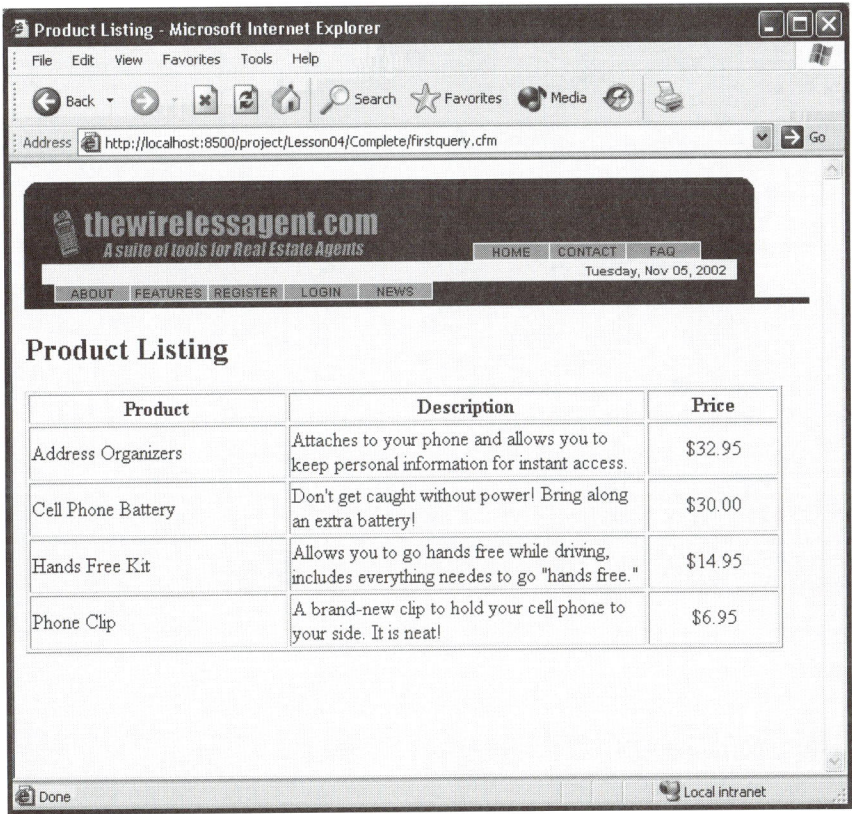

3) Back in firstquery.cfm, add the word DESC at the end of the ORDER BY line, like so:

```
<!--- Retrieve product information from database --->
<cfquery name="ProductQuery" datasource="Products">
  SELECT *
  FROM tblProducts
  ORDER BY ProductName DESC
</cfquery>
```

You can reverse the sort order by adding `DESC` after a column name in the `ORDER BY` part of a query. If the column contains textual information, the records will be sorted from Z to A instead of A to Z. If the column contains numeric information, the records with the highest values will be shown first, instead of last.

4) Save your work and reload the revised version of the page in your browser.

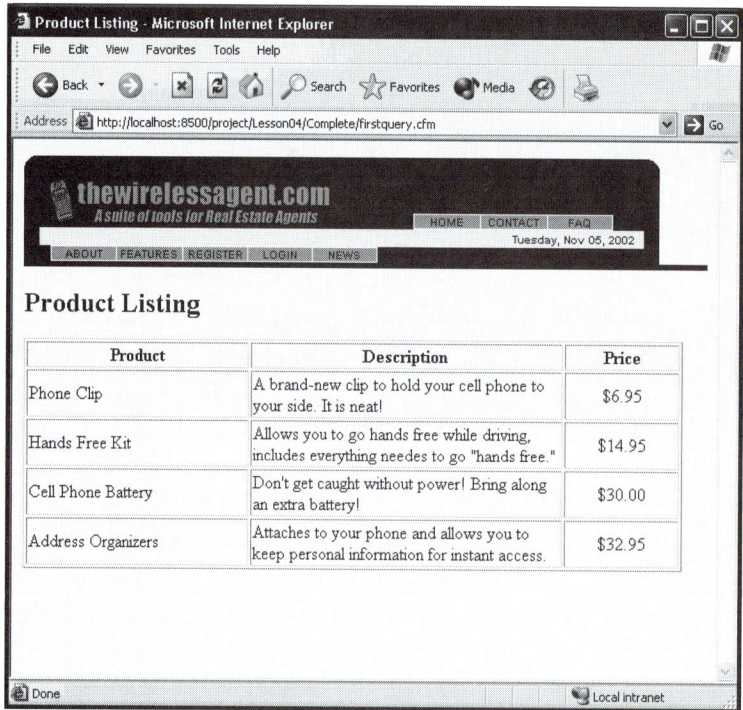

Now the products are shown in reverse alphabetical order.

5) If you wish, experiment with other sort orders.

For instance, you could try `ORDER BY ProductPrice` to sort the products by price (cheapest first).

You could also try `ORDER BY ProductPrice DESC` to sort them in the other direction (most expensive first).

6) When you're done experimenting, return the sort order to A-Z alphabetical order, using `ORDER BY ProductName`.

> **TIP** *As a general rule of thumb, it's always good to have an `ORDER BY` part in any query that will return more than one record. It never hurts to have the records appear in a predictable order.*

CREATING LINKS TO DETAIL PAGES

You've learned how to present database information as plain text, as bulleted lists, as drop-down boxes, and in HTML tables. All of these presentations have relied on the same basic `<cfquery>` and `<cfoutput>` techniques. You can use these same techniques to present the database information in the form of Web-style hyperlinks. The links, presumably, will bring users to a *detail page* that contains additional information about the record they clicked (in this case, a product). This detail page might also provide a picture of the item, a way to order the item or inquire about its availability, or whatever other function you want to provide.

1) With the firstquery.cfm open in Dreamweaver, use File > Save As to save it as productlist.cfm.

Make sure you save the new file in the same folder as the other files for this lesson.

2) Once again, replace the `<cfoutput>` block, this time with the following code:

```
<!---Output information about each product --->
<cfoutput query="ProductQuery">
  <a href="productdetail.cfm?ProductID=#ProductID#">#ProductName#</a><br>
</cfoutput>
```

3) Save your work, and view the new productlist.cfm page in a browser.

You will see that each product is now presented as a clickable link.

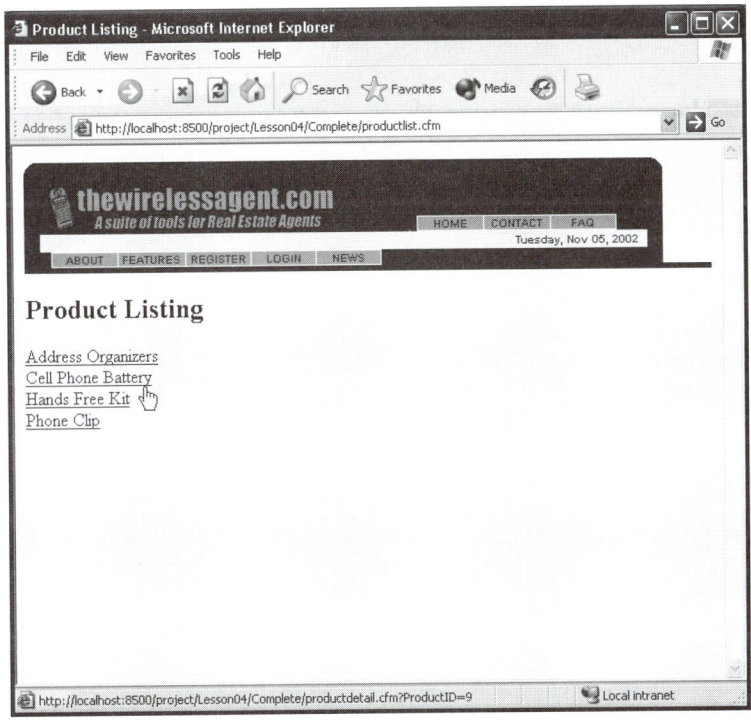

4) Try hovering your mouse over the links while watching the status bar at the bottom of your browser.

You will see that the ID number associated with each product has been incorporated into the URL for the corresponding hyperlink. The link for the Phone Clip product, for instance, has the following URL:

`http://localhost:8500/project/Lesson4/Start/productdetail.cfm?ProductID=1`

And the link for the Hands Free Kit has this URL:

`http://localhost:8500/project/Lesson4/Start/productdetail.cfm?ProductID=4`

Except for the ID number, the URLs are the same. The page that the link leads to (productdetail.cfm) can use this number to identify which product the user clicked on. You will create that page in the next exercise.

CREATING DETAIL PAGES

When a value (such as an ID number) is included in the URL using the ? mark and = sign syntax shown at the end of the last lesson, that value is usually referred to as a *URL parameter* or *URL variable*. The name of the parameter comes before the = sign, followed by the actual value of the parameter. Basically, this is a way to provide the page with variables that it can use internally.

The product list page you just finished creating includes a parameter called `ProductID` in the URL associated with each product. The page that the links lead to (sometimes called the *receiving page*) is then free to use the parameter for its own purposes. This is called *passing* the parameter.

If a parameter has been passed to a page, the ColdFusion code in that page can refer to the parameter as a variable. The variable is stored in the URL scope, so the best way to refer to the variable is in the form URL.variablename (for instance, `#URL.ProductID#`).

In this exercise, you will learn how easy it is to use URL parameters to create pages that respond differently, depending on the values passed to the page. You will quickly see how this simple technique becomes the basis for creating multi-paged, interactive Web sites.

1) **In Dreamweaver, use File > New, then Dynamic Page > ColdFusion to create a new ColdFusion document, and save it as productdetail.cfm.**

Make sure you save the new file in the same folder as the other files for this lesson.

2) **At the top of the new page, type the following:**

```
<!---This page requires a ProductID value in the URL --->
<cfparam name="URL.ProductID" type="numeric">
```

The `<cfparam>` tag is used to make sure that a particular variable or value is available when the page is visited. In this case, you want to make sure that a `ProductID` value is included in the URL so that the page knows which product to display information about. By adding this `<cfparam>` tag at the top of the page, you are declaring that the page expects a `ProductID` value, and can't do its job without it.

By specifying `type="numeric"`, you are telling ColdFusion to make sure that the ProductID value passed to the page is a number. This is a sensible check to add to your page, in case someone accidentally provides a value that includes letters or other symbols. If they do, ColdFusion will display an error message and stop processing the page right there at the `<cfparam>` tag, rather than allowing your code to continue executing.

TIP *It is a good idea to include a `<cfparam>` tag for each URL parameter that your page will require. Try to keep them at the top of the page so you can easily remind yourself what parameters the page expects.*

3) **Between the page's `<body>` tags, type the following code:**

```
<!---Include logo and navigation header at top of page --->
<cfinclude template="header.cfm">
```

You used this same code earlier, while building the firstquery.cfm page. It simply includes the logo and navigation header elements at the top of the page.

4) **Under the `<cfinclude>` line, type the following:**

```
<cfoutput>
  <p>You clicked product number #URL.ProductID#.
</cfoutput>
```

This will output the value of the `ProductID` parameter passed in the URL so it can be seen on the page. The point is simply to help you see how URL parameters can be treated just like the ordinary ColdFusion variables you create with `<cfset>`.

5) **Save your work, and then visit the productlist.cfm page (not the page you just finished) with your browser. Click on one of the links.**

The ID number of the clicked product will be displayed as part of the page. You can now click the Back button on your browser and click a different product link. As you would expect, the detail page changes depending on which product you pick, always displaying the corresponding number.

You clicked product number 4.

Don't close productdetail.cfm just yet.

RUNNING DYNAMIC QUERIES

Okay, so your product detail page now displays something specific about whatever product the user chooses: the ID number. That's pretty important as far as your application is concerned, but it probably isn't the kind of information that your site's visitors would expect. They probably want to see detailed information about product, like a full description, price, or availability.

ColdFusion makes it quite easy to create such a page, and you'll learn how to do it in this exercise. For the most part, the detail page is going to be made up of the same basic elements as the productlist.cfm page you created earlier. It's going to have a `<cfquery>` tag to retrieve information from the database, and a `<cfoutput>` block that displays the information using # sign syntax to indicate column names.

The only real difference is that the `<cfquery>` tag is going to use the `ProductID` parameter passed in the URL to tell the database to retrieve just one record from the database (that is, just the selected product), rather than all records.

1) In productdetail.cfm, make some room under the `<cfparam>` tag by pressing Enter a couple of times.

You'll place your new `<cfquery>` tag in the empty space you just created.

2) Place the cursor on one of the new blank lines, and then click the cfquery button on the CFML Basic tab of the Insert toolbar.

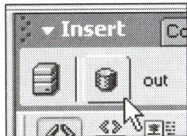

The Tag Editor dialog for the `<cfquery>` tag appears.

TIP *This is just an alternate way of inserting a `<cfquery>` tag into a ColdFusion page. If, after you try using this dialog, you find that you prefer typing the tag by hand, you are free to do that from now on.*

3) In the Query Name field, type *DetailQuery*.

This will cause the `<cfquery>` tag you are creating to have a `name="DetailQuery"` attribute. In the firstquery.cfm page you created earlier in this lesson, you used `name="ProductQuery"`. You'll use this name later when you want to display the information retrieved by the query. The name can be anything you want, but it's helpful to always use a name that suggests what type of information is being retrieved.

4) In the Data Source field, type *Products*.

This causes the `<cfquery>` to have a `datasource="Products"` attribute. Remember, Products is the data source you created at the beginning of this lesson. It's just a convenient way to refer to the products.mdb database file.

5) **In the SQL field, type the following code:**

```
SELECT *
FROM tblProducts
WHERE ProductID = #URL.ProductID#
```

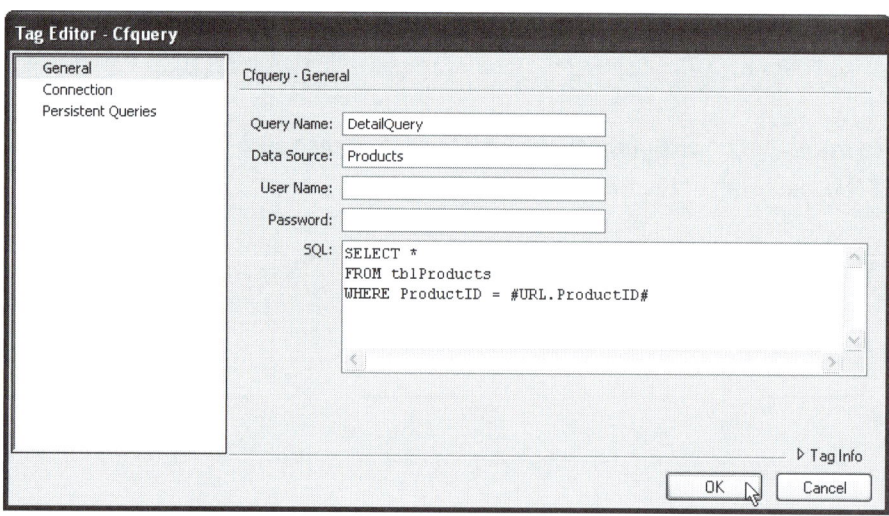

6) **Click OK.**

The completed `<cfquery>` tag is inserted into your document. This `<cfquery>` tag is quite similar to the one you saw earlier. This one specifies a different name for the **name** attribute, and contains an additional line in the SQL portion of the tag (the part between the `<cfquery>` tags).

```
1 <!--- This page requires a ProductID value in the URL --->
2 <cfparam name="URL.ProductID" type="numeric">
3
4 <cfquery name="DetailQuery" datasource="Products">
5 SELECT *
6 FROM tblProducts
7 WHERE ProductID = #URL.ProductID#
8 </cfquery>
```

You add a **WHERE** portion (also called a **WHERE** *clause*) to a query whenever you want to specify which rows get retrieved from a database table. Without a **WHERE** clause, a query will always retrieve every row in the table. With a **WHERE** clause, only those rows that match your criteria will be retrieved. In this case, the page is interested in retrieving only one row: whichever record matches the ID number passed in the URL.

7) Still in productdetail.cfm, replace the existing `<cfoutput>` block with the following:

```
<!---Display the product details --->
<cfoutput query="DetailQuery">
  <h2>#ProductName#</h2>
  <p>#ProductDesc#</p>
  <p>
    Price: #DollarFormat(ProductPrice)#<br>
    Status: #ProductStatus#<br>
    Number in Stock: #ProductQty#<br>
  </p>
</cfoutput>
```

Given what you've learned earlier in this lesson, this code should look pretty familiar at this point. You know that because this `<cfoutput>` block includes a `query` attribute, you can use any of the columns returned by the `DetailQuery` recordset using # sign syntax. You also know that ColdFusion will loop over each of the records returned by `DetailQuery`.

However, the nature of `DetailQuery` is such that it will never return more than one record. Every record in the tblProducts table has its own ID number, so it's simply not possible for the query to return multiple records. Therefore, this `<cfoutput>` block will execute only once, displaying the information about the selected product. Which is exactly what this page calls for!

8) Under the `<cfoutput>` block, add a link back to the product link page, like so:

```
<!---Link back to product selection page --->
<a href="productlist.cfm">Return to Product List</a>
```

9) Save your work, then go back to the productlist.cfm page and click on a product name.

The product detail page appears, displaying the details about whatever product you clicked. You can then use the Return to Product List link (or the back button on your browser) to return to the list of products, where you can try clicking some other product.

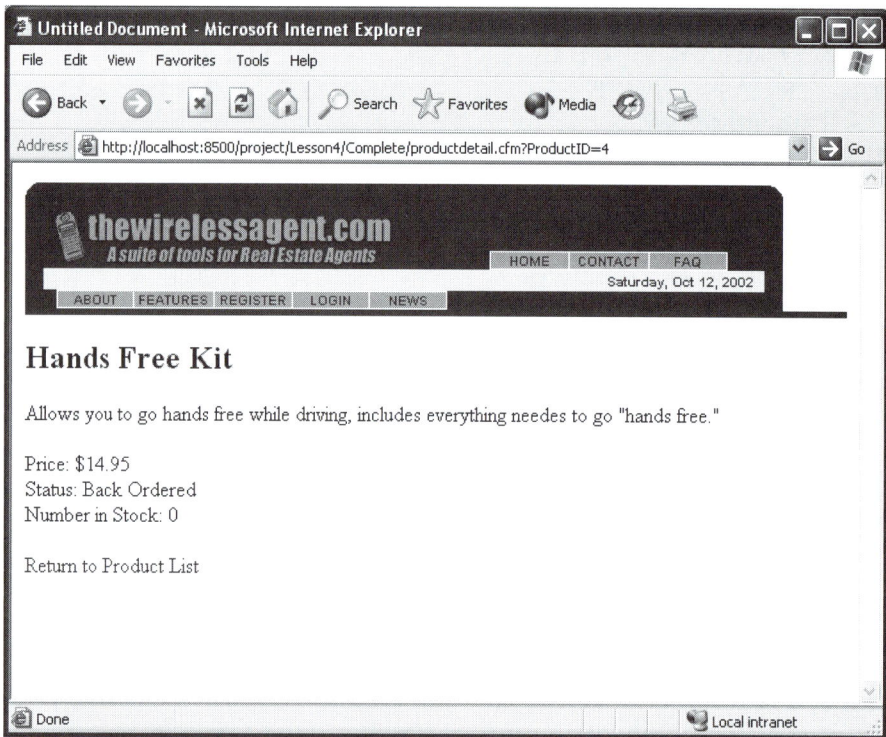

Congratulations! You have finished creating a simple set of master-detail pages, enabling users to browse through the information in a database using an intuitive, Web-friendly interface.

NOTE *Sometimes people will refer to a set of pages of this kind as a* drill-down application, *because users conceptually drill down from a top level (in this case, the product list page) down to more detailed levels (in this case, the product detail page). More sophisticated drill down applications might allow users to drill down through three or four levels of detail, rather than just two.*

WHAT YOU HAVE LEARNED

In this lesson, you have:

- Created a data source (pages 70–74)
- Explored the information in a database using Dreamweaver's Database panel (pages 75–80)
- Queried a database (pages 80–84)
- Output the results of a query (pages 84–92)
- Changed how records are sorted using **ORDER BY** (pages 92–94)
- Created a set of data drill-down pages for product details (pages 95–102)

creating search forms

LESSON 5

Forms are important elements of many Web sites. They can be used for so many different purposes—search forms, signup forms, shopping checkout forms, and so on—that they have become standard fare on today's Web. They are so ubiquitous, in fact, that most users now have an intuitive understanding of how to fill out all but the most complicated forms without any special instructions. The next two lessons will help you understand the role that HTML forms can serve in your ColdFusion applications. This lesson will show you how to build a search form, and the next lesson will show you how to create forms for creating and editing product records.

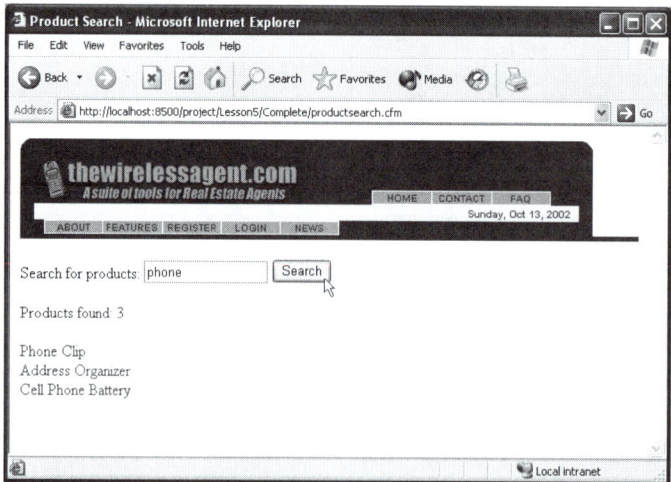

In this lesson, you create an increasingly sophisticated search interface for the products available on the fictitious Wireless Agent site. Before long, you will be well on your way to understanding what's needed to create search facilities for your own projects. Along the way, you will learn a good deal about working with forms in ColdFusion.

WHAT YOU WILL LEARN

In this lesson, you will:

- Learn the basics of HTML forms
- Post form data to an action page for processing
- Display search results
- Learn about `<cfif>` and conditional processing
- Create one- and two-page search interfaces
- Combine concepts to produce advanced search pages

APPROXIMATE TIME

This lesson takes approximately one hour and 30 minutes to complete.

LESSON FILES

Starting files:

Lesson05\Start\productdetail.cfm
Lesson05\Start\searchaction.cfm
Lesson05\Start\searchform.cfm

Completed project:

Lesson05\Complete\advproductsearch.cfm
Lesson05\Complete\productdetail.cfm
Lesson05\Complete\productsearch.cfm
Lesson05\Complete\searchaction.cfm
Lesson05\Complete\searchform.cfm

CREATING A BASIC HTML FORM

The ability to create forms for users to interact with has been a feature of HTML since the first days of the Web. They are obviously essential for any site that is designed to collect and respond to information provided by users. As such, they are perhaps the single most important feature of HTML—the one that really made it possible for the Web to evolve into such an important part of today's world.

The fact that the syntax for creating HTML forms has remained nearly unchanged since its original inception—even though forms are so important and so widely used—is a testament to how flexible and powerful that syntax really is. Using just a few simple tags like `<form>`, `<input>`, `<select>`, and `<option>`, you can create a form that asks the user to provide just about any type of information. Usually, you will instruct the form to submit the user's entries to ColdFusion, where you can process or respond to the entries in whatever way is appropriate.

The most commonly-used form elements include:

- Text entry fields, for entering text
- Drop-down lists, for selecting from a list of options
- Radio buttons, also for selecting from a (usually smaller) list of options
- Check boxes, for supplying yes/no or on/off types of values
- Submit buttons, for actually submitting the form entries to the server

Your first form-related exercise will be the creation of a search form. The form will allow users to search for products in the `tblProducts` table from this book's sample database.

1) Open Dreamweaver MX, if it's not open already. Choose File > Open and then select the searchform.cfm file from the wwwroot\Project\Lesson05\Start folder.

As you can see, this is a very simple file. Aside from the usual HTML syntax that you'd expect to see on any empty page, the only special code is a `<cfinclude>` tag that includes the Wireless Agent logo and navigation elements at the top of the page (you used the `<cfinclude>` tag to do the same thing in Lesson 4).

2) Under the `<cfinclude>` line, type the following code:

```
<!---Begin search form --->
<form action="searchaction.cfm" method="post">
</form>
```

LESSON 5

This pair of `<form>` tags creates the beginnings of an HTML form. It isn't able to do anything yet because it doesn't contain any text fields, check boxes, or other elements, but it's a start. The `action` attribute tells the browser to submit whatever information the user provides to a ColdFusion page called searchaction.cfm (which you will create in the next exercise).

NOTE *The `method="post"` attribute tells the browser how exactly to communicate with ColdFusion when the user submits the form. The differences between `post` and the other possible value, `get`, is beyond the scope of what you're learning in this book. For now, just accept that the `method="post"` attribute should always be part of any `<form>` tag that you want to use with ColdFusion. If you want more details, please consult a general HTML reference or guide.*

3) Between the `<form>` tags, add a text field for entering search keywords, like so:

```
<!---Text field for entering search criteria --->
Search for products:
<input type="text" name="Keywords" size="15">
```

This sets up your first form field—a simple text box. The purpose of this field is to collect the keywords that the user would like to search for in the product list. The `name` attribute is important because it's the handle by which you will reference the user's entries later.

4) Under the `<input>` tag, add a submit button for performing the search, like so:

```
<!---Submit button for performing search --->
<input type="submit" value="Search">
```

```
 9  <!--- Include logo and navigation header at top of page --->
10  <cfinclude template="header.cfm">
11
12  <!--- Begin search form --->
13  <form action="searchaction.cfm" method="post">
14
15    <!--- Text field for entering search criteria --->
16    Search for products:
17    <input type="text" name="Keywords" size="15">
18
19    <!--- Submit button for performing search --->
20    <input type="submit" value="Search">
21
22  </form>
```

This creates a submit button for the search form; the button is labeled with the word *Search*. When the user presses the button, the information is submitted to whatever page is specified in the `action` attribute of the `<form>` tag. In this case, that page is called searchaction.cfm, which you will create in the next exercise.

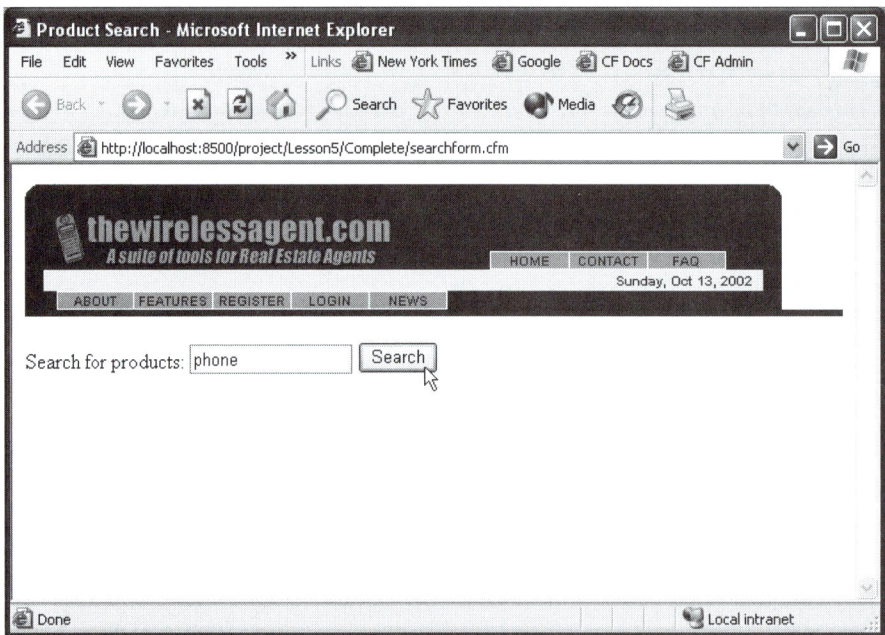

NOTE *Most browsers will also submit the form if the user presses the Enter key while their cursor is within the text entry field. Pressing Enter is generally considered to be equivalent to pressing a submit button.*

That is all you need to create a basic search form. If you view the page at this point, you will see the search form, but submitting it will result in a "Not Found" type of message, because the page that it submits its information to does not yet exist. Next, you will learn how to create that page.

CREATING AN ACTION PAGE

In the last exercise, you created a form that submits its entries to a page called searchaction.cfm. When the user submits the form, the browser will visit the searchaction.cfm page, supplying it with the user's entries as it does so. This is called *posting* the form. The receiving page (that is, the page specified in the form's `action` attribute) is often called the *action page*. The action page can be written with any server-side language that you wish, though of course the examples in this book will create the action page with ColdFusion.

ColdFusion makes it really easy to create action pages that respond to form criteria. All of the user's entries are made available to your code as variables in a special variable scope called `FORM`. The variables in the `FORM` scope correspond to the names of the input elements in the form the user is submitting. In the case of the search form you created in the last exercise, there is just one named form element—the text input field called `Keywords`—which means that the user's entry will be available in a variable called `FORM.Keywords`. You can use it just like any other variable: display the value of this variable in a `<cfoutput>` block, use it within a `<cfquery>` block to execute a dynamic query, and so on.

This exercise will show you how to build an action page for the search form you just created. You will see that this action page is nearly identical to the productlist.cfm page you created in Lesson 3. The main difference is that you will ask the database to return records based on the user's search criteria, rather than by ID number. Let's get started.

1) Open the Lesson05\Start\searchaction.cfm file in Dreamweaver.

It's worth noting that this file is also very simple when you start out. It also doesn't contain anything special other than the `<cfinclude>` tag for the common page header.

2) At the very top of the page, add the following code:

```
<!---This page expects a form parameter named Keywords --->
<cfparam name="FORM.Keywords" type="string">
```

This `<cfparam>` tag is very similar to the one you added to the productdetail.cfm page in Lesson 4. It makes it clear that the page's logic depends on a form field called `Keywords`. Assuming that this page is executed in the manner in which it was intended (that is, by submitting the form in productsearch.cfm), that will always be the case. If the page is executed in some other way (for instance, if someone happens to type the URL for the page directly into their browser's address field), ColdFusion will display an error message as soon as it reaches the `<cfparam>` tag.

3) Under the `<cfparam>` tag, type the following code:

```
<!---Find matching products --->
<cfquery name="SearchQuery" datasource="products">
  SELECT ProductID, ProductName
  FROM tblProducts
  WHERE ProductName LIKE '%#FORM.Keywords#%'
</cfquery>
```

This query is similar to the one at the top of the productdetail.cfm page from Lesson 4. Both queries incorporate a ColdFusion variable in the `WHERE` part of the query in order to create a dynamic query (one that changes depending on what the user does). Instead of basing the criteria on the ID number for a particular product, though, this one attempts to obtain records based on the words in the ProductName column of the tblProducts table. So, unlike the previous query (which could never return more than one record), this query might return one, two, or any other number of records. It could also return zero records, depending on what the user enters for the search keywords.

Another important difference in this query is the use of the `LIKE` operator in the `WHERE` clause. The `LIKE` operator, which is a standard feature of SQL, allows you to match records using simple wildcards. There are a few different wildcards you can use with `LIKE`, but the one you will most likely use in your ColdFusion pages is the % wildcard. You can use the % sign syntax shown here to create queries that return records based on partial matches.

If, for instance, a user enters *phone* in the search form and submits the form, ColdFusion will use the following SQL code to search the database:

```
SELECT ProductID, ProductName
FROM tblProducts
WHERE ProductName LIKE '%Phone%'
```

In plain English, this SQL code means "retrieve the ID number and name of any product that contains the word *phone* somewhere in the name." The actual word *phone* might be at the very start of the name, at the end of the name, or anywhere in between.

TIP *You could also add a* `ORDER BY` *line to this query to control the sort order of the records that match the user's search words. You learned about* `ORDER BY` *at the end of Lesson 4.*

4) After the `<cfinclude>` line, type the following code:

```
<!---Display number of matches --->
<cfoutput>
  <p>Your search for #FORM.Keywords# found
  #SearchQuery.RecordCount# matches.</p>
</cfoutput>
```

Every query recordset has a RecordCount value associated with it. You can always display the number of records retrieved by a query by outputting its `RecordCount` value as shown here. Later, you will learn how to use the `RecordCount` value to display different messages based on the number of records found (for instance, a "no matches found" type of message when the query retrieves zero records).

5) After the `<cfoutput>` block you just added, type the following code:

```
<!---Output information about each product --->
<cfoutput query="SearchQuery">
  <a href="productdetail.cfm?ProductID=#ProductID#">#ProductName#</a><br>
</cfoutput>
```

This is almost exactly the same `<cfoutput>` block that was used in the productlist.cfm file from Lesson 4. It creates a hyperlink for each product in the `SearchQuery` recordset (the records that match the user's criteria). If the user clicks a link, they are brought to a detail page for the corresponding product. The productdetail.cfm page referred to in this code is the same as the one you saw earlier (also in Lesson 4).

At this point, you can test out the search tool by visiting the productsearch.cfm page (not the one you just created) in your browser. Type a word into the search field and click the Search button (or just hit the Enter key on your keyboard). The searchaction.cfm page appears, displaying whatever records are appropriate, if any. If you click on one of the matched records, you are brought to that product's details page (just as in Lesson 4).

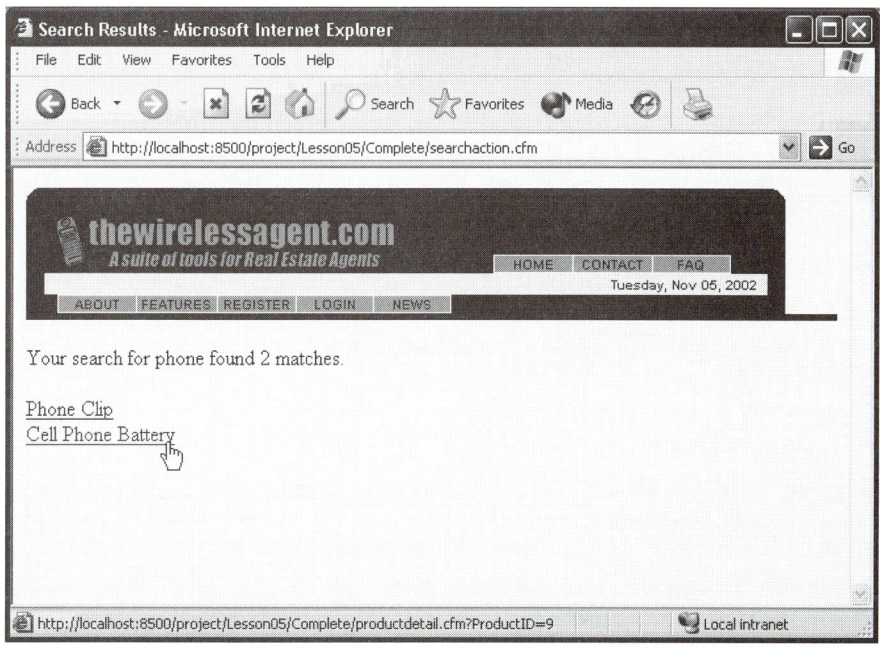

MATCHING ON MORE THAN ONE FIELD

The product search facility now works, but it can still be improved. One obvious enhancement would be to have it search the product descriptions as well as the product names. This exercise will show you how to run searches against multiple fields (columns) in the database.

1) In searchaction.cfm, change the WHERE clause to the following:

```
WHERE (  (ProductName LIKE '%#FORM.Keywords#%')
    OR (ProductDesc LIKE '%#FORM.Keywords#%')  )
```

```
<!--- Find matching products --->
<cfquery name="SearchQuery" datasource="products">
  SELECT ProductID, ProductName
  FROM tblProducts
  WHERE (    (ProductName LIKE '%#FORM.Keywords#%')
         OR (ProductDesc LIKE '%#FORM.Keywords#%') )
</cfquery>
```

In plain English, this **WHERE** clause means "find any records where the product name contains the user's keywords, or where the description contains the keywords."

Whenever you use the **OR** keyword, you should use sets of parentheses as shown here, to make sure the database understands exactly what you are trying to accomplish. Always put a set of parentheses around each **LIKE** condition, and then put an additional set of parentheses around the entire set of **OR** conditions (assuming that you want them to be considered as a group, which you usually do).

NOTE *Actually, the parentheses aren't really so important unless you are combining* **OR** *conditions with* **AND** *conditions in the same query (you will see* **AND** *conditions shortly), at which point the database might misunderstand your intentions if the parentheses are missing. However, you can't go wrong by adding the parentheses whenever you use* **OR***. It's a good habit to get into.*

2) Save your work, and then test the search form again.

The search facility will now find any products that match the keyword you type, whether that keyword is in the product name or the description.

You can base the search on as many fields as you wish, assuming that the fields all contain words (rather than numbers or dates). For example, if there was an additional column called ProductNotes, you could have the page find matches in any of the three columns by using this **WHERE** clause:

```
WHERE (  (ProductName LIKE '%#FORM.Keywords#%')
    OR (ProductDesc LIKE '%#FORM.Keywords#%')
    OR (ProductNotes LIKE '%#FORM.Keywords#%')
```

DISPLAYING A NO RECORDS FOUND MESSAGE

It's easy to add code to the search action page so that it displays one message (the number of records found) when at least one match from the database is retrieved, and another message (perhaps an encouragement to try different keywords) when no matches are retrieved. This is a common feature of most search pages, and one that your users will probably expect to see.

To make ColdFusion display different messages or take different actions depending on some kind of condition (in this case, the number of records retrieved by a database query), you will usually use a CFML tag called `<cfif>`. You haven't seen the `<cfif>` tag in action yet, but it's time you did. It's easy to use, powerful, and well suited for many different situations. This exercise will show you how to use `<cfif>` to make the search result page seem more professional.

1) In Dreamweaver, open the searchaction.cfm file if it's not open already. Remove the first `<cfoutput>` block (the one that displays the number of records found).

You will be replacing this message with two different messages, adding `<cfif>` logic along the way to tell ColdFusion which message to display in which situations.

2) Under the `<cfinclude>` tag, type the following code:

```
<!---If no matches were found --->
<cfif SearchQuery.RecordCount is 0>
```

This `<cfif>` tag tells ColdFusion to execute the following code only when the `SearchQuery.RecordCount` variable is equal to zero. In other words, the code that follows this `<cfif>` tag should only be used when the user's search keywords fail to return any records.

3) After the `<cfif>` line you just added, type the following message:

```
<!---Display a "no matches found" message --->
<p>No products were found that match your keywords
("<cfoutput>#FORM.Keywords#</cfoutput>").<br>
Please try a different search.</p>
```

Because it is preceded by the `<cfif>` tag, this message will only appear when the user's search returns no records.

4) After the message you just added, type the following:

```
<!---If at least one match was found --->
<cfelse>
```

As its name implies, the `<cfelse>` tag tells ColdFusion what to do if the condition in the preceding `<cfif>` tag is not met. In this case, the code that follows this `<cfelse>` tag will execute when `SearchQuery.RecordCount` is anything other than zero (that is, when at least one record is retrieved).

5) After the `<cfelse>` you just added, type the following message:

```
<!---Display the number of records found --->
<p>Products found:
<cfoutput>#SearchQuery.RecordCount#</cfoutput></p>
```

This code simply displays the number of records retrieved by the query, by outputting its `RecordCount` property.

6) After the `<cfoutput>` block that displays the matches (that is, just before the closing `</body>` tag), add the following:

```
</cfif>
```

This ends the conditional portion of the page; anything after this `</cfif>` will be included in the page regardless of the number of records found.

7) Indent the two portions of code (before and after the `<cfelse>`) to make the code easier to read.

```
20  <!--- Include logo and navigation header at top of page --->
21  <cfinclude template="header.cfm">
22
23  <!--- If no matches were found --->
24  <cfif SearchQuery.RecordCount is 0>
25
26    <!--- Display a "no matches found" message --->
27    <p>No products were found that match your keywords
28    ("<cfoutput>#FORM.Keywords#</cfoutput>").<br>
29    Please try a different search.</p>
30
31  <!--- If at least one match was found --->
32  <cfelse>
33
34    <!--- Display the number of records found --->
35    <p>Products found:
36    <cfoutput>#SearchQuery.RecordCount#</cfoutput></p>
37
38    <!--- Output information about each product --->
39    <cfoutput query="SearchQuery">
40      <a href="productdetail.cfm?ProductID=#ProductID#">#ProductName#</a><br>
41    </cfoutput>
42
43  </cfif>
```

TIP *Dreamweaver makes it easy to indent code. Just highlight the lines you want to indent (for instance, the lines between the opening* `<cfif>` *and the* `<cfelse>` *tag), and then press the Tab key or Shift+Ctrl+>. The selected lines of code will be indented for you. To reverse the change (that is, to unindent the code), press Shift-Tab or Shift+Ctrl+<.*

8) Save your work, and then try using the search tool again.

If you search for a word that is not in the list of products, you will see the "No products were found" message.

On the other hand, if you search for a word that returns at least one match (such as *phone*), you will see the second message.

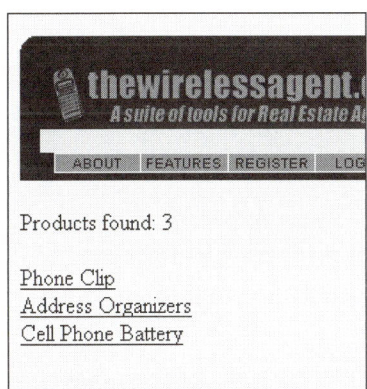

NOTE *As you can see, three records have been retrieved from the database based on a search for the word* phone, *even though the word* phone *doesn't actually appear when the search results are displayed. The search interface will find the word* phone *in a product description or product name, even though it's only the product name that is being displayed here. Just click on the link for each product in the search results to get to the product detail page, which also displays the description.*

EXPERIMENTING WITH COMPARISON OPERATORS

You have just learned how to use *conditional processing* to control the flow of execution within your ColdFusion pages. ColdFusion provides a few different ways to perform conditional processing, and you will learn more about them in subsequent lessons. Whenever you want a certain chunk of code to be executed only under certain conditions, wrap that chunk with a `<cfif>` block. If you want a different chunk of code to be executed when the first condition is not met, add a `<cfelse>` tag within the `<cfif>` block.

In the example you just worked on, the condition was described as:

```
SearchQuery.RecordCount is 0
```

The role of the `is` keyword here is fairly clear. It tells ColdFusion that the code in the `<cfif>` block should be executed if the two values on either side of the `is` (here, the number of records found and the number zero) are equivalent. Used in this way, the `is` keyword is actually one of a small group of special words called *comparison operators*.

Commonly used comparison operators include:

- `is`, which tests if the two values are the same
- `eq`, which is a synonym for `is`
- `is not`, which tests if the two values are different
- `neq`, which is a synonym for `is not`
- `gt`, which tests if the first value is greater than the first
- `lt`, which tests if the first value is less than the first
- `gte`, which tests if the first value is greater than or the same as the first
- `lte`, which tests if the first value is less than or the same as the first

These are the comparison operators that you are likely to need in the majority of situations. There are some other operators not included here; see the ColdFusion documentation for the definitive list.

In the page you just created, the `<cfif>` and `<cfelse>` logic used this basic structure:

```
<cfif SearchQuery.RecordCount is 0>
  ...not found message...
<cfelse>
  ...display records...
</cfif>
```

If you wish, try rearranging the code so that it uses the following basic structure, instead:

```
<cfif SearchQuery.RecordCount is not 0>
   …display records…
<cfelse>
   …not found message…
</cfif>
```

The page will behave in the same way in either case; they are really two ways of explaining the same idea to ColdFusion. There are two differences between the two versions of the logic. The first difference is the use of **is not** instead of **is**. The second difference is the fact that the position of the two messages has been swapped. By changing both of these things at the same time, the changes effectively cancel each other out. You're left with the same basic behavior: the "not found" message appears when there aren't any records to display, and the "display records" message appears when there are.

If you wish, you can rearrange the logic yet again, so that it looks like this:

```
<cfif SearchQuery.RecordCount gt 0>
   …display records…
<cfelse>
   …not found message…
</cfif>
```

This version of the logic uses the **gt** (greater than) operator instead of **is** or **is not** to get the job done, but the overall effect is, once again, the same. Similarly, you could rearrange the code one last time, like so:

```
<cfif SearchQuery.RecordCount lt 1>
   …not found message…
<cfelse>
   …display records…
</cfif>
```

That final version is probably the least intuitive—when asked to explain the concept of zero, "one less than one" isn't the answer that most people would come up with off the top of their heads! But it will work exactly the same way. The point to these little experiments is only to make you see how flexible ColdFusion's **<cfif>** tag and comparison operators are, and how that means there is often more than one way to skin a cat.

Okay, enough theory. On with the lesson!

COMBINING THE FORM AND ACTION PAGES

The version of the search page you have at this point works just fine, but there's one more thing you can do to improve its usability. Instead of displaying the search form and the search results on two separate pages, you can have both elements appear on the same page. That way, the search form will always be visible, even after a search. If the user's search doesn't retrieve the records they were expecting, they can refine their search right away, without having to use the Back button to return to a separate search form.

This exercise will show you how to combine the two pages you have created so far into one convenient search page.

1) Save the existing searchform.cfm file as productsearch.cfm (File > Save As).

Make sure to save it in the same folder as the other files from the lesson.

> **NOTE** *If Dreamweaver asks you about updating links in documents, answer* no. *Later on, when you are working on your own files, you can let Dreamweaver handle this for you. For now, let's do everything manually so you understand exactly what's going on.*

2) Change the `action` attribute of the `<form>` tag to productsearch.cfm (the name of your newly created file).

Before, the search form submitted the user's entries to a separate page. Now the browser will submit the entries back to the same page instead. When the user submits the form, the productsearch.cfm page will be executed again, and this time the user's search words will be available in `FORM.Keywords`.

> **NOTE** *Forms that submit their entries to the same page in this fashion are often called* self-submitting forms. *They are sometimes a tiny bit harder to write, but often more convenient for users.*

3) Copy the `<cfparam>` line from the top of searchaction.cfm and paste it at the top of the new productsearch.cfm page.

This is our way of saying that this new combined page will be using a form parameter called Keywords, just as the previous searchaction.cfm page did.

4) Add a `default=""` attribute to the `<cfparam>` tag you just pasted, so that it looks like this:

```
<cfparam name="FORM.Keywords" type="string" default="">
```

When you add a `default` attribute to a `<cfparam>` tag, you are telling ColdFusion to assign the default value to the variable if it doesn't exist already. In this case, the default value is an empty string, which means that the `FORM.Keywords` variable will always exist. If a specific value is submitted by the browser, then that value will be used. Otherwise, the variable will hold the default value (the empty string). This is a very handy way to deal with form or URL parameters that may or may not be specifically passed to a page.

5) **Add a `value="#FORM.Keywords#"` attribute to the form's `<input>` tag and wrap `<cfoutput>` tags around it, like so:**

```
<cfoutput>
  <input type="text" name="Keywords" size="15" value="#FORM.Keywords#">
</cfoutput>
```

The `value` attribute is part of the standard HTML `<input>` tag. It pre-fills the text field with whatever value you specify, so that the value is already showing when the page appears in a browser. In this case, the net effect is this: the search field will be blank when it first appears on the page, but when the page reloads after the user submits the form, the search field will retain whatever keywords the user has entered. This is a common usability feature on many search engines and other Web sites—your search results usually include the original search field, with your search words still present in the field.

TIP *Remember, the `<cfoutput>` tags are necessary any time you want ColdFusion to include the values of # sign variables in the final HTML source code it sends back to the browser.*

6) **Under the closing `</form>` tag, add the following code:**

```
<!---Stop here if the search field is blank --->
<cfif FORM.Keywords eq "">
  <cfabort>
</cfif>
```

```
16  <!--- Begin search form --->
17  <form action="productsearch.cfm" method="post">
18
19    <!--- Text field for entering search criteria --->
20    Search for products:
21    <cfoutput>
22      <input type="text" name="Keywords" size="15" value="#FORM.Keywords#">
23    </cfoutput>
24
25    <!--- Submit button for performing search --->
26    <input type="submit" value="Search">
27
28  </form>
29
30  <!--- Stop here if the search field is blank --->
31  <cfif FORM.Keywords eq "">
32    <cfabort>
33  </cfif>
```

This is the first time you're seeing the `<cfabort>` tag. As its name implies, the `<cfabort>` tag simply causes ColdFusion to stop processing the page. Any code after the `<cfabort>` tag does not get executed at all.

The `<cfabort>` tag is perfect for this situation. When the user first visits the search page, the `FORM.Keywords` parameter will be empty. This will cause the `<cfabort>` tag to execute, which stops the processing of the page. In other words, everything after this `<cfif>` block will execute only when the user types something into the search field and submits the form.

7) Copy the `<cfquery>` block from searchaction.cfm and paste it under the code you just added.

Since the query follows the `<cfabort>` code you just added, the query will only be run if the user has actually specified keywords to search for.

8) Copy the large `<cfif>` block (including the `<cfelse>` part and everything in between) from searchaction.cfm and paste it under the query.

You're now copying the code that actually displays the records retrieved by the query, or that displays a "no matches found" type of message if the query retrieves zero records.

```
30  <!--- Stop here if the search field is blank --->
31  <cfif FORM.Keywords eq "">
32    <cfabort>
33  </cfif>
34
35  <!--- Find matching products --->
36  <cfquery name="SearchQuery" datasource="products">
37    SELECT ProductID, ProductName
38    FROM tblProducts
39    WHERE (    (ProductName LIKE '%#FORM.Keywords#%')
40            OR (ProductDesc LIKE '%#FORM.Keywords#%')  )
41  </cfquery>
42
43  <!--- If no matches were found --->
44  <cfif SearchQuery.RecordCount is 0>
45
46    <!--- Display a "no matches found" message --->
47    <p>No products were found that match your keywords
48    ("<cfoutput>#FORM.Keywords#</cfoutput>").<br>
49    Please try a different search.</p>
50
51  <!--- If at least one match was found --->
52  <cfelse>
```

9) Save your work and test out the new productsearch.cfm page in your browser.

You can now run your searches and see the results all on the name page.

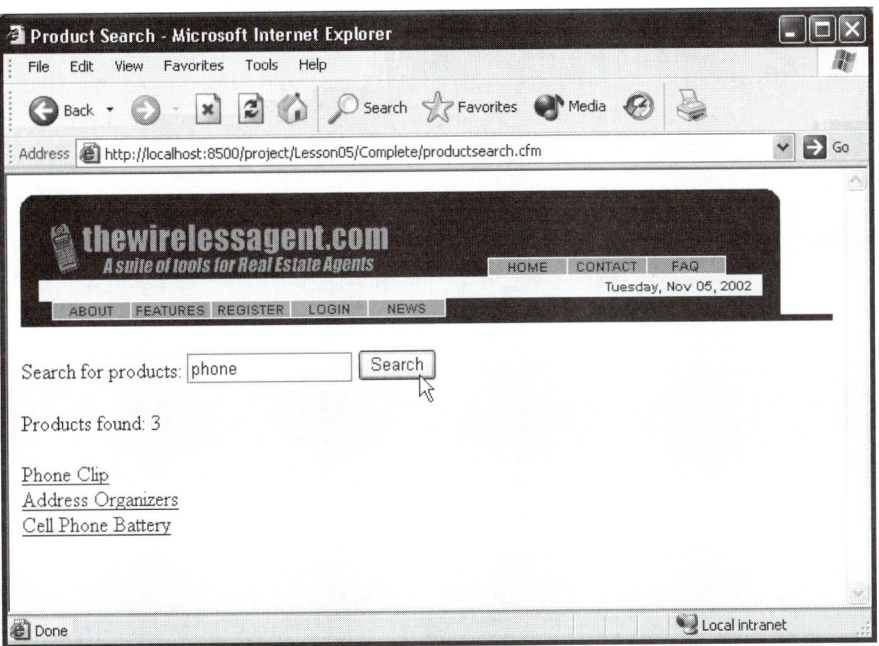

AUTO-FOCUSING THE SEARCH FIELD

As another usability improvement, you can use a bit of JavaScript to "focus" the text field on the search form when the page loads in the browser. In this context, the term *focus* basically means to activate the text field, so that the cursor is already in the field when the page appears. This keeps the user from having to click on the search field before typing their search keywords.

This exercise will show you how to add the necessary JavaScript code to the product search page. Unfortunately, there isn't space here to explain the code, or even to go into a proper explanation of what JavaScript is. For now, you will just need to accept that JavaScript is another mini-language that you can use to manage certain aspects of the browser's behavior (such as controlling form fields, opening popup windows, and so on). If you're not familiar with it, we encourage you to check out a JavaScript reference guide for more information.

1) In productsearch.cfm, add an `onload` attribute to the opening `<body>` tag, like so:

```
<body onload="document.forms[0].Keywords.focus()">
```

The code within the `onload` attribute is simple JavaScript syntax for setting focus to a text field or similar form element. Again, there isn't space to get into all the specifics here, but in plain English, this attribute basically means "when this page loads, activate the Keywords element in the first form within the document."

NOTE *JavaScript code is case-sensitive, so it's important that you capitalize everything within the `onload` attribute exactly as shown here. Also, it's important that the name attribute of the form's text `<input>` field be spelled `Keywords` (with a capital K).*

2) **Save your work and reload the productsearch.cfm page in your browser.**

When the page loads, the cursor will automatically be placed in the search field, ready for the user to type a query.

CREATING AN ADVANCED SEARCH PAGE

Many Web sites provide an advanced search page that allows users to add additional criteria to their search, thereby honing in more precisely on the records they are looking for. In this exercise, you'll add some advanced options to your existing search form; you'll learn how to add form fields that will allow the user to enter a price range (a minimum price, maximum price, or both). Additionally, the advanced version of the form will include a check box that allows the user to search only for products that are currently in stock.

1) **Use File > Save As to save the productsearch.cfm file as advproductsearch.cfm.**

Make sure to save the new file in the same folder as the other files for this lesson.

2) **Change the value of the form's `action` attribute to *advproductsearch.cfm*.**

Because the form on this page is designed to be self-submitting, you want the `action` attribute to match the name of the file.

3) **Under the existing `<cfparam>` at the top of the page, add the following lines:**

```
<!---Additional form parameters --->
<cfparam name="FORM.MinPrice" type="string" default="">
<cfparam name="FORM.MaxPrice" type="string" default="">
<cfparam name="FORM.InStockOnly" type="string" default="">
```

```
1  <!--- This page contains a form parameter named Keywords --->
2  <cfparam name="FORM.Keywords" type="string" default="">
3
4  <!--- Additional form parameters --->
5  <cfparam name="FORM.MinPrice" type="string" default="">
6  <cfparam name="FORM.MaxPrice" type="string" default="">
7  <cfparam name="FORM.InStockOnly" type="boolean" default="no">
8
9  <html>
```

4) Under the submit button in the existing form, add the following:

```
<!---Additional text fields for min/max prices --->
<cfoutput>
  <p>Price range:
  $<input type="text" name="MinPrice" size="5"
    <cfif IsNumeric(FORM.MinPrice)>value="#FORM.MinPrice#"</cfif>>
  to
  $<input type="text" name="MaxPrice" size="5"
    <cfif IsNumeric(FORM.MaxPrice)>value="#FORM.MaxPrice#"</cfif>>
</cfoutput>
```

```
29  <!--- Submit button for performing search --->
30  <input type="submit" value="Search">
31
32  <!--- Additional text fields for min/max prices --->
33  <cfoutput>
34    <p>Price range:
35    $<input type="text" name="MinPrice" size="5"
36      <cfif IsNumeric(FORM.MinPrice)>value="#FORM.MinPrice#"</cfif>>
37    to
38    $<input type="text" name="MaxPrice" size="5"
39      <cfif IsNumeric(FORM.MaxPrice)>value="#FORM.MaxPrice#"</cfif>>
40  </cfoutput>
```

These additional input fields work the same way as the `Keywords` field, except that the `value` attribute is only pre-filled with the user's previous entry if that entry was a numeric value. This snippet of code uses ColdFusion's built-in `IsNumeric()` function to accomplish this minor feat. The net effect is this: if the user enters a valid number for the minimum or maximum price field (such as `10` or `20`), that value will re-appear in the same field when the page reloads after a form submission. If, on the other hand, the user enters a non-numeric value (such as a word or some other garbage entry), the entry is ignored.

5) **Under the fields you just added, type the following:**

```
<br>
<input type="checkbox" name="InStockOnly" value="yes"
  <cfif FORM.InStockOnly>checked</cfif>>In stock
<hr>
```

```
37      to
38      $<input type="text" name="MaxPrice" size="5"
39        <cfif IsNumeric(FORM.MaxPrice)>value="#FORM.MaxPrice#"</cfif>>
40    </cfoutput>
41
42    <br>
43    <input type="checkbox" name="InStockOnly" value="yes"
44      <cfif FORM.InStockOnly>checked</cfif>>In stock<hr>
45  </form>
```

This creates a standard HTML check box element within the form. If the user checks the box and submits the form, the browser will submit the value of the check box (in this case, yes) to ColdFusion. If the user leaves the box unchecked, then no value for `InStockOnly` is submitted to the server, in which case the default value of the corresponding `<cfparam>` (at the top of the page) kicks in. In any case, the value of the `FORM.InStockOnly` will be Yes if the check box is checked, No if it is not.

6) **Within the `<cfquery>` block, add the following criteria:**

```
<!---If the user wants to see in-stock products only --->
<cfif FORM.InStockOnly eq "yes">
  AND ProductQty > 0
</cfif>
```

```
52  <!--- Find matching products --->
53  <cfquery name="SearchQuery" datasource="products">
54    SELECT ProductID, ProductName
55    FROM tblProducts
56    WHERE (    (ProductName LIKE '%#FORM.Keywords#%')
57          OR (ProductDesc LIKE '%#FORM.Keywords#%')  )
58
59    <!--- If the user wants to see in-stock products only --->
60    <cfif FORM.InStockOnly eq "yes">
61      AND ProductQty > 0
62    </cfif>
63  </cfquery>
```

If the "in stock" check box is checked when the user submits the form, this `<cfif>` block executes, adding an additional condition to the query's criteria. Only those records that have at least one item in stock will be retrieved.

NOTE *It's worth noting that the SQL operator for* greater than *in queries is* >, *whereas the equivalent CFML operator (for use in* `<cfif>` *tests) is* `gt`.

7) **Also within the `<cfquery>` block, add the following:**

```
<!---If user provided a minimum price --->
<cfif IsNumeric(FORM.MinPrice)>
  AND ProductPrice >= #FORM.MinPrice#
</cfif>
<!---If user provided a maximum price --->
<cfif IsNumeric(FORM.MaxPrice)>
  AND ProductPrice <= #FORM.MaxPrice#
</cfif>
```

```
52  <!--- Find matching products --->
53  <cfquery name="SearchQuery" datasource="products">
54    SELECT ProductID, ProductName
55    FROM tblProducts
56    WHERE (    (ProductName LIKE '%#FORM.Keywords#%')
57            OR (ProductDesc LIKE '%#FORM.Keywords#%')   )
58
59    <!--- If the user wants to see in-stock products only --->
60    <cfif FORM.InStockOnly eq "yes">
61      AND ProductQty > 0
62    </cfif>
63
64    <!--- If user provided a minimum price --->
65    <cfif IsNumeric(FORM.MinPrice)>
66      AND ProductPrice >= #FORM.MinPrice#
67    </cfif>
68
69    <!--- If user provided a maximum price --->
70    <cfif IsNumeric(FORM.MaxPrice)>
71      AND ProductPrice <= #FORM.MaxPrice#
72    </cfif>
73  </cfquery>
```

These `<cfif>` blocks use the `IsNumeric()` function again to test whether the user has specified a minimum or maximum price for his or her search. If so, these `<cfif>` blocks add the corresponding criteria to the SQL query's `WHERE` clause.

So, if the user types Phone into the search field, 5 for the minimum price, 20 for the maximum price, and checks the "in stock" check box, ColdFusion would end up using the following SQL syntax to retrieve records from the database:

```
SELECT ProductID, ProductName
FROM tblProducts
WHERE ( (ProductName LIKE '%Phone%') OR (ProductDesc LIKE '%Phone%') )
AND ProductQty > 0
AND ProductPrice >= 5
AND ProductPrice <= 20
```

8) Save your work, then use F12 to bring the revised form up in your browser.

This advanced form contains blanks for the search keywords, plus a minimum and maximum price. In addition, there is a checkbox for searching in-stock products only. Feel free to experiment with the form, using different values for the minimum/maximum prices and so on.

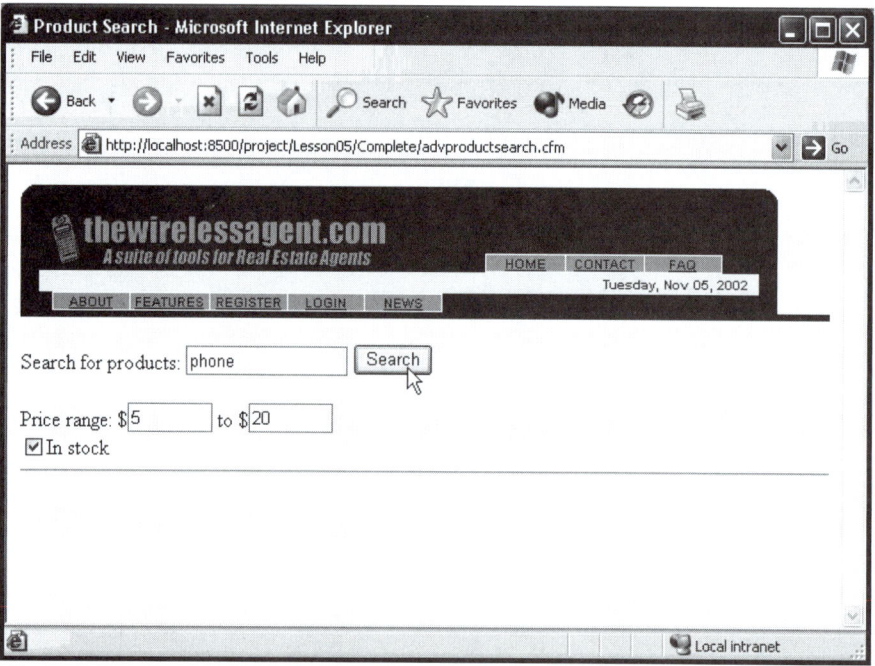

NOTE *You must type something into the text field in order to conduct a search, but the minimum/maximum fields and the in-stock checkbox are optional.*

WHAT YOU HAVE LEARNED

In this lesson, you have:

- Mastered the basic steps of simple form creation (pages 106–108)
- Processed form submissions in action pages (pages 108–112)
- Used `<cfif>` to create pages that adapt to different conditions (pages 113–117)
- Learned to repopulate form fields with previously submitted entries (pages 118–121)
- Learned to create search forms that respond to multiple search criteria (pages 122–126)

building data entry pages

LESSON 6

In Lessons 4 and 5, you learned how to retrieve information from a database, and how to create search forms for that same information. These are significant features for nearly any Web site, of course, but providing the means to make changes to the information in the database takes a site's power and usefulness to another level. That is the point at which your Web application becomes an active participant in the collection and maintenance of your company's data.

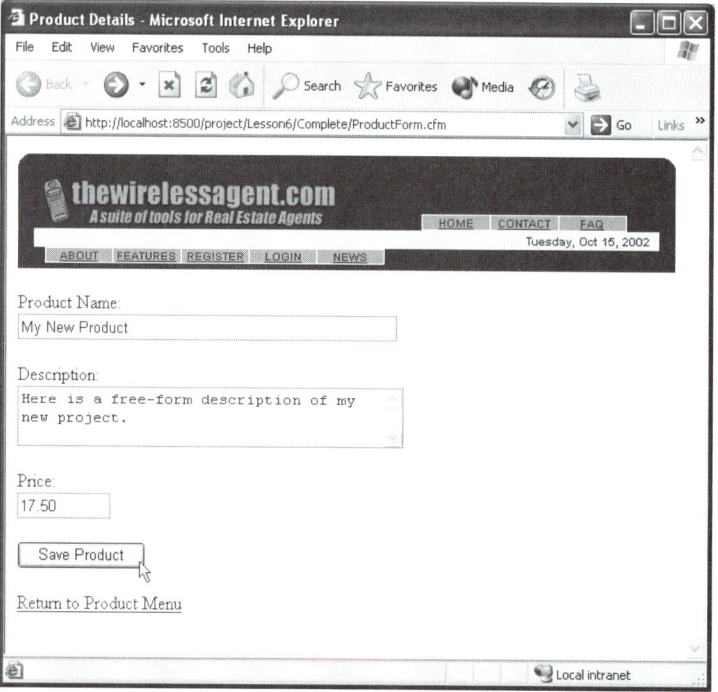

ColdFusion makes it easy to create Web-based interfaces for editing the information stored in a database table.

For example, let's say you want to change the price of an item in your catalog, or remove a customer or change his address. It used to be that you had to get into the database to make these kinds of changes. Now you can do them through a simple Web interface created with ColdFusion—you don't have to do them directly in the database. When you update information through the Web interface page, the changes would then be reflected throughout the site immediately. These options give you better control over your site's dynamic content and the information critical to its operation.

In this lesson you will be adding, updating, and removing items from the product database for the Wireless Agent Web site. This ability allows you to keep the product database content fresh and up to date.

WHAT YOU WILL LEARN

In this lesson, you will:

- Update records in a database
- Delete records from a database
- Insert records into a database
- Use validation rules to check form entries

APPROXIMATE TIME

This lesson takes approximately one hour and 30 minutes to complete.

LESSON FILES

Starting Files:

Lesson06\Start\ProductDetail.cfm
Lesson06\Start\ProductMenu.cfm

Completed Project:

Lesson06\Complete\ProductAction.cfm
Lesson06\Complete\ProductDelete.cfm
Lesson06\Complete\ProductDetail.cfm
Lesson06\Complete\ProductForm.cfm
Lesson06\Complete\ProductMenu.cfm

CREATING A PRODUCT MENU FOR UPDATING

Your first task will be to create a product menu for adding, editing, or deleting product records in the database. This will be a sort of "home base" for users who want to make any kind of edits to the product list. The good news is that you can create this product menu by making a few small additions to your existing productlist.cfm page. Let's get started.

NOTE *Assume that the users of the pages in this lesson are in-house users that are authorized to make changes to the database (rather than random visitors from the Internet at large). In Lesson 7, you will learn how to make sure that only the appropriate people are able to access these pages by requiring your users to log in.*

1) In Dreamweaver, open ProductMenu.cfm from the wwwroot\Project\Lesson06\ Start folder on your computer's hard drive.

As it stands, this file is the same as the productlist.cfm page from Lesson 4. The page queries the tblProducts table from the products.mdb database, displaying each product as a clickable link.

2) Wrap `<strong>` tags around the existing product link, and add a `<p>` tag, as follows:

```
<!---Link to view product details --->
<p>
<strong>
  <a href="ProductDetail.cfm?ProductID=#ProductID#">#ProductName#</a><br>
</strong>
```

TIP *Dreamweaver makes it easy to add `<strong>` tags (which instruct the browser to display the text using a bold font). Just highlight the text you want to affect (in this case, the `<a>` line), and then press the Bold button on the Text tab of the Insert toolbar. You can also use the Ctrl+B keyboard shortcut to do the same thing.*

3) Within the `<cfoutput>` block that displays the product links, add this Edit link:

```
<!---Link to edit product information --->
<a href="ProductForm.cfm?ProductID=#ProductID#">Edit</a>
```

As you can see, this link is very similar to the product detail link that you worked with in the previous step. Both pass the current product's ID number as a URL parameter. The only difference is the page that the link leads to—this new link leads to a page called ProductForm.cfm, which will give the user a form to edit the product information with. You will create that page later in this lesson.

4) Under the Edit link you just inserted, add this Remove link:

```
<!---Link to remove product from table --->
<a href="ProductDelete.cfm?ProductID=#ProductID#">Remove</a>
```

This link will invoke the ProductDelete.cfm page, which you will also create later in this chapter.

```
24  <!--- Output information about each product --->
25  <cfoutput query="ProductQuery">
26    <!--- Link to view product details --->
27    <p>
28    <strong>
29      <a href="ProductDetail.cfm?ProductID=#ProductID#">#ProductName#</a><br>
30    </strong>
31
32    <!--- Link to edit product information --->
33    <a href="ProductForm.cfm?ProductID=#ProductID#">Edit</a>
34
35    <!--- Link to remove product from table --->
36    <a href="ProductDelete.cfm?ProductID=#ProductID#">Remove</a>
37  </cfoutput>
```

5) Save your work and view the new product menu with your browser.

The edit and remove links won't work yet, of course, because the ProductForm.cfm and ProductDelete.cfm files haven't been created. When those pages are complete, though, this page will serve as a simple, easy place from which people can make changes.

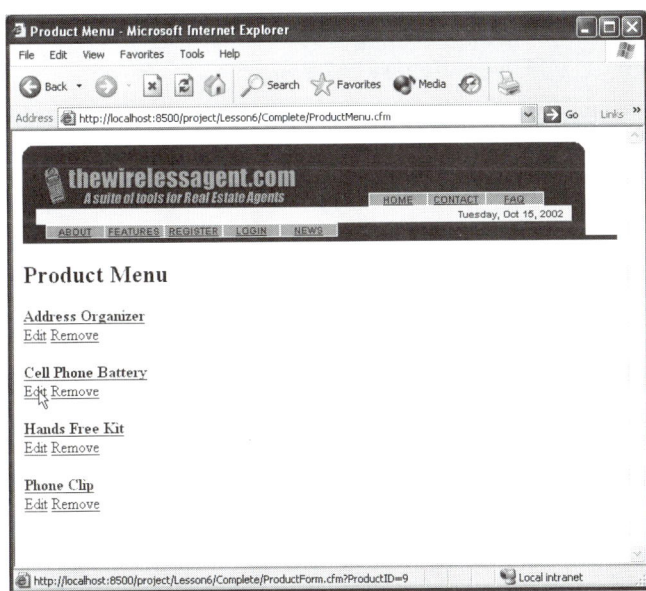

TIP *Remember, you can use the F12 key in Dreamweaver to quickly view the page you're working on in a browser.*

CREATING THE PRODUCT EDIT FORM

With the product menu in place, your next task is to create a form for editing individual product records. This page will be called *ProductForm.cfm* and will use the product ID number passed to it in the URL to retrieve the current product's information from the database. The page will then display an edit form with blanks for the product's name, description, and price. The blanks will be pre-filled with the current information about the product from the database.

If you think about it, this task isn't much different conceptually from what the Product Detail page (what you are brought to if you click the product name in the menu page you just created) already does. They both run a query based on the product ID passed in the URL, and then display the product information. The only difference is that one displays the information as a normal, text-based Web page, the other as an HTML form.

Since the two pages are so similar in terms of what they have to do, this exercise will use the ProductDetail.cfm page as a starting point.

1) In Dreamweaver, open the ProductDetail.cfm page (in the Lesson06\Start folder).

This is the same page that was originally created in Lesson 4.

2) Using File > Save As, save the page as ProductForm.cfm.

Make sure to save this file in the same folder.

3) Erase all the code between the existing `<cfoutput>` tags.

You will replace these lines with HTML form code.

4) Within the `<cfoutput>` block, add the following code:

```
<form action="ProductAction.cfm" method="post">
</form>
```

```
27  <!--- Display the product details --->
28  <cfoutput query="DetailQuery">
29    <form action="ProductAction.cfm" method="post">
30    </form>
31  </cfoutput>
```

This form will submit the user's entries to a ColdFusion page called ProductAction.cfm. That page will commit the user's form entries to the database. (The page doesn't exist yet; you will be creating it in the next exercise.)

TIP *If you want, you can use the Form button from the Forms tab of the Insert toolbar to create this* `<form>` *block instead of typing it manually. When the Form tag editor dialog appears, just enter* ProductAction.cfm *in the Action field, and select Post from the Method drop-down.*

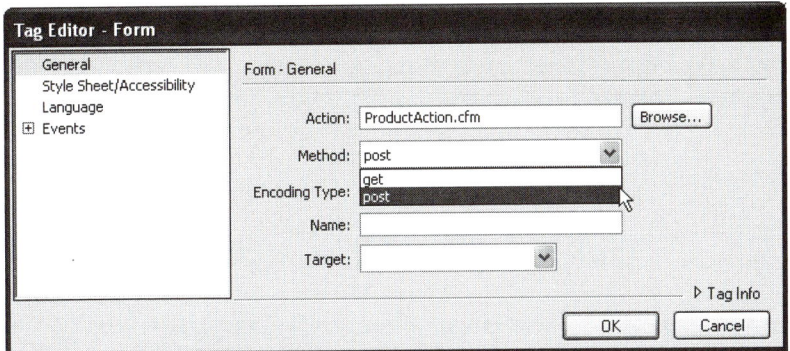

5) **Within the** `<form>` **block, add the following code:**

```
<!---Make ProductID available to action page --->
<input
  type="hidden"
  name="ProductID"
  value="#URL.ProductID#">
```

In addition to the visual form fields you have already worked with (such as text entry fields and checkboxes), the forms feature of HTML also includes the idea of a hidden form field. As the name implies, *hidden* fields are not visible when a form is displayed in a Web browser, so the user has no way to edit the information on screen. However, the value of the hidden field will be sent to the server along with all the other fields when the form is actually submitted.

Hidden fields are typically used (by a page or set of pages) as a simple way to "remember" small pieces of information while the form is being edited. In this case, the hidden field is being used to remember the ID number of the product that the user is currently modifying. When ColdFusion receives the user's submitted values in the form's action page, the hidden value will be available as a variable called `FORM.ProductID`, which the page can use to update the correct product record.

Think of the product list menu as Point A, the form as Point B, and the form's action page (which will save the user's changes to the database) as Point C. The product ID was passed from Point A to Point B as a URL parameter. The hidden field will pass the value from Point B to Point C.

6) After the hidden field, add the following text entry field:

```
<!---Text input field for product name --->
<p>Product Name:<br>
<input
  type="text"
  name="ProductName"
  size="50"
  maxlength="50"
  value="#HTMLEditFormat(ProductName)#">
```

NOTE *Just for fun, try using the Text Field button on the Forms tab of Dreamweaver's Insert bar (instead of typing this `<input>` tag manually). The Input tag editor dialog box will appear, where you can enter the name, size, maximum length, and value quickly and easily.*

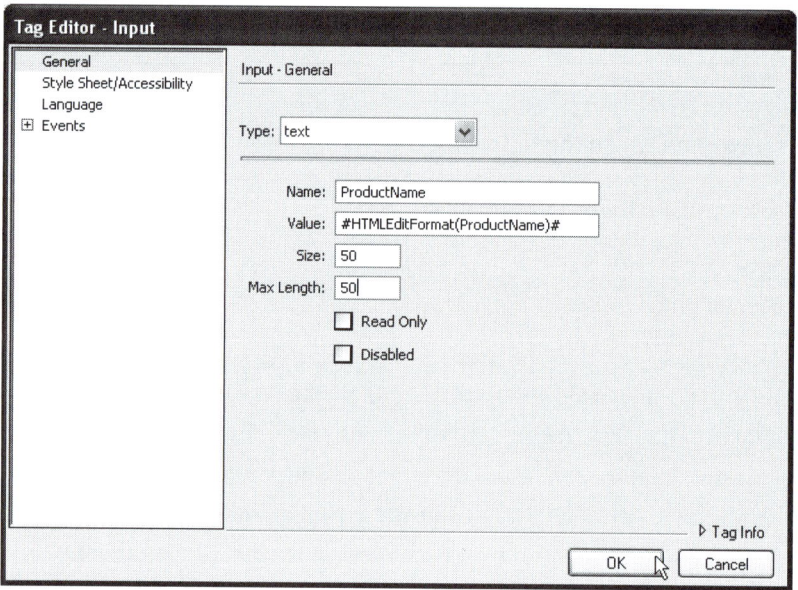

This text entry field will become a ColdFusion variable named `FORM.ProductName` when the form is submitted to its action page. Note that the `maxlength` attribute has been set to 50 to keep the user from entering a product name that is too long. The `value` attribute is populated with the value of the `ProductName` column from the `DetailQuery` recordset, so the current product name will be displayed in the edit field when the form first appears. ColdFusion's built-in `HTMLEditFormat()` function is wrapped around the `ProductName` variable, just in case the name currently stored in the database contains any characters that have special meaning to HTML (in particular, quotation marks).

NOTE *Always use the* `HTMLEditFormat()` *function when outputting database information that might contain quotation marks or angle brackets. The function will automatically replace these special characters with the corresponding HTML escape sequences (such as* `&quot;` *and* `&lt;`*). Otherwise, problems may arise if a user includes a quotation mark or angle bracket in the name or description of a product.*

7) **After the text field for the product name, add the following code:**

```
<!---Text area field for product description --->
<p>Description:<br>
<textarea
  name="ProductDesc"
  rows="3"
  cols="40"
  wrap="soft">#HTMLEditFormat(ProductDesc)#</textarea>
```

This creates a *text area* field for the product description. Text areas are just like normal text entry fields, except they are designed for text that can span multiple lines because of its length. Note the value of the field goes between opening and closing `<textarea>` tags, rather than in a value attribute. The `rows` and `cols` attributes control the physical size of the text area.

NOTE *The* `wrap="soft"` *attribute tells the browser to allow words to wrap while the user is typing, but to submit the text all on one line when the form is submitted. This is the way you want the wrapping to work in most cases. For details, please consult an HTML reference.*

8) **After the text area you just created, add the following code:**

```
<!---Text entry field for product price --->
<p>Price:<br>
<input
  type="text"
  name="ProductPrice"
  size="8"
  value="#HTMLEditFormat(ProductPrice)#">
```

This creates a text field for the product's price. It is essentially identical to the field for the product's name, which you created in Step 6.

9) **Finish the form by adding a submit button:**

```
<!---Submit button for committing data to database --->
<p><input type="submit" value="Save Product">
```

```
104      <!--- Text area field for product description --->
105      <p>Description:<br>
106      <textarea
107        name="ProductDesc"
108        rows="3"
109        wrap="soft"
110        cols="40">#HTMLEditFormat(ProductDesc)#</textarea>
111
112      <!--- Text entry field for product price --->
113      <p>Price:<br>
114      <input
115        type="text"
116        name="ProductPrice"
117        size="8"
118        value="#HTMLEditFormat(ProductPrice)#">
119
120      <!--- Submit button for committing data to database --->
121      <p><input type="submit" value="Save Product">
122
123    </form>
124  </cfoutput>
```

This creates a submit button labeled Save Product. When the user presses this button, the browser submits the user's entries to the ProductAction.cfm page (which you will create in the next exercise).

10) **Save and test your work.**

You can't visit the page you just created by simply visiting its URL (for instance, by hitting the F12 key in Dreamweaver), because it needs the ID number of the product you intend to edit. Instead, bring up the ProductMenu.cfm page in your browser, then click on one of the Edit links. The form you just created will appear, with the current information for the product filled in.

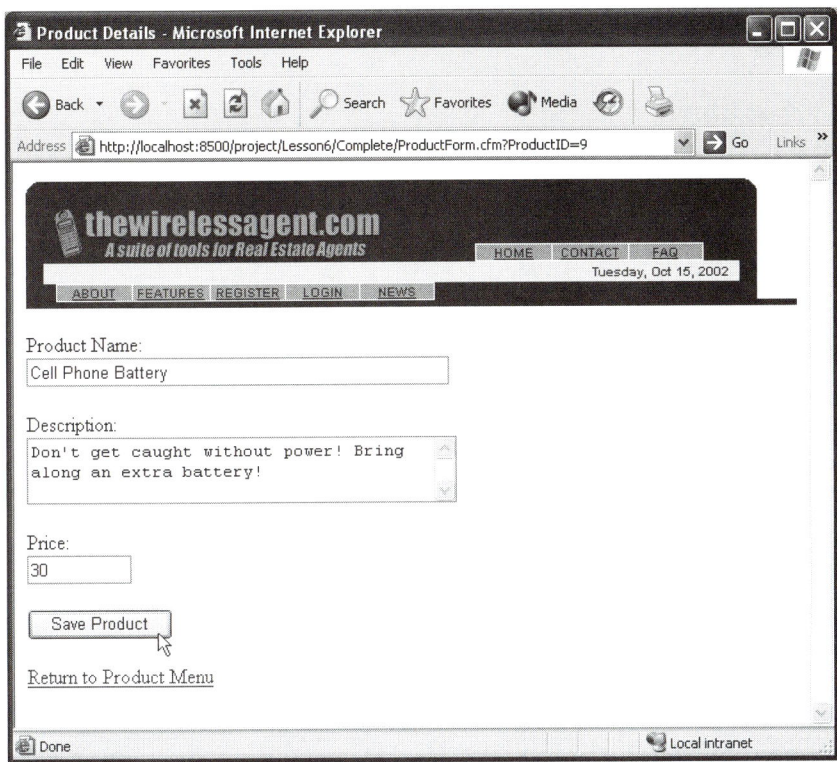

NOTE *If you try to submit the form with the Save Product button at this point, it won't work because the form's action page (ProductAction.cfm) hasn't been created yet. You'll create that page in the next exercise.*

PERFORMING THE UPDATE

Okay, users can now select a product to edit and make whatever changes they want on an on-screen form. Now all you need to do is create the ProductAction.cfm page to which the form submits the edited information. This page's job will be to update the product's record in the database with the user's entries.

There are two basic ways to perform database updates with ColdFusion:

- Automatically, with the `<cfupdate>` tag
- Manually, with an SQL `UPDATE` statement you write yourself in a `<cfquery>` block

For straightforward updating tasks, you can use the super-convenient `<cfupdate>` tag, which requires almost no typing on your part. For more complex updating tasks, where you might want to massage the user's entries or combine or cross-reference them with other information in some way, you can use `<cfquery>`, which gives you more control. You will learn how to use both in this lesson.

TIP *Think of `<cfupdate>` as a shortcut for writing an UPDATE query on your own.*

Let's try the `<cfupdate>` method first.

1) Use File > New in Dreamweaver to create a new ColdFusion file.

Remember, choose Dynamic Page > ColdFusion within the New File dialog so that you create a ColdFusion file instead of an ordinary HTML file.

2) Erase all code from the new file, so that it is completely empty.

Because this page will only perform an action (updating the database), rather than displaying anything, you don't want it to include the usual set of `<html>`, `<body>`, and other HTML tags.

3) At the top of the new file, add the following `<cfupdate>` tag:

```
<!---Update the product record in the database --->
<cfupdate datasource="products" tablename="tblProducts">
```

Believe it or not, that's all you need to do. ColdFusion will connect to the data source (in this case, the Access database for this book), determine the names of the columns in the database table, and match the fields from the form up with the names of the table columns. It then constructs the appropriate SQL UPDATE syntax and executes it on your behalf.

4) After the `<cfupdate>` tag, add the following:

```
<!---Send the user back to the product menu page --->
<cflocation url="ProductMenu.cfm">
```

```
1  <!--- Update the product record in the database --->
2  <cfupdate datasource="products" tablename="tblProducts">
3
4  <!--- Send the user back to the product menu page --->
5  <cflocation url="ProductMenu.cfm">
```

The `<cflocation>` tag instructs the browser to return to the ProductMenu.cfm page once the `<cfupdate>` operation is complete. If it weren't for this `<cflocation>` tag, the user would just see a blank white screen after the update was complete, since there is no HTML code on this page to display any kind of message or other information.

5) Save the new file as ProductAction.cfm (in the same folder as the other files for this lesson).

At this point, the update functionality is ready to go. Return to the update form in your browser and change the product name, description, or price (or all three). Now submit the form. ColdFusion will update the product record in the tblProducts table, and then return you to the product menu page you created at the beginning of this lesson. If you changed the name of the product, you will see the new name reflected right away in the product menu. You can click on the name of the product to go to the product's details page, which will also reflect the updated information.

DELETING RECORDS FROM A DATABASE

To delete a record from a database table, you use SQL's `DELETE` statement within the body of a `<cfquery>` block. In this exercise, you will create the ProductDelete.cfm page, which contains the code to make the Delete links on the product menu page actually work.

> **NOTE** *Be very careful when allowing users to delete records via a Web interface. SQL doesn't provide an "undo" command for `DELETE` operations. Once a record has been deleted, the idea is for it to be gone forever. Depending on the database software you are using, it may be possible to restore the information from the database's transaction log, but that is generally an involved process.*

1) Using File > New in Dreamweaver, create a new ColdFusion document. Remove all code from the new file, so that it is completely empty.

Again, this page will only be performing an action (deleting the appropriate record from the database), rather than displaying anything, so it shouldn't contain the usual set of HTML tags.

2) Add the following `<cfparam>` tag to the top of the new file:

```
<!---This page requires a ProductID value in the URL --->
<cfparam name="URL.ProductID" type="numeric">
```

This `<cfparam>` tag is identical to the ones at the top of the ProductDetail.cfm and ProductForm.cfm pages. It ensures that the ID number of the product to be deleted is provided to the page as a URL parameter.

3) Under the `<cfparam>` tag, add the following `<cfquery>` tag:

```
<!---Remove the product from the database --->
<cfquery datasource="products">
  DELETE FROM tblProducts
  WHERE ProductID = #URL.ProductID#
</cfquery>
```

This tag contains standard SQL `DELETE` syntax for removing a record from a database table. As you can see, the syntax is easy to use. Just use the words `DELETE FROM`, followed by the name of the table from which to delete the record(s), and then, in the `WHERE` clause, specify which records to delete.

NOTE *The criteria you provide in the `WHERE` clause can involve any number of conditions (separated by `AND` and `OR` logic, as in the advproductsearch.cfm page from Lesson 5). However, when you're deleting a specific record, you will almost always be using the record's ID number alone, as shown here.*

4) Add a `<cflocation>` tag to send the user back to the product menu page, as follows:

```
<!---Send the user back to the product menu page --->
<cflocation url="ProductMenu.cfm">
```

This is just like the `<cflocation>` that you added at the end of the previous exercise (the ProductAction.cfm page). It simply returns the user to the list of products after the `DELETE` operation is complete.

```
1  <!--- This page requires a ProductID value in the URL --->
2  <cfparam name="URL.ProductID" type="numeric">
3
4  <!--- Remove the product from the database --->
5  <cfquery datasource="products">
6    DELETE FROM tblProducts
7    WHERE ProductID = #URL.ProductID#
8  </cfquery>
9
10 <!--- Send the user back to the product menu page --->
11 <cflocation url="ProductMenu.cfm">
```

5) Save the file as ProductDelete.cfm (in the same folder as the other files you've been working with).

That's all you need to do. You can now test out the delete functionality by going back to the product menu page and trying

TIP *Be careful! Clicking the Delete link will delete the record right away, with no confirmation or other warning.*

INSERTING INFORMATION INTO A DATABASE

Okay, so your users can now modify and delete existing records, but what about adding new product records? After all, one of the most important aspects of a database application is the ability to add new information to it. This exercise will show you how to add a simple record-insertion capability to the pages you've created so far.

NOTE *There are many ways to approach the insertion of new records. In particular, some sites will want the form for inserting a record to be different from the one used to update an existing record. For most situations, however, it is usually sufficient to use the same Web form for inserts and updates. Many developers find this preferable, in fact, since it means that they don't have to maintain two different form pages. This exercise assumes that you want to use the same form to insert new records and update existing ones.*

1) In the Product Menu page (ProductMenu.cfm), add the following code just above the `<cfoutput>` block:

```
<!---New Product button for inserting database record --->
<form action="ProductForm.cfm">
  <input type="submit" value="New Product">
</form>
```

This creates an extremely simple HTML form that contains only a single submit button, marked New Product. The only reason we're using a form here is to show you that you can use forms to create simple navigational buttons for certain kinds of situations. Many people will respond to a button differently than a normal hyperlink, so there may be times when you find it useful to use this technique.

```
19  <!--- Title this section of the page --->
20  <h2>Product Menu</h2>
21
22  <!--- New Product button for inserting database record --->
23  <form action="ProductForm.cfm">
24    <input type="submit" value="New Product">
25  </form>
26
27  <!--- Output information about each product --->
28  <cfoutput query="ProductQuery">
29    <!--- Link to view product details --->
```

If you would prefer that users use a normal hyperlink instead of a button to insert a record, you could the following link code instead:

```
<a href="ProductForm.cfm">New Product</a>
```

In any case, the important thing to note here is that the ProductForm.cfm page will now be linked to *without* supplying a URL parameter called `ProductID`. But the ProductForm.cfm page requires a `ProductID` parameter in the URL in order to function properly, and will display an error message if the parameter is missing. Therefore, you will need to make a couple of minor changes to that page, so that it interprets the lack of a `ProductID` parameter as a signal that the user wants to insert a new record.

2) In ProductForm.cfm, add a `default="0"` attribute to the `<cfparam>` at the top of the page, like so:

```
<!---This page looks for a ProductID value in the URL --->
<cfparam name="URL.ProductID" type="numeric" default="0">
```

Without the `default` attribute, ColdFusion would have displayed an error message if the page were visited without a `ProductID` parameter in the URL. Now it will just set the `URL.ProductID` variable to zero whenever the parameter is not provided explicitly.

3) Also in ProductForm.cfm, add this code just after the `<cfquery>` block:

```
<!---If the user wants to create a new record --->
<cfif URL.ProductID eq 0>
  <cfset QueryAddRow(DetailQuery)>
</cfif>
```

```
1  <!--- This page looks for a ProductID value in the URL --->
2  <cfparam name="URL.ProductID" type="numeric" default="0">
3
4  <!--- Get data about this product from the database --->
5  <cfquery name="DetailQuery" datasource="Products">
6    SELECT *
7    FROM tblProducts
8    WHERE ProductID = #URL.ProductID#
9  </cfquery>
10
11 <!--- If the user wants to create a new record --->
12 <cfif URL.ProductID eq 0>
13   <cfset QueryAddRow(DetailQuery)>
14 </cfif>
15
```

This `<cfif>` test checks to see if the value of the `URL.ProductID` variable is currently zero. If so, that is an indication that the parameter was not provided explicitly to the page, which in turn is an indication that the user got to the page via the New Product button (as opposed to the Edit link for one of the existing products).

If the `<cfif>` test determines that the user is inserting a new record, a ColdFusion function called `QueryAddRow()` is used to add a new, blank row to the `DetailQuery` recordset. Why? Well, consider what is going to happen when the `<cfquery>` tag (just above this code) is executed. Remember, the query looks like this:

```
6    SELECT *
7    FROM tblProducts
8    WHERE ProductID = #URL.ProductID#
```

Since the `URL.ProductID` variable is zero, the query is going to attempt to retrieve all records that have a product ID number of zero. Of course, none of them do, and none of them ever will, so the query will always return an empty recordset (that is, a recordset that has all the usual columns but no rows of actual data). The `QueryAddRow()` function is then used to add a single blank row to the recordset. After this code executes, the recordset contains exactly one row, just as if a record had been successfully retrieved from the database. The only difference is that the values for the product name, description, and all other fields are blank (that is, the value of each column is an empty string).

NOTE *This is a trick to essentially fool the rest of the page into behaving as if a record has been retrieved from the database. For instance, when the page gets to the place where it is meant to pre-fill the product name and description fields with the corresponding values in the recordset, it will faithfully do so—but since those values are all blank, the result will be an empty form, all ready for the new record's information. There are other ways to achieve this same effect; this is simply one of the simplest and easiest to put into place.*

4) Put a `<cfif>` test around the form's hidden field, as follows:

```
<!---Make ProductID available to action page --->
<cfif URL.ProductID neq 0>
  <input
    type="hidden"
    name="ProductID"
    value="#URL.ProductID#">
</cfif>
```

This will cause the hidden field to *not* be included in the form when the user is inserting a new record. Thus, when the form is submitted, no `ProductID` value will be supplied to the form's action page (ProductAction.cfm). That page will be able to interpret the absence of the `ProductID` as a signal that the user is submitting information that should be used to create a new record.

5) **At the very top of ProductAction.cfm, add the following `<cfif>` test:**

    ```
    <cfif IsDefined("FORM.ProductID")>
    ```

6) **Add a `<cfelse>` tag after the existing `<cfupdate>` tag.**

    The `<cfupdate>` tag should now be sandwiched between the `<cfif>` and the `<cfelse>`.

7) **Under the `<cfelse>`, add the following `<cfupdate>` tag:**

    ```
    <!---Update the product record in the database --->
    <cfinsert datasource="products" tablename="tblProducts">
    ```

    NOTE *As used here, the attributes for the `<cfinsert>` tag are the same as for `<cfupdate>`. The `tablename` attribute tells ColdFusion which table to insert the new record into, and the `datasource` attribute tells ColdFusion which database the table is a part of. Sometimes, you may also want to use the `formfields` attribute as well; see the ColdFusion documentation for details.*

8) **Add a closing `</cfif>` tag after the `<cfinsert>` you just added.**

    ```
    <cfif IsDefined("FORM.ProductID")>
       <!--- Update the product record in the database --->
       <cfupdate datasource="products" tablename="tblProducts">

    <cfelse>
       <!--- Insert a new product record to the database --->
       <cfinsert datasource="products" tablename="tblProducts">

    </cfif>

    <!--- Send the user back to the product menu page --->
    <cflocation url="ProductMenu.cfm">
    ```

    This concludes the code needed to make the page work for both inserts and updates.

9) **Save your work in all three files, and then test out the insert functionality.**

    You should be able to insert a new record by clicking the New Product button on the product menu page, and then filling out the form and clicking the form's submit button. After the new record is inserted, you will be returned to the product menu page (where the new product should be showing). You can then view, edit, or delete the new record just like any of the other products.

ADDING VALIDATION RULES

Your form-based interface for updating and inserting records is coming along nicely. The only real problem with it is the fact that it doesn't do any kind of *validation* of the user's entries. Validation is the process of making sure that information is appropriate for the way it's intended to be used. In the case of form entries, validation basically means performing simple checks to make sure that form fields aren't left blank, or that certain fields contain only numbers, dates, or whatever other type of information is appropriate.

ColdFusion MX provides two easy ways to add validation to your forms:

- With server-side validation rules
- With client-side validation, powered by JavaScript

Developers can choose which of these methods to use, or can use them in conjunction with each other. Let's work on the server-side validation option first.

VALIDATING FORM ENTRIES ON THE SERVER SIDE

This exercise will show you how to tell ColdFusion to check the user's entries after the user submits the form (but before any attempt is made to send the information to the database).

1) In Dreamweaver, open the ProductForm.cfm page, if it's not open already.

This is the product-editing page that you created earlier in the lesson. You will now add validation rules to the form so that the user is prevented from leaving the name, price, or other fields blank.

2) After the opening `<form>` tag (before the existing hidden field), insert the following lines:

```
<!---Add server-side validation rules --->
<input type="hidden" name="ProductName_required">
<input type="hidden" name="ProductDesc_required">
<input type="hidden" name="ProductPrice_required">
```

```
27  <!--- Display the product details --->
28  <cfoutput query="DetailQuery">
29    <form action="ProductAction.cfm" method="post">
30
31      <!--- Add server-side validation rules --->
32      <input type="hidden" name="ProductName_required">
33      <input type="hidden" name="ProductDesc_required">
34      <input type="hidden" name="ProductPrice_required">
```

When the form is submitted, these values will be passed to ColdFusion along with the other form fields. When ColdFusion receives a form field that ends in `_required`, it takes this as a signal that the corresponding form field should be considered to be *required* (that is, can't be left blank). For instance, when ColdFusion receives the `ProductName_required` field, it will inspect the user's entry for the `ProductName` field. If the user has left the product name blank, ColdFusion displays a simple message that instructs the user to fix the entry and re-submit the form.

So, by adding these three hidden fields, you have just ensured that the user will not be able to leave the product name, description, or price blank.

NOTE *The validation rules are applied (and any error message is displayed) before the code in the form's action page is executed. This means that you can write the action page with confidence, knowing that it will not be executed if the user provides incomplete or incorrect entries.*

3) After the three hidden fields you just added, add one more, like so:

```
<input type="hidden" name="ProductPrice_float">
<input type="hidden" name="ProductPrice_range" value="min=0">
```

```
31    <!--- Add server-side validation rules --->
32    <input type="hidden" name="ProductName_required">
33    <input type="hidden" name="ProductDesc_required">
34    <input type="hidden" name="ProductPrice_required">
35    <input type="hidden" name="ProductPrice_float">
36    <input type="hidden" name="ProductPrice_range" value="min=0">
```

This hidden field ends in `_float`, rather than in `_required`. While the previous hidden fields told ColdFusion to make sure users aren't able to leave fields blank, this one makes sure that the user's entry for the `ProductPrice` field is a valid floating-point number. (If you don't remember the exact definition of a floating-point number from high school math, the basic idea is that the number can contain a decimal point, with any number of digits to the right.) The `_float` validation rule is handy whenever you are collecting a price or other currency-based value from users.

The `_range` validation rule can be used to make sure that a numeric value isn't too small or too big. Just as an example, the hidden field shown here insists that the price of the product is at least zero. If the user tries to enter a negative number for the price, the validation rule will kick in and display a message to the user when the form is submitted.

NOTE *ColdFusion also supports some other validation rules not shown in this lesson: `_integer`, `_time`, `_date`, and `_eurodate`. See the ColdFusion documentation for details.*

4) Save your work, and then test the revised form in your browser.

If you submit the form without filling in all the values properly, ColdFusion will display a message explaining what exactly needs to change before the form can be submitted. You can then use your browser's Back button to return to the form and fix your entries.

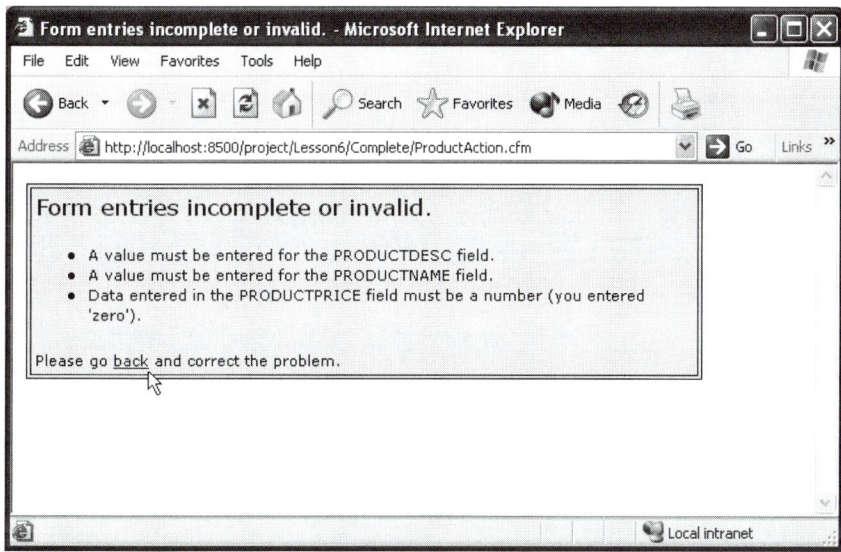

TIP *You can customize the look of the message that appears when a validation rule is not obeyed (for instance, a field being left blank), using the `<CFERROR>` tag. Consult the ColdFusion documentation for details about `<CFERROR>`.*

NOTE *You can also customize the text of the validation message for each field, by supplying a `value` attribute to the `_required` or `_float` hidden fields. The ColdFusion documentation explains the details.*

VALIDATING FORM ENTRIES ON THE CLIENT SIDE

The validation rules you just learned about are checked *after* the user submits the form. ColdFusion also provides a simple way to add *client-side validation* to your forms. The idea behind client-side validation is to check the user's entries *before* the form is submitted.

To add ColdFusion's client-side validation to your pages, you need to use the `<cfform>` tag instead of the normal HTML `<form>` tag. Then, for any fields to which you want to apply client-side validation, you change the `<input>` to `<cfinput>`, adding a few additional attributes as you go. ColdFusion uses the attributes you supply to these tags to add special JavaScript code to your form for you. So, even though the user's form entries will be checked for consistency by JavaScript, you don't have to know anything about JavaScript to get the job done. Pretty nifty, eh?

NOTE *There is more to the client-side validation feature than can be covered in this short lesson, but the following exercise will get you started by introducing you to the most commonly used attributes.*

1) **Still in ProductForm.cfm, change the opening and closing `<form>` tags to `<cfform>` tags.**

   You can leave the attributes of the tags alone, so the only change you're making here adding the letters `cf` to the tag name. Changing the tags to `<cfform>` tells ColdFusion to add its special JavaScript code to the form on the fly as it is processing the page. You need to use `<cfform>` to be able to include `<cfinput>` tags, which are how you specify which form fields should be checked using client-side validation.

   ```
   27  <!--- Display the product details --->
   28  <cfoutput query="DetailQuery">
   29    <cfform action="ProductAction.cfm" method="post">
   ```

2) **Change the `<input>` field for the product name to `<cfinput>` and add `required` and `message` attributes, like so:**

   ```
   <cfinput
     type="text"
     name="ProductName"
     size="50"
     maxlength="50"
     value="#HTMLEditFormat(ProductName)#"
     required="yes"
     message="Please don't leave the product name blank.">
   ```

   The `required` attribute tells ColdFusion to add JavaScript code to the form that ensures the user hasn't left the field blank (in which case the user would be shown the message provided in the `message` attribute). You can leave the `message` attribute out if you wish, but the default message that ColdFusion uses when you do isn't as user-friendly.

3) **Make similar changes to the input field for the product price, like so:**

```
<cfinput
  type="text"
  name="ProductPrice"
  size="8"
  value="#HTMLEditFormat(ProductPrice)#"
  required="yes"
  validate="float"
  message="Please enter a number for the product's price.">
```

This code adds a `validate="float"` attribute to make sure that the user enters a valid number.

NOTE *In addition to* float, *you can also use* date, eurodate, time, integer, telephone, zipcode, creditcard, social_security_number, *and* regular_expression. *Details are available in the ColdFusion documentation.*

4) **Save your work and test the new version of the form.**

If you fail to enter the correct information before attempting to submit the form, a JavaScript-powered message box appears, displaying the validation message you provided to the `message` attribute of the `<cfinput>` tag. Once you've fixed the problem(s) in the form, it will be submitted normally.

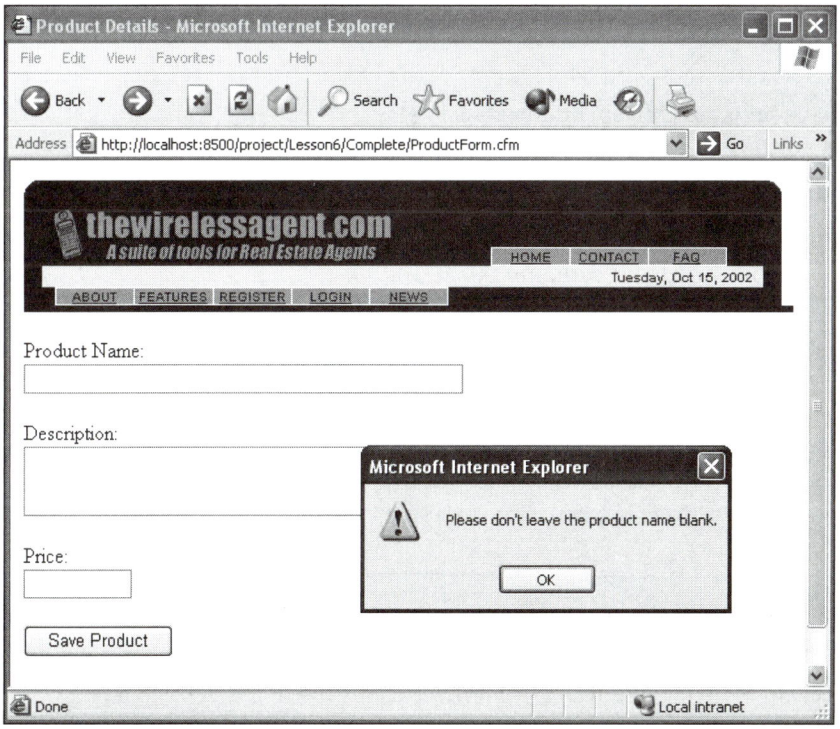

NOTE *By definition, the client-side validation checks will be sidestepped if the user (or a company firewall) has disabled JavaScript in their browser. The server-side validation rules will still work, though, so it's a good idea to use both when you can.*

NOTE *ColdFusion doesn't provide a built-in client-side validation mechanism for `<textarea>` fields in the same way it does for simple text input fields. You can add such validation on your own using JavaScript, but that's beyond the scope of what can be covered in this lesson. The server-side validation rule you added earlier does work with `<textarea>` fields.*

OPTIONAL: USING SQL'S UPDATE AND INSERT STATEMENTS

NOTE *This exercise is optional. You don't necessarily need to know how to work with `INSERT` and `UPDATE` to build ColdFusion applications. If you wish, you can skip this section for now and come back to it if you have a specific need or curiosity later.*

Earlier in this lesson, you learned how to use the `<cfupdate>` and `<cfinsert>` tags to update existing records or insert new records into a database. When you use these tags, ColdFusion writes and executes SQL `UPDATE` and `INSERT` statements for you behind the scenes. It's also possible to use `UPDATE` and `INSERT` in ordinary `<cfquery>` tags, which gives you complete control over the exact SQL that ColdFusion uses to interact with the database.

It's not possible to explain everything about SQL `UPDATE` and `INSERT` statements here, but this exercise will show you how to convert the existing `<cfupdate>` and `<cfinsert>` tags in your code to the corresponding `<cfquery>` tags.

1) If it's not open already, open the ProductAction.cfm page in Dreamweaver.

This is the page that processes the user's requests to insert or modify product records in the database. You created it earlier in this lesson.

2) Add the following `<cfparam>` lines at the very top of the page:

```
<!---This page expects the following form fields --->
<cfparam name="FORM.ProductName" type="string">
<cfparam name="FORM.ProductDesc" type="string">
<cfparam name="FORM.ProductPrice" type="numeric">
```

For security reasons, it is always strongly advised that you use `<cfparam>` to establish the names and expected data types (`string`, `numeric`, `datetime`, or the like) of all form variables the page will be dealing with. Without the `<cfparam>` checks, it is possible that a hacker could do mean things to your database by including SQL commands in the URL.

NOTE *This security issue is a bit too involved to explain properly here; it is discussed in more detail in Security Bulletin ASB99-04, available at www.macromedia.com/security.*

3) **Above the existing `<cfupdate>` tag (within the `<cfif>` block), add one more `<cfparam>` for the product ID:**

```
<!---Product IDs are expected to be numeric --->
<cfparam name="FORM.ProductID" type="numeric">
```

This `<cfparam>` serves the same basic purpose as the ones you added in the last step. However, since the product ID is provided to this page only when the user is performing an update (as opposed to an insert), this line needs to be within the portion of the page that is especially for updates. That's why it is positioned within (or protected by, if you will) the `<cfif>` block.

4) **Now replace the `<cfupdate>` tag with the following `<cfquery>` block:**

```
<!---Update the product record in the database --->
<cfquery datasource="products">
  UPDATE tblProducts
  SET ProductName = '#FORM.ProductName#',
    ProductDesc = '#FORM.ProductDesc#',
    ProductPrice = #FORM.ProductPrice#
  WHERE ProductID = #FORM.ProductID#
</cfquery>
```

```
 7  <cfif IsDefined("FORM.ProductID")>
 8    <!--- <cfupdate datasource="products" tablename="tblProducts"> --->
 9
10    <!--- Product IDs are expected to be numeric --->
11    <cfparam name="FORM.ProductID" type="numeric">
12
13    <!--- Update the product record in the database --->
14    <cfquery datasource="products">
15      UPDATE tblProducts
16      SET ProductName = '#FORM.ProductName#',
17        ProductDesc = '#FORM.ProductDesc#',
18        ProductPrice = #Val(FORM.ProductPrice)#
19      WHERE ProductID = #FORM.ProductID#
20    </cfquery>
21
```

This is the basic form of a typical **UPDATE** query. The word **UPDATE** is followed by the table name, then the word **SET**, followed by a series of column names and updated values. Values for normal text columns are surrounded by single quotation marks; numeric values are not. The **WHERE** clause specifies which row to alter.

NOTE *Be careful! If you forget to add the* **WHERE** *clause, all rows of the table will be updated with the new values. There's no easier way to get yourself in big trouble.*

TIP *Instead of replacing the* **<cfupdate>** *tag, you might want to just put ColdFusion comment tags around it, so that you can still see the "old way" of updating the record in your code. Developers often refer to this as commenting out a line of code. You can use the Comment button on the CFML Basic tab of Dreamweaver's Insert toolbar to quickly comment out the tag.*

5) Replace the `<cfinsert>` tag with the following code:

```
<!---Insert a new product record to the database --->
<cfquery datasource="products">
  INSERT INTO tblProducts (
    ProductName, ProductDesc, ProductPrice
  ) VALUES (
    '#FORM.ProductName#', '#FORM.ProductDesc#', #FORM.ProductPrice#
  )
</cfquery>
```

```
<cfelse>
  <!--- <cfinsert datasource="products" tablename="tblProducts"> --->

  <!--- Insert a new product record to the database --->
  <cfquery datasource="products">
    INSERT INTO tblProducts (
      ProductName, ProductDesc, ProductPrice
    ) VALUES (
      '#FORM.ProductName#', '#FORM.ProductDesc#', #Val(FORM.ProductPrice)#
    )
  </cfquery>
</cfif>

<!--- Send the user back to the product menu page --->
<cflocation url="ProductMenu.cfm">
```

This is a fairly typical **INSERT** query. The words **INSERT INTO** are followed by the table name, then a set of parentheses that contains a list of column names. Then the word **VALUES** is followed by another set of parentheses that contains a list of values. Again, values for normal text columns are surrounded by single quotation marks; numeric values are not.

6) Save your work and test the insert and update functionality.

Inserts and updates will continue to work in the same way they did before. The difference is that here, you wrote the SQL code yourself, rather than having ColdFusion write it for you on the fly. As you've seen, doing things this way requires more work on your part than just using `<cfinsert>` and `<cfupdate>`. So what was the point of this exercise?

The answer is that there are all sorts of special circumstances where there will be added benefit in writing the `INSERT` and `UPDATE` code yourself. For instance, you could use conditional logic (such as `<cfif>` tags) in the body of the `<cfquery>` tag to create slightly different SQL code depending on some sort of criteria important to your application. You can also use ColdFusion variables other than form variables (like URL variables or variables you create yourself with `<cfset>`) in the body of the query. In short, you get more control over what exactly happens behind the scenes when an update or insert takes place.

WHAT YOU HAVE LEARNED

In this lesson, you have:

- Created a "menu" page for modifying database information (pages 130–131)
- Created a form for editing and inserting database records (pages 132–136)
- Updated a database record with `<cfupdate>` (pages 137–138)
- Deleted a database record with SQL's `DELETE` statement (pages 139–140)
- Inserted a new database record with `<cfinsert>` (pages 141–144)
- Added server-side validation rules with hidden fields (pages 145–147)
- Added client-side validation rules with `<cfform>` and `<cfinput>` (pages 147–149)
- Learned about using SQL's `INSERT` and `UPDATE` instead of `<cfinsert>` and `<cfupdate>` (pages 150–153)

creating secured pages

LESSON 7

In the last chapter, you learned how to create a set of pages that allow users to edit the information in a database table. The actual example files only allowed edits to a list of products, but you could obviously apply the same ideas to create similar editing pages for lists of customers, mailing lists, purchase orders, or just about any other type of information. No matter what the underlying database tables track, Web-based editing pages are almost always welcomed with open arms, since they are so familiar and easy for users to understand.

So far, though, there's one big piece missing: security. The product menu and product editing examples from the last chapter are completely insecure. The only thing you would need to know to get into those pages is the URL, which just about anyone could stumble across. It's fairly clear that the pages should prompt the user for a user name and password, to make sure that only the appropriate people can make changes to your data.

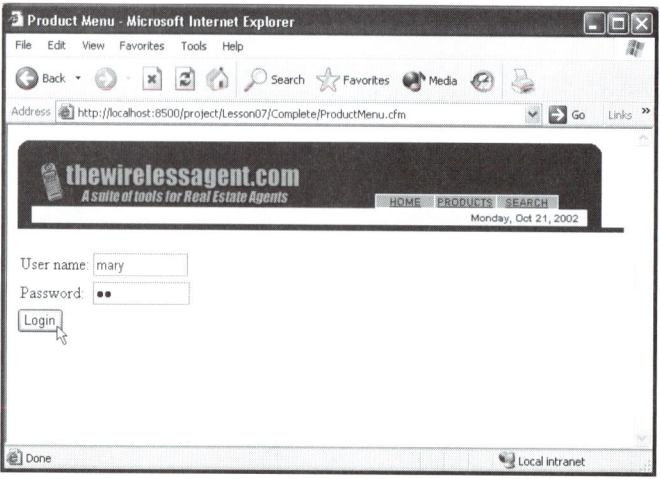

The new ‹cflogin›, ‹cflogout›, and related tags and functions make it easy to add password protection to your pages.

Luckily, ColdFusion MX includes a brand-new set of tags and functions that make it really easy to add a reasonable amount of security to your applications. These login-related tags and functions make up a kind of framework that is straightforward enough to handle simple projects easily, yet flexible enough to allow you to address more complicated demands as well. This lesson will get you started with this new security framework.

WHAT YOU WILL LEARN

In this lesson you will:

- Learn about the `<cflogin>` framework of tags and functions
- Create a form for users to log in with
- Determine whether a user name and password are valid
- Apply password protection to individual pages
- Use security roles to give different levels of access to different people

APPROXIMATE TIME

This lesson will take approximately one hour and 30 minutes to complete.

LESSON FILES

Starting Files:
Lesson07\Start\LoginForm.cfm
Lesson07\Start\ProductAction.cfm
Lesson07\Start\ProductDelete.cfm
Lesson07\Start\ProductDetail.cfm
Lesson07\Start\ProductForm.cfm
Lesson07\Start\ProductList.cfm
Lesson07\Start\ProductMenu.cfm

Completed Project:
Lesson07\Complete\ForceUserToLogin.cfm
Lesson07\Complete\Header.cfm
Lesson07\Complete\LoginForm.cfm
Lesson07\Complete\Logout.cfm
Lesson07\Complete\ProductAction.cfm
Lesson07\Complete\ProductDelete.cfm
Lesson07\Complete\ProductDetail.cfm
Lesson07\Complete\ProductForm.cfm
Lesson07\Complete\ProductList.cfm
Lesson07\Complete\ProductMenu.cfm
Lesson07\Complete\LogoutButton.swf

NOTE *While you will not need to open and edit all of the files listed in the Start folder, they must all be present (and in the same folder) for the examples to work properly.*

INTRODUCING THE <CFLOGIN> FRAMEWORK

Before ColdFusion MX, most developers added security to their pages by creating a login form to collect a user name and password from the user, then checking the user's entries against valid user names and passwords in a database table. If the user name and password were valid, the user's logged-in status was maintained using session variables. This technique worked well; but it had one problem: every developer had to figure out how to do it on their own.

NOTE *You haven't learned much about session variables yet. They are covered in Lesson 8. For now, just think of them as a way of remembering something about a user (for instance, their name or favorite color, or whether they have logged in) for a short period of time.*

ColdFusion MX introduces a new set of tags and functions to help standardize the process of handling user logins, thus making it easier than ever to add integrated password protection to your pages. If you use this new framework to secure your pages (rather than creating your own code based on session variables or something similar), you will be implementing security in the same basic way as many other ColdFusion MX developers, using a reasonable set of best practices.

Additionally, if you use the <cflogin> framework to secure your pages, you are well on your way to having the password protection work together with advanced ColdFusion MX features, such as integration with Flash MX (via the Flash Remoting Service) and ColdFusion Components (CFCs). Please consult the ColdFusion MX documentation for more information about these features and how they interact with the <cflogin> framework.

NOTE *The ColdFusion documentation refers to these tags and functions as* user security language elements. *This book refers to the tags and functions as the* cflogin framework.

CREATING THE LOGIN FORM

Let's start with the simplest part: the creation of a login form that collects a user name and password from the user.

1) In Dreamweaver MX, open LoginForm.cfm from the Lesson07\Start folder.

Because you have already created several forms at this point, the majority of this one has been pre-built for you to save time. Of course, you can customize the look of the form in whatever way you please.

> **NOTE** You'll notice that the form uses `<cfform>` tags (as opposed to regular `<form>` tags). This allows the form to use ColdFusion's client-side validation feature, which you learned about in Lesson 6.

2) **Add a text field for the user name, similar to the following:**

> **NOTE** The comment is already in place, so you just need to add the `<cfinput>` tag underneath.

```
<!---Text field for username goes here --->
<cfinput
  type="text"
  name="username"
  size="10"
  required="yes"
  message="Please don't leave the username blank.">
```

This field simply collects a user name from the user. When the form is submitted, the user's entry will be available in the `FORM.Username` variable.

3) **Add a password field for the user's password, as follows:**

> **NOTE** Again, the comment shown below is already in the file, so you just need to add the actual `<cfinput>` tag.

```
<!---Text field for password goes here --->
<cfinput
  type="password"
  name="password"
  size="10"
  required="yes"
  message="Please don't leave the password blank.">
```

This `<cfinput>` tag uses a `type="password"` attribute to "mask" the user's entry when the form is actually filled out. You should use `type="password"` whenever you create form fields that collect passwords or any other type of information that should never be visible on screen.

> **NOTE** If you want, you could use `type="password"` in the user name field as well. That way, the user name wouldn't be visible onscreen either. You may choose not to do this because it can confuse some users, but it's important to understand that ColdFusion will receive the information the same way, regardless of the input's `type` attribute.

4) Add the following line to the very top of the page:

```
<!---This is the complete URL for the current page --->
<cfset ThisPageURL = "#CGI.SCRIPT_NAME#?#CGI.QUERY_STRING#">
```

This creates a variable called `ThisPageURL`, which contains the URL for the current page. This variable is created by combining two variables from ColdFusion's special `CGI` scope. The `CGI` scope is populated by the Web server at the beginning of every page request and contains a number of special values that can come in handy from time to time. This code uses two of the most commonly used CGI variables: `CGI.SCRIPT_NAME` and `CGI.QUERY_STRING`.

So, why are these variables being used? Well, as you will soon see, this login form may appear on any given page in your site. If a page requires a password, and the user hasn't provided it yet, this form will be shown at the top of whatever page the user requested. The idea is for the form to submit its information back to the same page, so that the user is left exactly where they wanted to be when the login operation is complete.

To make this possible, the `action` attribute of the form must be set on the fly, so that it matches the URL for the page on which the form is being included. The `CGI` variables used here make this possible. The `CGI.SCRIPT_NAME` variable always holds the name of the ColdFusion page being processed (that is, the portion of the URL after the http:// part, up to and including the .cfm in the filename). The `CGI.QUERY_STRING` variable holds the URL parameter portion of the URL (that is, the part of the URL after the question mark (?), if one exists; if not, the variable is an empty string).

In short, after this `<cfset>` tag executes, the `ThisPageURL` variable will hold the relative URL of the page currently being processed.

TIP *CFML is not case-sensitive, so you don't need to use uppercase letters when referring to `CGI` variables in your code, but it is conventional to do so.*

NOTE *The `CGI` scope simply reflects the set of CGI (Common Gateway Interface) variables set by the Web server. As such, the actual variables that will be available in the `CGI` scope will depend somewhat on the Web server software you are using (which might be Apache, Microsoft IIS, a Sun/Netscape server, ColdFusion's built-in development Web server, or the like). All modern Web servers will support the variables used here, but you should consult your Web server documentation to inform yourself about the complete list of variables it makes available to the `CGI` scope.*

5) Set the form's action attribute to `#ThisPageURL#` to make it self-submitting.

```
1  <!--- This is the complete URL for the current page --->
2  <cfset ThisPageURL = "#CGI.SCRIPT_NAME#?#CGI.QUERY_STRING#">
3
4  <!--- Begin login form --->
5  <cfform action="#ThisPageURL#" method="post" preservedata="yes">
```

Now, when the form is included in a page, its `action` attribute will always match the URL for the page it appears on; that is, the `action` will match the URL in the browser's address field.

TIP *If this form were using a regular `<form>` tag, you would need `<cfoutput>` tags to make ColdFusion notice the `#` signs. However, `<cfoutput>` is not needed when providing attribute values to tags that begin with `<cf>`.*

NOTE *The `<cfform>` tag used for this form also uses a `preservedata="yes"` attribute, which will cause the user's entries to automatically reappear if the form needs to be redisplayed right after it is submitted; in this case, that will happen whenever the user enters an incorrect user name or password. This attribute is a shortcut for having to populate the `value` attribute of the `<cfinput>` tags yourself. Consult the ColdFusion documentation for details.*

PRESENTING AND PROCESSING THE LOGIN FORM

Now that the login page has been created, all that's left is to create the code that displays the form when appropriate, and that checks to see whether the user name and password provided by the user are valid. This exercise will show you how to do this. Along the way, you will become familiar with the `<cflogin>` and `<cfloginuser>` tags.

1) In Dreamweaver, choose File > New, then Dynamic Page > ColdFusion to create a new ColdFusion document.

This page will check to see if the user has been logged in yet, presenting the login form if they have not.

TIP *If you want all new files to be ColdFusion documents by default, open the Preferences dialog by choosing Edit > Preferences, and then select the New Document category. Select ColdFusion in the Default Document Type drop-down menu, and uncheck the option marked Show New Document Dialog on Control+N. Now you can just use the Ctrl+N keyboard shortcut to create a new ColdFusion document in one quick step.*

2) Remove all code from the new file so that it is completely empty.

Because this file will be included within other pages (all of which are expected to be complete HTML pages), you don't want it to include the usual `<html>`, `<body>`, and other tags that indicate the beginning and end of a page.

3) Put a pair of `<cflogin>` tags at the top of the file, like so:

```
<!---Force the user to log in --->
<!---This block executes only if user has *not* logged in --->
<cflogin>
</cflogin>
```

The `<cflogin>` tag sits at the heart of ColdFusion MX's new user security framework. It will check to see if the current user has already logged in. If so, the code between the `<cflogin>` tags is skipped entirely, and page execution continues right after the closing `</cflogin>` tag.

If, however, the user has not yet logged in, the code between the `<cflogin>` tags executes. Presumably, the code between the tags will collect a user name, a password, or other credentials from the user, and verify their validity, but what you actually put between the tags is entirely up to you.

So, `<cflogin>` is really just a container for whatever logic you want to be executed when users need to log in. You will see how this works in a moment.

NOTE *Some people find the tag name `<cflogin>` to be somewhat confusing, since it implies that the tag is what actually logs the user in. That isn't the case (as you will see shortly, it's actually the `<cfloginuser>` tag that logs the user in). The purpose of the `<cflogin>` tag is simply to check whether or not the user has been logged in. If it helps, you can just pretend that the tag name is something like `<cflogincheck>` or `<cfifnotloggedin>`.*

NOTE *The `<cflogin>` tag accepts a number of optional attributes that you can use to tweak its behavior. The attributes are particularly useful if you want a user to be able to log in just once to gain access to several different ColdFusion applications on your server (or servers). Consult the ColdFusion documentation for details.*

4) Within the `<cflogin>` block you just created, add the following test:

```
<!---Display login form (unless user is currently submitting it) --->
<cfif IsDefined("FORM.Username") is False
  or IsDefined("FORM.Password") is False>
</cfif>
```

This code checks to see whether form variables called **Username** and **Password** are currently being submitted the browser. These variables will exist after the user fills out and submits the login form that you created in the last exercise. Therefore, if they do not exist, then the user is not currently trying to submit the form. So, the code in this `<cfif>` block executes whenever the user encounters a page that requires a login, unless she is currently submitting a user name and password.

5) **Within the `<cfif>` block you just created, add the following lines:**

```
<cfinclude template="LoginForm.cfm">
<cfabort>
```

```
1  <!--- Force the user to log in --->
2  <!--- This block executes only if user has *not* logged in --->
3  <cflogin>
4
5    <!--- Display login form (unless user is currently submitting it) --->
6    <cfif IsDefined("FORM.Username") is False
7       or IsDefined("FORM.Password") is False>
8      <cfinclude template="LoginForm.cfm">
9      <cfabort>
10   </cfif>
```

This tells ColdFusion to include the LoginForm.cfm file (which you created in the last exercise), thus displaying the login form to the user. The `<cfabort>` tag causes ColdFusion to stop processing the page immediately after including the login form. In other words, the login form is displayed, but whatever content the user requested (which is presumably sensitive) is not displayed.

6) **Under the `<cfif>` block, add the following:**

> **NOTE** *Remember, this code executes only if the user is currently submitting the login form.*

```
<!---Make sure both username and password are provided --->
<cfif FORM.Username IS "" OR FORM.Password IS ""

  <!---Display message and re-display login form --->
  <font color="red"><b>A user name and password are required.</b></font>
  <cfinclude template="LoginForm.cfm">
  <cfabort>
</cfif>
```

This code simply makes sure that the user hasn't left the user name or password fields empty. This block won't execute under normal circumstances, because the client-side validation you added to the form should keep the user from submitting the form without filling in both of the fields. This check is just here for extra safety, in case the user's browser has JavaScript disabled or if the user is trying to do something sneaky.

If either the user name or password has been left blank, this code displays a message to the user (in bold red type) and then re-displays the login form.

NOTE *The <cfabort> tag is used whenever the login form is displayed with <cfinclude>. In the end, it's the <cfabort> tags that make the security mechanism really do something useful. If you forget to add one of these <cfabort> tags, the user will end up seeing the content you were trying to protect, regardless of whether they log in.*

7) **Under the `<cfif>` block you just added, add the following query:**

```
<!---Attempt to find user in database --->
<cfquery name="LoginQuery" dataSource="products">
  SELECT * FROM tblLogin
  WHERE Username = '#FORM.Username#'
    AND Password = '#FORM.Password#'
</cfquery>
```

This query simply attempts to retrieve a record from the database table called tblLogin, based on the user name and password provided by the user. The tblLogin table has four columns: `LoginID`, `Username`, `Password`, and `SecurityRoles`. Unless you have edited the data in this table on your own, it includes three rows of data, as shown here.

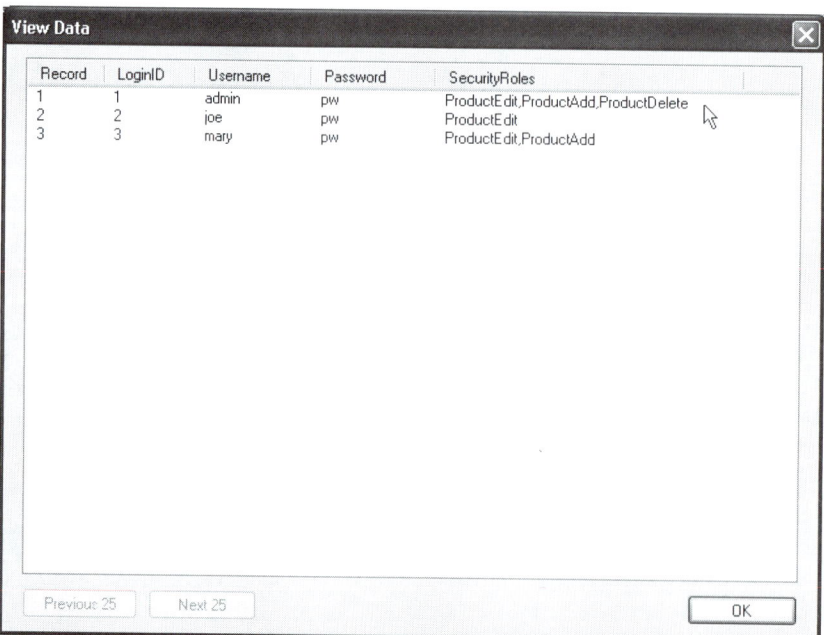

NOTE *Don't worry about the SecurityRoles column for now. You will deal with that toward the end of this lesson.*

If there is a record (that is, an authorized user) in the table with a user name and password that matches up with what the user provided in the login form, this query will return that record. If not, the query won't return anything; that is, the `LoginQuery` resultset will contain zero records.

8) After the query, add a `<cfif>` test that checks the status of the query, like so:

```
<!---If the user was found in database --->
<cfif LoginQuery.RecordCount is 1>
</cfif>
```

If the `LoginQuery` contains a record, that means that the user name and password provided on the login form are valid. It's easy to check if a query contains a record: just check if its `RecordCount` property is equal to 1. So, the code in this `<cfif>` block will execute only if the user should be considered "authorized" to view the protected pages on the site.

9) Within the `<cfif>` block you just added, insert a `<cfloginuser>` tag, as follows:

```
<!---Tell ColdFusion to consider user to be logged in --->
<cfloginuser
  name="#FORM.Username#"
  password="#FORM.password#"
  roles="">
```

```
26      WHERE Username = '#FORM.Username#'
27        AND Password = '#FORM.Password#'
28    </cfquery>
29
30
31    <!--- If the user was found in database --->
32    <cfif LoginQuery.RecordCount is 1>
33
34      <!--- Tell ColdFusion to consider user to be logged in --->
35      <cfloginuser
36        name="#FORM.Username#"
37        password="#FORM.password#"
38        roles="">
39
```

The purpose of the `<cfloginuser>` tag is to tell ColdFusion to consider the present user to be successfully logged in. This is basically the simplest way to use the tag. The tag takes three attributes, all required: `name`, `password`, and `roles`. This code provides the user's user name and password to the **name** and **password** attributes, respectively; ColdFusion uses these values internally to track the user's status from page to page. For now, you are leaving the **roles** attribute blank (you'll fill it in later in this lesson).

TIP *This is a bit advanced, but here goes. If you want, you can supply the user's ID number instead of their user name to the* **name** *attribute (in this case, that would mean* **name="#LoginQuery.LoginID#"**). *That way, the* **GetAuthUser()** *function (discussed later in this lesson) becomes a handy way of tracking the user's ID number.*

NOTE *It's assumed that each combination of* **name** *and* **password** *is unique in the database table, which is a reasonable enough requirement for user names and passwords. If not, the* **<cflogin>** *framework may not work correctly.*

10) Under the `<cflogin>` tag you just added, insert a `<cfelse>` tag, like so:

```
<!---If user was not found based on username/password --->
<cfelse>
```

The code between the `<cfelse>` and the closing `</cfif>` tag will execute only when no records are retrieved by the `LoginQuery` query. In other words, the code that follows executes only when the user provides an incorrect user name or password.

11) After the `<cfelse>` tag, insert the following code:

```
<!---Display message and re-display login form --->
<font color="red"><b>Invalid username or password.</b></font>
<cfinclude template="LoginForm.cfm">
<cfabort>
```

```
31  <!--- If the user was found in database --->
32  <cfif LoginQuery.RecordCount is 1>
33
34    <!--- Tell ColdFusion to consider user to be logged in --->
35    <cfloginuser
36      name="#FORM.Username#"
37      password="#FORM.password#"
38      roles="">
39
40    <!--- If user was not found based on username/password --->
41    <cfelse>
42      <!--- Display message and re-display login form --->
43      <font color="red"><b>Invalid username/password.</b></font>
44      <cfinclude template="LoginForm.cfm">
45      <cfabort>
46  </cfif>
47  </cflogin>
```

This code simply displays a message to the user, explaining that the user name and password they entered is not valid, and then re-displays the login form.

12) Use File > Save As to save the new file as *ForceUserToLogin.cfm*.

Make sure to save the file in the same folder as the other files for this lesson.

You are almost ready to test out the new login functionality; you just need to decide which of your pages should require users to log in.

ADDING PASSWORD PROTECTION TO INDIVIDUAL PAGES

In the last exercise, you created a ColdFusion file called ForceUserToLogin.cfm, which contains all the logic needed to present users with the login form when called for, and to process user names and passwords submitted with the form. All you need to do now is to include this file into any pages that you wish to be protected by the new security measures. This exercise will show you how to do that. As you will see, it's really very simple.

1) Open the ProductMenu.cfm file in Dreamweaver.

This is the same page that you created in Lesson 6. Because this page provides the launch pad from which users make changes to the database, it makes sense to add password security to this page first.

2) Locate the `<cfinclude>` tag that includes the Header.cfm file.

Because you want the product menu page to look nice, even when it needs to display the login form, you will include the login logic *after* the site's usual logo and navigation header.

3) After that `<cfinclude>` tag, add another one for the login logic, like so:

```
<!---Only authenticated users may access this page --->
<cfinclude template="ForceUserToLogin.cfm">
```

```
16  <body>
17
18  <!--- Include logo and navigation header at top of page --->
19  <cfinclude template="Header.cfm">
20
21  <!--- Only authenticated users may access this page --->
22  <cfinclude template="ForceUserToLogin.cfm">
23
24  <!--- Title this section of the page --->
25  <h2>Product Menu</h2>
```

4) Open the ProductForm.cfm file (in the same folder), and make the same addition there.

Place the new `<cfinclude>` line right after the one that includes the page header, just as you did in ProductMenu.cfm. You would also make the same change to any other pages that you wanted to be password-protected.

> **TIP** *If you wanted all pages to be password protected, you could simply create an Application.cfm file and place the `<cfinclude>` line there.*

5) Add an identical `<cfinclude>` tag to the tops of ProductAction.cfm and ProductDelete.cfm.

```
<!--- Only authenticated users may access this page --->
<cfinclude template="ForceUserToLogin.cfm">

<!--- This page expects the following form fields --->
<cfparam name="FORM.ProductName" type="string">
```

These pages don't actually display anything on their own; as you probably remember, they just make the appropriate change to the database, then send the user back to the product menu page. But you still want to add the same `<cfinclude>` tag to them so that people can't invoke their functionality without providing an appropriate user name and password.

> **NOTE** *In any case, the `<cfinclude>` tag that includes the login logic should always come before the sensitive part of the page—as close to the top of the file as possible. For pages that display content, it should precede the sensitive information. For pages that perform actions but don't display content, the tag might as well be at the very top of the file.*

6) Save your work in all of the files, and then test out the ProductMenu.cfm page in your browser.

> **TIP** *In Dreamweaver MX, you can use File > Save All to save all open files in one fell swoop.*

When the page first appears, it displays the login form.

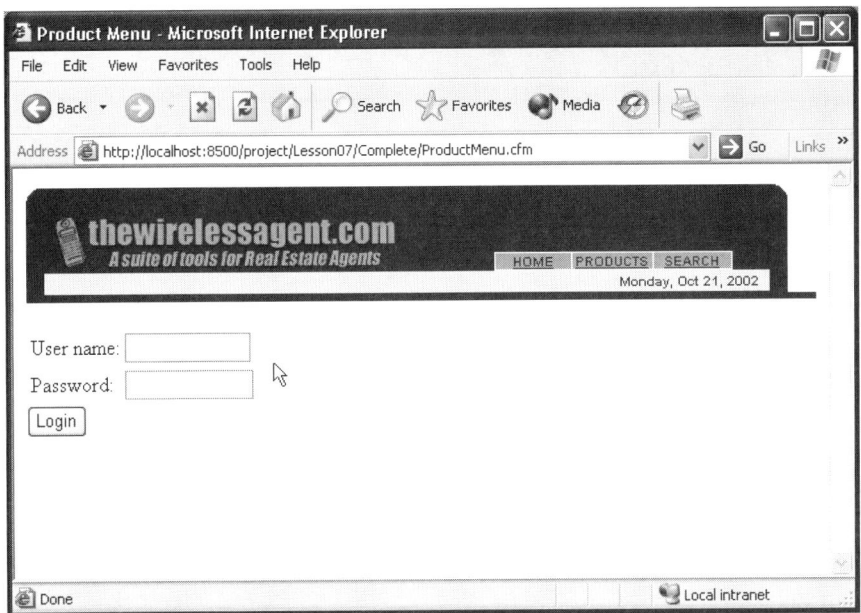

The login behaves as you would expect: if you provide a user name or password that is not valid, the page lets you know and re-displays the login form so you can try again.

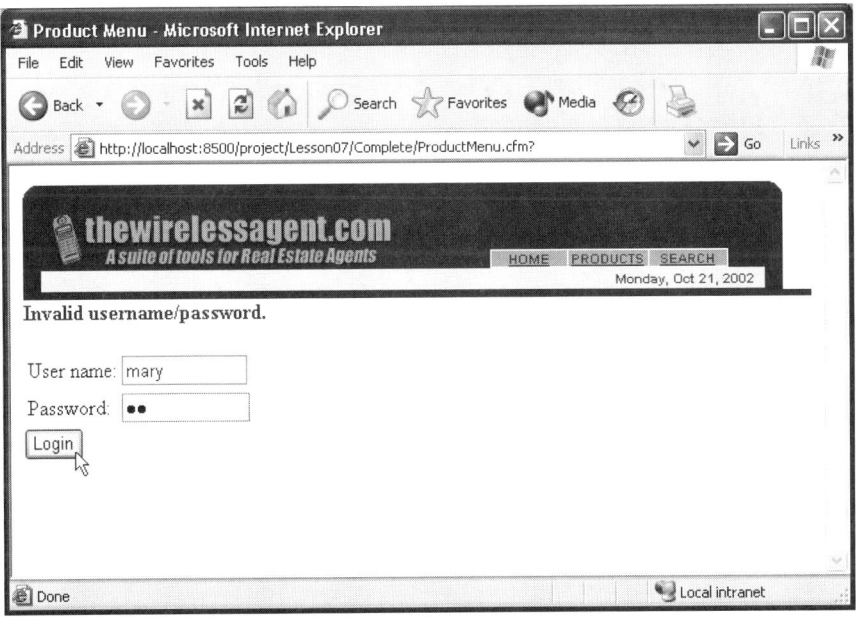

If you provide a valid user name and password, the page reloads—this time without the login form. The page will now behave as it did when you created it in Lesson 6, providing links to edit or delete each product in the tblProducts table of the example database.

NOTE *The valid user names in our example database are Admin, Joe, and Mary. The password is* pw *for all three user names. Of course, you could change the passwords or add new login records at any time by opening the table in Access and editing the data in the tblLogin table directly.*

NOTE *ColdFusion MX uses a cookie to remember that a user has been logged in, so cookies need to be enabled in your browser for the login functionality to work properly.*

PROVIDING A WAY TO LOG OUT

As it stands, users can simply close their browsers to be considered logged out. If a user then reopens the browser and returns to one of the password-protected pages, he would need to re-enter his user name and password. You might want to provide a way for users to log themselves out without closing the browser. This exercise will show you how to create a Log Out link that users can click at any time.

1) At the bottom of ForceUserToLogin.cfm, after the closing `</cflogin>` tag, add the following code:

NOTE *The location of this code (at the bottom of the file) means it will be processed only for users who have already logged in successfully.*

```
<!---Provide a link for user to log out --->
<table align="right" width="100">
  <tr>
    <td align="center">
      User: <strong><cfoutput>#GetAuthUser()#</cfoutput></strong><br>
    </td>
  </tr>
</table>
```

NOTE *The only lines in this code snippet that are of any technical consequence are the two lines within the* `<td>` *tag. The surrounding* `<table>`, `<tr>`, *and* `<td>` *code items exist only to place the Log Out link at the top-right corner of the page, using normal HTML table syntax. Consult an HTML reference or guide for details.*

This code uses a new function that you haven't seen before: the `GetAuthUser()` function. This is related to the `<cflogin>` and other tags that you have been learning about in this lesson. Its purpose is simple: to return the user name of the person who is currently logged in. Whatever value was provided to the `name` attribute of the `<cfloginuser>` tag can be retrieved at any time using the `GetAuthUser()` function.

NOTE *Here, the* `GetAuthUser()` *function is being used simply to display the current user's user name, as a user-friendly reminder to the user that they are currently logged in. However, you could use the function to do more sophisticated things, such as run a query to get further information about the user based on his user name.*

Next, you will add a Log Out link under the user's user name. And since you already know how to create plain old links, this time we'll create a Flash button to do the job.

2) Make a blank line within the `<td>` tag you just added, after the `User:` line.

```
45    </cfif>
46  </cflogin>
47
48  <!--- Provide a link for user to log out --->
49  <table align="right" width="100">
50    <tr>
51      <td align="center">
52        User: <strong><cfoutput>#GetAuthUser()#</cfoutput></strong><br>
53        |
54      </td>
55    </tr>
56  </table>
```

Make sure to leave the cursor on the new, blank line. You will tell Dreamweaver MX to insert a Flash button there.

3) Choose Insert > Interactive Images > Flash Button.

The Insert Flash Button dialog appears.

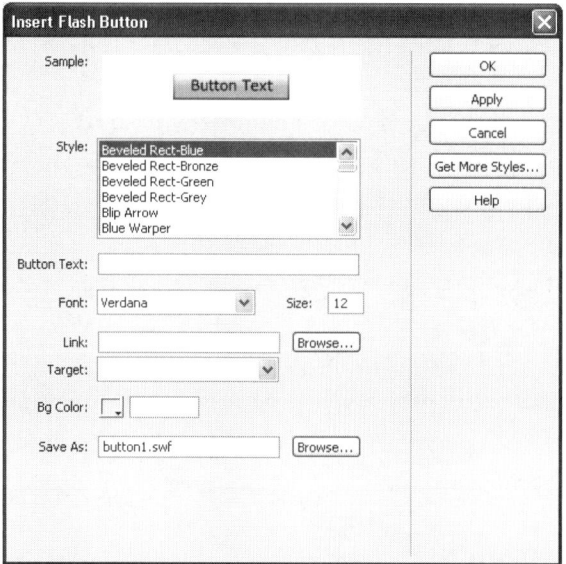

4) In the Button Text field, type *Log Out*.

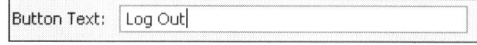

Whatever text you enter here will appear on the face of the button. You can use this Dreamweaver feature to quickly create buttons for all sorts of things.

5) In the Link field, type *Logout.cfm*.

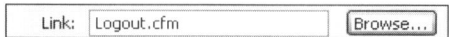

You haven't created the Logout.cfm page yet, but if it did already exist, you could simply select it using the Browse button.

6) In the Save As field, type *LogoutButton.swf*.

All Flash movies (including simple ones like the button you are creating) have a .swf extension.

7) Click OK to create the Flash button.

That's all you need to do. Dreamweaver MX creates the Log Out button as a Flash movie called LogoutButton.swf, and inserts the appropriate HTML code to make the button appear on your page.

8) Choose File > New, then Dynamic Page > ColdFusion to create a new ColdFusion document.

This will become the Logout.cfm page referred to by the button you just added.

9) Add a `<cflogin>` tag at the very top of the new page, like so:

```
<!---Log the user out of the application --->
<cflogout>
```

As the name suggests, the `<cflogout>` tag tells ColdFusion that the user should no longer be considered logged in. As such, it has the exact opposite purpose as `<cfloginuser>`. The `<cflogout>` tag is easy to use, because it takes no arguments. As soon as it is encountered in a ColdFusion page, the `cflogin` variable ceases to exist, and code in any `<cflogin>` blocks will no longer be skipped.

10) Within the new page's `<body>` tags, add the following lines:

```
<!---Include logo and navigation header at top of page --->
<cfinclude template="Header.cfm">
<!---Display message for user --->
<p><strong>You have been logged out.</strong><br>
```

This code simply includes the usual page header at the top of the page, then notifies the user that he or she has been logged out of the secured portion of the site.

11) Under the lines you just added, insert the code for the following two links:

```
<!---Link to re-enter the protected area --->
<p>To return to the secure product menu,
<a href="ProductMenu.cfm">click here</a>.<br>
(you will have to log back in)</p>
<!---Link to enter the non-protected area --->
<p>To go to the product list,
<a href="ProductList.cfm">click here</a>.<br>
(no password is required)</p>
```

```
1  <!--- Log the user out of the application --->
2  <cflogout>
3
4
5  <html>
6  <head>
7  <title>System Logout</title>
8  <meta http-equiv="Content-Type" content="text/html; charset=iso-8859-1">
9  </head>
10
11 <body>
12
13 <!--- Include logo and navigation header at top of page --->
14 <cfinclude template="Header.cfm">
15 <!--- Display message for user --->
16 <p><strong>You have been logged out.</strong><br>
17
18 <!--- Link to re-enter the protected area --->
19 <p>To return to the secure product menu,
20 <a href="ProductMenu.cfm">click here</a>.<br>
21 (you will have to log back in)</p>
22 <!--- Link to enter the non-protected area --->
23 <p>To go to the product list,
24 <a href="ProductList.cfm">click here</a>.<br>
25 (no password is required)</p>
26
27 </body>
28 </html>
```

This code presents two links to the user: one to return to the top-level secure page (in this case, the product menu page), and another to proceed to an unsecured page. Of course, you could provide the user with whatever links you wanted; alternatively, you could use `<cflocation>` to send the user straight to the page of your choosing (perhaps your site's home page, for example).

12) Save your work, and then test out the ProductMenu.cfm page again in your browser.

Once you log in, you will find that your login name appears at the top right corner of any secured page. The Flash-powered Log Out button appears under your user name.

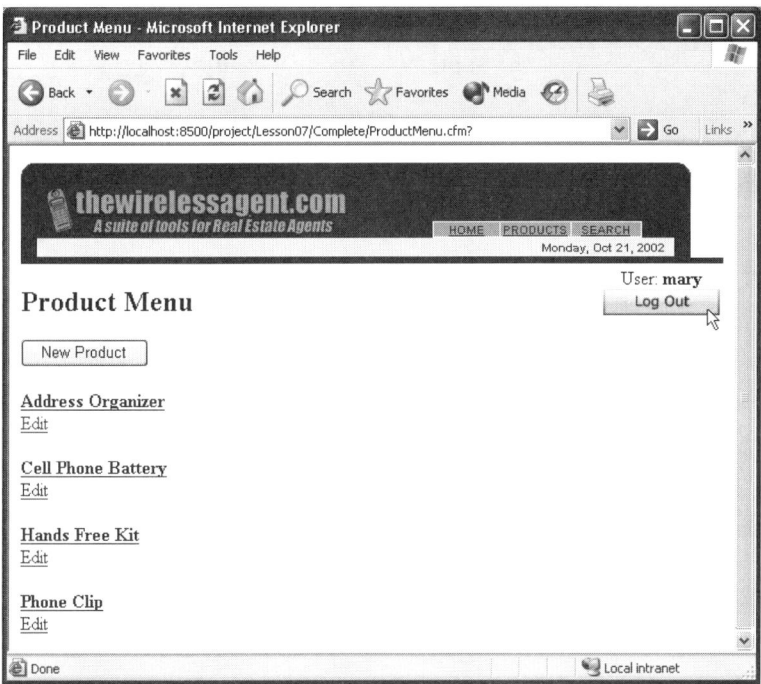

If you click the button, you are logged out of the system and presented with the two links you added in the last step. If you decide to follow the link back to the secured area (or if you return to a secured page using a bookmark or by typing its URL directly into your browser's address field), you will be re-prompted for your user name and password.

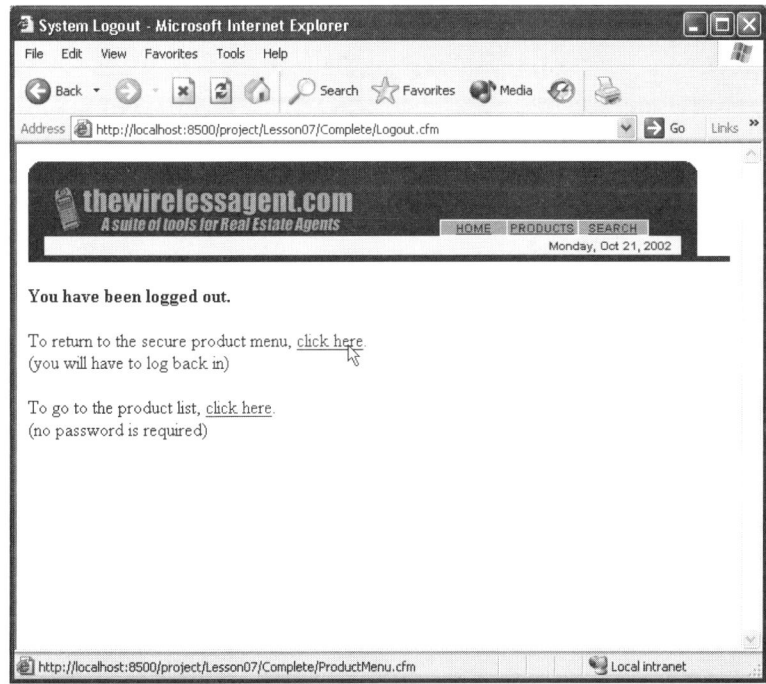

IMPLEMENTING PER-USER PRIVILEGES WITH ROLES

Okay, you have learned how to create a simple but effective security system for sensitive pages. Many times, this user-name-and-password combination will be as far as you need to go. However, you should know that the `<cflogin>` framework in ColdFusion MX also supports the concept of *security roles*, which you can use to create pages that allow some users to see more than others.

In other words, "let anyone with a password into the site" doesn't have to be your only policy choice. Instead, you can create pages that allow one level of access to some users, and a different level of access to others. This exercise will show you one way of using ColdFusion MX's concept of security roles to implement per-user privileges in your pages.

NOTE *So, what exactly is a role? It's really anything you want it to be. Think of a role as a named attribute that your pages can use to determine what to show to whom. Depending on the type of application you are building, roles are usually used in a way that is generally synonymous with the concept of* user groups *(administrators, power users, and the like) or with the concept of* privileges *(editing privileges, deleting privileges, the privilege to cancel an order, and so on). This exercise treats roles according to the latter definition, in which each role name corresponds to a specific privilege.*

1) Re-open the ForceUserToLogin.cfm file in Dreamweaver, if it's not open already.

You need to make just one small change to this file to add role-based security to your pages.

2) Add a `roles="#LoginQuery.SecurityRoles#"` attribute to the `<cfloginuser>` tag.

```
30  <!--- If the user was found in database --->
31  <cfif LoginQuery.RecordCount is 1>
32
33      <!--- Tell ColdFusion to consider user to be logged in --->
34      <cfloginuser
35        name="#FORM.Username#"
36        password="#FORM.password#"
37        roles="#LoginQuery.SecurityRoles#">
38
39      <!--- If user was not found based on username/password --->
40  <cfelse>
```

The `roles` attribute tells ColdFusion which security roles are applicable to a particular user. You can designate any number of roles for any given user; just supply the role names as a comma-separated list.

In this case, that list will come from the `LoginQuery` recordset, which in turn comes directly from the tblLogin table in the database. This table includes a column called SecurityRoles. The column contains a comma-separated list of role names for each login record, as shown below:

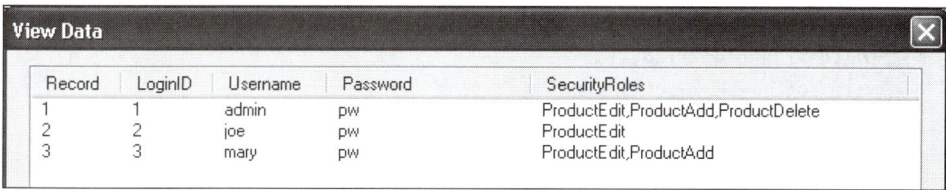

As you can see, the Admin login has been assigned three security roles: ProductEdit, ProductAdd, and ProductDelete. On the other hand, Joe can only edit existing products but can't delete them or add new ones, and it looks like Mary can add and edit products but can't delete them. In a moment, you'll see how to enforce these rules in your code.

NOTE *Role names can be whatever you want, but it is clearly best to make sure the names are meaningful and self-explanatory. To ensure clarity, it is a good idea to create each role name out of at least two English words.*

When this `<cfloginuser>` tag is encountered, the `roles` attribute will be set to whatever roles are currently in the login record in the database. ColdFusion will automatically keep that list of roles associated with the user as he or she moves from page to page in your application.

NOTE *The role information is being kept as a comma-separated list to keep this lesson's examples nice and simple, but the practice of keeping multiple pieces of information in a single database column is generally frowned upon. A more correct (or "normalized") approach would be to have an additional table in the database (perhaps called tblLoginSecurityRoles) that mapped each user to their security roles, using one row for each user/role combination. Unfortunately, the specifics of designing this type of normalized table relationship is beyond the scope of this book. You can find out more about the advantages of using several tables to express this type of "one to many" data relationship in a book or Web site that discusses SQL or database design.*

3) Open the ProductMenu.cfm page in Dreamweaver, if it's not open already.

This is the page that provides links and buttons for users to add, edit, and remove products from the database.

4) Locate the `<form>` block that displays the New Product button.

You will now add code to make sure that only users that have the **ProductAdd** role are given the option to insert a new product record.

5) Surround the `<form>` with a `IsUserInRole()` condition, so it looks like this:

```
<cfif IsUserInRole("ProductAdd")>
  <form action="ProductForm.cfm">
    <input type="submit" value="New Product">
  </form>
</cfif>
```

This code uses one final login-related function that you haven't seen before: the `IsUserInRole()` function. This function is very easy to use. You simply supply it with a role name. The function returns value of True or False, based on whether or not that role was associated with the current user when he or she logged in.

The code inside this `<cfif>` block executes only if the user has been assigned the **ProductAdd** role (or privilege, if you prefer). If the user is not associated with the role, the block is skipped entirely. In this case, that means that the New Product button is only shown to people who have the **ProductAdd** privilege. Perfect!

6) Surround the Edit link with a similar `<cfif>` for the `ProductEdit` role, like so:

```
42  <!--- Link to edit product information --->
43  <cfif IsUserInRole("ProductEdit")>
44    <a href="ProductForm.cfm?ProductID=#ProductID#">Edit</a>
45  </cfif>
```

You have now told ColdFusion to provide the Edit link only for those users who have been granted the **ProductEdit** role in the database.

7) Similarly, surround the Remove link with a `<cfif>` for the `ProductDelete` role, like so:

```
47  <!--- Link to remove product from table --->
48  <cfif IsUserInRole("ProductDelete")>
49    <a href="ProductDelete.cfm?ProductID=#ProductID#">Remove</a>
50  </cfif>
51  </cfoutput>
```

Likewise, this change tells the page to display the Remove link only for those users who are associated with the **ProductDelete** role.

8) Open the ProductAction.cfm page.

This is the file that actually does the work of inserting new product records, or updating existing records. You will now add `IsUserInRole()` tests (similar to the ones you just added to ProductMenu.cfm) to make sure that the user's security role is verified whenever this action page is visited.

9) Surround the `<cfupdate>` tag with a `<cfif>` for the `ProductEdit` role, like so:

```
10  <cfif IsDefined("FORM.ProductID")>
11    <!--- Update the product record in the database --->
12    <cfif IsUserInRole("ProductEdit")>
13      <cfupdate datasource="products" tablename="tblProducts">
14    </cfif>
```

This `<cfif>` test ensures that the `<cfupdate>` tag will be skipped if the user isn't associated with the ProductEdit role. No error message will be displayed; the user's demand is simply ignored.

> **NOTE** *Normally, a user would never get to this page if they didn't have the privilege, but you should still double-check the role at the last minute before allowing your code to anything important like make a permanent change to a database.*

10) Similarly, surround the `<cfinsert>` tag with a `<cfif>` for the `ProductAdd` role, like so:

```
16  <cfelse>
17    <!--- Insert a new product record to the database --->
18    <cfif IsUserInRole("ProductAdd")>
19      <cfinsert datasource="products" tablename="tblProducts">
20    </cfif>
21
22  </cfif>
```

Again, the idea here is to make sure that the portion of the code that actually performs the product-adding action is available only to users that have the appropriate privilege.

11) Open the ProductDelete.cfm page in Dreamweaver.

This is the file that does the work of deleting a record from the database when the user clicks the product's Remove link on the product menu page.

12) Surround the `<cfquery>` block with a `<cfif>` for the `ProductDelete` role, like so:

```
7  <!--- Remove the product from the database --->
8  <cfif IsUserInRole("ProductDelete")>
9    <cfquery datasource="products">
10     DELETE FROM tblProducts
11     WHERE ProductID = #URL.ProductID#
12   </cfquery>
13 </cfif>
14
15 <!--- Send the user back to the product menu page --->
16 <cflocation url="ProductMenu.cfm">
```

If an authorized user attempts to visit the ProductDelete.cfm page (either by following a link, or by typing the URL directly into their browser's Address field), this `<cfif>` test will prevent the page from actually making any change to the database.

13) Open the ProductForm.cfm page in Dreamweaver.

This is the page that contains the HTML form for adding new product records or editing existing records.

14) Add the following code, directly after the `<cfinclude>` for the ForceUserToLogin.cfm file:

```
<!---Check security roles before proceeding --->
<cfif URL.ProductID eq 0>
  <cfif IsUserInRole("ProductAdd") eq False>
    Sorry, you aren't allowed to add products.
    <cfabort>
  </cfif>
<cfelse>
  <cfif IsUserInRole("ProductEdit") eq False>
    Sorry, you aren't allowed to edit products.
    <cfabort>
  </cfif>
</cfif>
```

NOTE *Remember, when the `URL.ProductID` variable is 0, that is an indication that the user is trying to add a new product record. Refer back to Lesson 6 if you need to refresh your memory about how this logic works.*

If the user is trying to insert a new product record, this code checks to see if the user has the `ProductAdd` privilege (role). If not, a simple message is displayed, and then the `<cfabort>` tag is used to stop all further processing. A similar message is displayed if the user is trying to edit an existing record but doesn't have the `ProductEdit` privilege. In either case, the form will not be displayed to users who don't have the authorization to see it.

15) Use File > Save All to save all your work, and then re-visit the ProductMenu.cfm page in your browser.

If you log in using the Admin user name, you will have full access to the New Product, Edit, and Remove elements of the page, and will be able to carry out all operations normally. If you then log out (either using the Log Out button or by closing and reopening the browser) and revisit the page again, this time as the user Mary, you will be able to insert and edit products, but not remove them—the Remove link for each product will be automatically missing. If you log in as Joe, you will only have access to the Edit functionality; the New Product and Remove elements will be missing.

NOTE *It's not just the links that are withheld from unauthorized users: the actual functionality is withheld as well. For instance, if you log out, and then attempt to visit the ProductForm.cfm page directly, you will be denied access if you log in as a user who does not have the* `ProductAdd` *privilege (such as Joe).*

WHAT YOU HAVE LEARNED

In this lesson, you have:

- Created a login form (pages 156–158)
- Used `<cflogin>` and `<cfloginuser>` to accept and process login credentials (pages 159–165)
- Created an attractive Flash-powered button with Dreamweaver MX (pages 169–170)
- Used the `<cflogout>` tag to provide users with a way to log out (pages 168–173)
- Added `IsUserInRole()` tests to role-based security to enforce per-user privileges (pages 174–179)

using session variables

LESSON 8

The common standards that make the Web possible—specifically, HTML and HTTP—are *stateless*, meaning that the basic standards don't make any attempt to keep track of the individual users who are visiting a Web site at a given time. What this means in practice is that Web servers treat each page request on its own. Every time a user visits one of your pages, it's as if she dials in to the Internet, opens her browser, visits that one page, and then closes her browser and her Internet connection—and then goes through that whole process again to visit the next page on your site, and so on.

Of course, the typical user doesn't go through all that every time she types in a new Web address, clicks a link, or submits a form. As far as the user is concerned, all

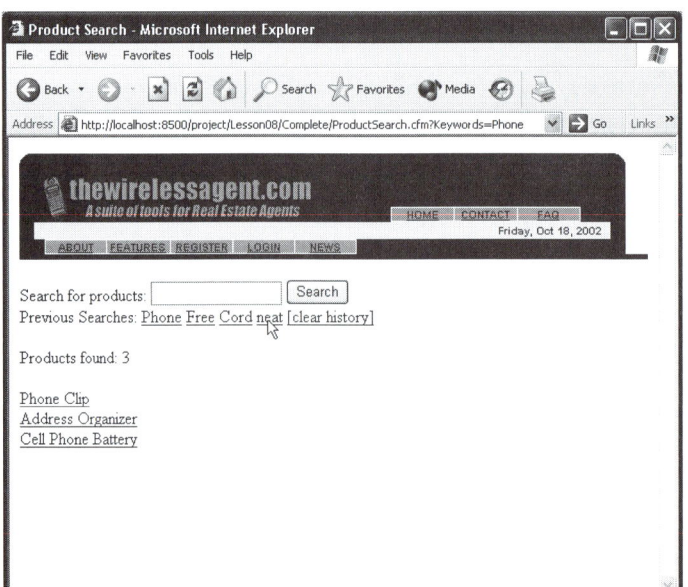

ColdFusion's session management features make it easy to create pages that remember information during a user's visit. In this lesson they will be used to retain a search history for each user. They can also be used to maintain shopping carts, wish lists, or shipping information—anything that should be remembered in the short term for each of your visitors.

consecutive interactions with your site seem to be part of a single "session" or "visit." Opinions vary among users about what constitutes the end of the session: some say it's when they navigate to another site; others that it's when they close their browser. But just about anyone thinks of their interactions with the Web in terms of visits, or sessions—not isolated page requests. It's just the nature of the beast.

The point is that there is a conceptual rift between the typical user's idea of a session versus what is actually built into the infrastructure of the Web (which is basically nothing). The problem of closing that gap is something that is typically filled in by server-side Web application servers such as Active Server Pages, Java Server Pages, PHP, and of course ColdFusion. Each of these products provides some kind of mechanism for tracking a user's progress as she moves through the various pages of your site. These mechanisms are usually referred to as *session tracking* or *session management* features.

ColdFusion's session management features are particularly simple, elegant, and powerful. The idea is simple: the ColdFusion server assigns a unique number to each user the first time they visit one of your pages, and keeps that number associated with the user for the duration of the user's visit. The server is able to use the number internally to "connect the dots" of the user's individual page requests. All the page requests associated with a given number can thus be thought of as belonging to a single, unified session, and can share or track values between themselves accordingly. *Voilà*, sessions!

The great news is that you don't really have to know any of these details to use ColdFusion's session management features. The server takes care of all that for you. This lesson will introduce you to the session-based functionality available to you in ColdFusion MX. It's actually quite a bit of fun…all sorts of ideas will pop into your head as you work though these exercises. Ready, set, go!

NOTE *ColdFusion's session management features expect that the ColdFusion server will be able to set cookies to keep track of your users. This means that the examples in this lesson will not work if you (or someone else) has disabled cookies in your browser. So, if you find that the pages you build in this lesson are not working properly, make sure that your browser's options or preferences are not set to disable or block cookies. With most modern browsers, you will be able to tell the browser to accept cookies from your own machine (localhost) even if you don't want it to accept cookies from the Internet at large.*

WHAT YOU WILL LEARN

In this lesson you will:

- Learn about session management and the `SESSION` variable scope
- Use the `<cfapplication>` tag to enable session variables
- Use session variables to retain histories of your users' searches
- Work with arrays to remember a numbered set of values
- Get a short introduction to application variables

APPROXIMATE TIME

This lesson will take approximately two hours to complete.

LESSON FILES

Starting Files:

Lesson08\Start\ProductSearch.cfm

Completed Project:

Lesson08\Complete\Application.cfm
Lesson08\Complete\ProductSearch.cfm

NOTE *There are a few additional files in the Start and Complete folders that allow the examples for this chapter to work. For instance, the header.cfm and ProductDetail.cfm files (which you have used many times at this point) are re-used once again by this lesson's examples.*

GETTING STARTED WITH SESSION VARIABLES

The centerpiece of ColdFusion's session management feature is the concept of a *session variable*. You create session variables just like any other type of variable (for instance, with a `<cfset>` tag as explained in Lesson 3, or with a `<cfparam>` tag). The difference is that session variables don't cease to exist when the page finishes executing. Once set, they are stored in ColdFusion's memory and made available to all subsequent page requests from the same user for the remainder of the user's visit (you'll learn more about how a "visit" is defined shortly).

Not surprisingly, session variables are stored in a special variable scope called `SESSION`. You can set a variable called, say, `SESSION.FavoriteColor` to remember the user's favorite color, or `SESSION.LastSearch` to remember the user's most recent search criteria. The values of these variables will be retained automatically between the user's page requests; you can display or use them at any time during the user's visit.

The first step in using session variables is to "turn them on" with a CFML tag you haven't seen yet: the `<cfapplication>` tag. This exercise will show you how to use `<cfapplication>` to enable ColdFusion's session management feature.

1) In Dreamweaver MX, use File > New to create a new ColdFusion document.

Remember, to create a ColdFusion document, you choose *Dynamic Page*, and then *ColdFusion* from the New Document dialog.

2) Save the file as Application.cfm, in the same folder as the other files you'll be working on in this lesson.

Typically, that folder is C:\CFusionMX\wwwroot\Project\Lesson08\Start.

NOTE *It's important to spell Application.cfm exactly as shown, with a capital A. Otherwise, ColdFusion servers installed on non-Windows machines won't recognize it as a special file.*

You learned about the special Application.cfm file toward the end of Lesson 3, but you haven't heard much else about it since. As a reminder, whenever you name a file Application.cfm, ColdFusion will automatically execute all code in the file right before it executes any other page from the same folder (or nested subfolders). In other words, it's a lot like putting the following `<cfinclude>` tag at the very top of every single page in your site:

```
<cfinclude template="Application.cfm">
```

In Lesson 3, you used Application.cfm to create simple variables that could be used in any page. The idea was straightforward: by putting a series of ordinary `<cfset>` lines in Application.cfm, the variables would effectively be re-created for each page request. The values are always the same, and can't really be changed without editing the Application.cfm file itself (the code in a page can change one of these variables, but the new value doesn't become visible to successive page requests—the value just snaps back to the one specified in Application.cfm). Simple and limited as it is, this method of creating a globally available variable is nonetheless very helpful.

As you will soon see, session variables are more sophisticated, because they can be changed at any time by any page. The new value is then reflected in all other page requests from the same user during the same visit. Each user will have his or her own private copies of each session variable.

3) Delete all code from the new file.

Because the Application.cfm file is automatically called for every page request, you generally don't want there to be any HTML code in it. This isn't a hard and fast rule, but in most situations, you only want "invisible" operations (like setting variables) to take place in Application.cfm, rather than text or code output of any kind.

4) Place the following `<cfapplication>` tag at the top of the file:

```
<!---Turn on session management --->
<cfapplication
  name="WirelessAgentSite"
  sessionmanagement="yes">
```

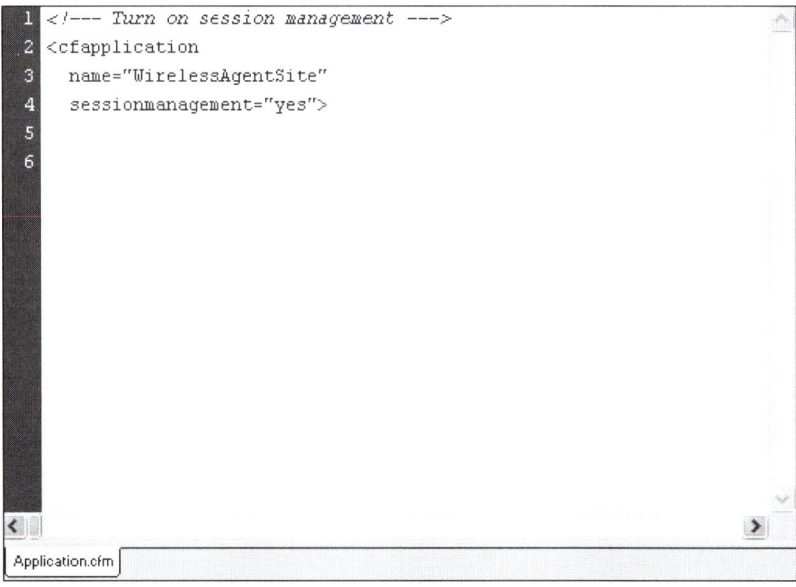

To enable session variables, you typically use `<cfapplication>` with the two attributes shown here. The `name` attribute can be anything you want, but must be unique; that is, no other `<cfapplication>` tag on the same ColdFusion server should use the same name, unless you want session variables to be shared between the two sets of pages. So don't use a name that's too generic, like `site` or `web`. Instead, use a descriptive name, preferably one made up of two or three words, like `WirelessAgentSite`.

The `sessionmanagement="yes"` attribute is what actually turns on ColdFusion's session variable feature. As soon as you place a `<cfapplication>` tag with this attribute in your Application.cfm file, then any page in the same folder (or subfolders, or sub-subfolders, and so on) can create and use variables in the `SESSION` scope. ColdFusion will display an error message if a page attempts to use the `SESSION` scope and this step hasn't been completed.

NOTE *You can also use `<cfapplication>` to turn on client variables by adding a `clientmanagement="yes"` attribute. Client variables are similar conceptually to session variables, but they are designed to be retained for a longer period of time (several days or months, rather than for just the current visit) and are therefore stored differently on the server. You can read more about the differences between session and client variables in the ColdFusion documentation, but they are generally very similar in terms of how you actually use them in your ColdFusion pages.*

5) Save your work.

There isn't anything to test out at this point, so there is no point in visiting the Application.cfm page with your Web browser. In fact, if you try to do so, ColdFusion will display an error message saying that Application.cfm cannot be visited directly. The Application.cfm file is only meant to be used in its special capacity as an automatically included file. You're not meant to access it directly (in other words, you're not meant to enter its URL in a browser's Address field).

USING A SESSION VARIABLE TO REMEMBER SEARCH KEYWORDS

In this exercise, you will learn to use a simple session variable to remember a user's search keywords for the remainder of their visit. You will start with the product search form that you created in Lesson 5. You will then add code that saves the value of the `FORM.Keywords` variable as a session variable called `SESSION.PriorSearchKeywords`. The code updates the session variable whenever the user conducts a new search, and retrieves the value whenever the user returns to the search form.

1) Open the ProductSearch.cfm page from the Lesson08\Start folder.

This is the same search page you created in Lesson 5.

2) Remove the `<cfparam>` tag at the top of the page.

You will be replacing this `<cfparam>` tag with some custom logic of your own.

3) In the place of the `<cfparam>`, add the following `<cfif>` block:

```
<!---If the FORM.Keywords variable does not exist --->
<!---(that is, if the user is not submitting the form) --->
<cfif IsDefined("FORM.Keywords") eq False>
</cfif>
```

This `<cfif>` block will execute if the `FORM.Keywords` variable does not exist. If you were to add a `<cfset FORM.Keywords = "">` line inside this `<cfif>` block, it would serve the same purpose as the `<cfparam>` tag you just replaced. That's close to what you'll be doing next.

4) Within the `<cfif>` block, add the following:

```
<!---If the user has already searched during this session --->
<cfif IsDefined("SESSION.PriorSearchKeywords")>
  <cfset FORM.Keywords = SESSION.PriorSearchKeywords>
<cfelse>
  <cfset FORM.Keywords = "">
</cfif>
```

The idea here is to check for the existence of a session variable called `PriorSearchKeywords`. If the variable exists, the `<cfif>` condition kicks in and copies the value from the session variable and places it into the `FORM.Keywords` variable. If the variable doesn't exist, the `FORM.Keywords` variable is simply set to an empty string.

```
1  <!--- If the FORM.Keywords variable does not exist --->
2  <!--- (that is, if the user is not submitting the form) --->
3  <cfif IsDefined("FORM.Keywords") eq False>
4
5    <!--- If the user has already searched during this session --->
6    <cfif IsDefined("SESSION.PriorSearchKeywords")>
7      <cfset FORM.Keywords = SESSION.PriorSearchKeywords>
8    <cfelse>
9      <cfset FORM.Keywords = "">
10   </cfif>
11
12 </cfif>
13
```

In plain English, this whole `<cfif>` block means "if the user has already run a search earlier in this session, use the previous search keywords as the default; otherwise, just use an empty string as the default."

5) **Still in ProductSearch.cfm, add the following code, right before the `<cfquery>` tag:**

    ```
    <!---Remember keywords for remainder of user's session --->
    <cfset SESSION.PriorSearchKeywords = FORM.Keywords>
    ```

```
28  </form>
29
30  <!--- Stop here if the search field is blank --->
31  <cfif FORM.Keywords eq "">
32    <cfabort>
33  </cfif>
34
35  <!--- Remember keywords for remainder of user's session --->
36  <cfset SESSION.PriorSearchKeywords = FORM.Keywords>
37
38  <!--- Find matching products --->
39  <cfquery name="SearchQuery" datasource="products">
40    SELECT ProductID, ProductName
41    FROM tblProducts
```

When the user actually submits the form to perform a search, this line of code will execute just before the actual search is carried out. This `<cfset>` line copies the current value from the `FORM.Keywords` variable, storing it in the `SESSION.PriorSearchKeywords` variable. In other words, it saves the user's search keywords for later. If the user returns to the page later in the same visit, the `IsDefined()` test you added in Step 4 will kick in, causing the `FORM.Keywords` variable to "remember" the saved keywords. Which, in turn, means that the saved keywords will appear pre-filled in the search field when the page appears in the browser.

6) **Save your work and test out the revised page with your browser.**
Run a search, follow one of the links in the search results page, and then return to the search page using the "Return to search results" link. You'll find that your search

criteria are still visible in the search field, and the page has actually re-run your search such that your results are still visible.

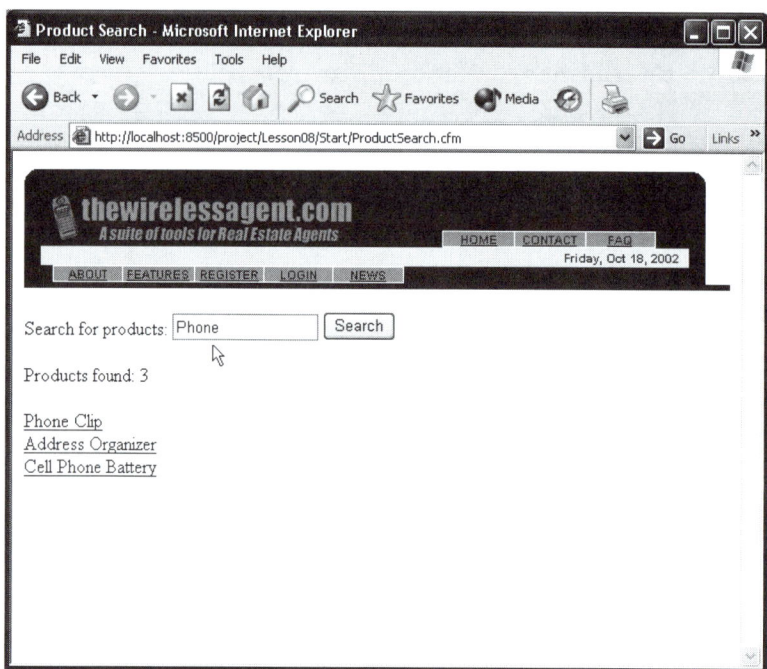

Now, without closing your browser, try going to some other site (it doesn't matter which one). Then return to the ProductSearch.cfm page, but don't use the Back button. Return to it by re-typing its URL into the browser's address field. Hey, check it out! The session variable still exists, and is still reflected the page's search field and results. In fact, you can even close the browser entirely, re-open it, revisit the page, and *still* see the search information retained on the page.

NOTE *The session variable will remain in ColdFusion's memory until the end of the user's session (or until the ColdFusion server is restarted). You'll learn how the end of a user's session is defined in the next section.*

ADJUSTING WHEN SESSION VARIABLES ARE DISCARDED

By default, session variables are maintained in ColdFusion's memory until the user fails to make another page request for 20 minutes or more. Because of the inherently stateless nature of the Web (as mentioned in the introduction to this session), ColdFusion is never explicitly told when the user leaves a site. The best it can do is keep track of how much time has passed since each user's last page request. Once 20 minutes pass without another page request from a user, ColdFusion assumes that the user is done working with the site for now and discards the session information from its memory. A session that has been discarded in this fashion is often said to have *timed out*.

If a user happens to return, say, 22 minutes after their last page request (perhaps they had to answer the phone or deal with a crying baby, who knows?), they will find that their session variables have disappeared. That's bound to be disconcerting or inconvenient in certain situations—but it's still your call to control it as you see fit. For example, if the nature of your site's pages is such that your users routinely spend longer than 20 minutes between page requests (maybe you publish very long articles that might take 45 minutes or an hour to read), you can adjust the timeout using ColdFusion Administrator.

You can also tell ColdFusion to discard the user's session when they close their browser. This exercise will show you how to adjust this behavior as well.

1) Open the ColdFusion Administrator and enter your administrator password.

Remember, you can open the Administrator using the Programs > Macromedia ColdFusion MX > ColdFusion Administrator shortcut on the Windows Start menu.

2) **Click on Memory Variables in the left-hand navigation area.**

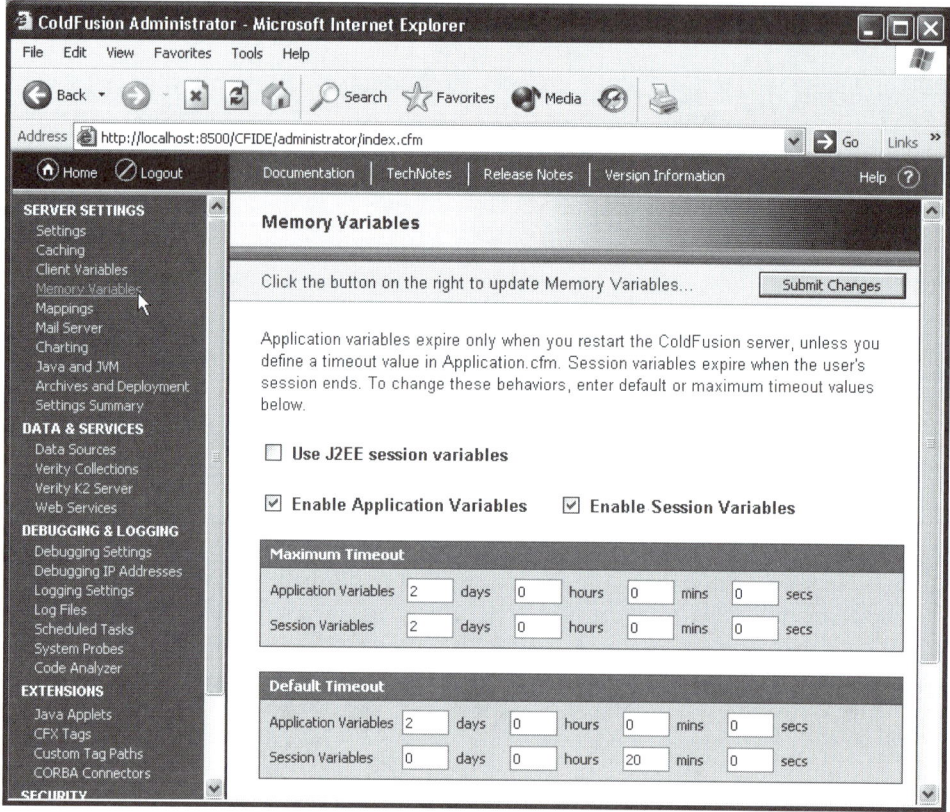

The Memory Variables section of the Administrator contains settings for session variables, plus another special variable scope that you aren't specifically learning about in this book: application variables. The application variable scope is designed for values that need to be stored in the server's memory, and may change over time, but are to be shared amongst all users of the application.

NOTE *Typically, application variables are used for things like hit counters and other "system status" types of values, though they can be used for just about any type of information. In general, the Application scope is only needed in relatively advanced situations. Consult the ColdFusion documentation for details.*

3) **Check the Use J2EE Session Variables option.**

☑ Use J2EE session variables

This option tells ColdFusion to handle session variables in such a way that each user's session variables will be discarded when the user closes their browser. If the user reopens the browser and visits your pages again, they will be using a fresh session. Any session variables that existed for the user before they closed the browser will no longer be reflected.

NOTE *Actually, it would be somewhat more accurate to say that the user's session variables are abandoned when the browser is closed. The user's original session variables will still remain in the server's memory until it times out (that is, after 20 minutes or whatever timeout interval you specify in the Administrator). When the user reopens the browser and returns to your site, they will be given a second session, which itself will remain in memory until it is allowed to time out. The distinction probably doesn't matter much on a practical level, but it's important to understand that ColdFusion always relies on a timeout to actually remove sessions from its memory. The J2EE option just allows users to effectively disconnect themselves from sessions ahead of time by closing their browsers.*

4) **In the *Default Timeout* area at the bottom of the page, enter *5* for the number of minutes for session variables.**

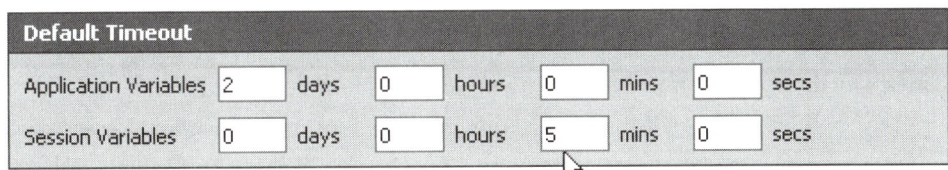

This decreases the timeout for session variables from 20 minutes to 5 minutes. You could, alternatively, increase the timeout to 45 minutes or an hour. You'll be able to see the effect of the change more easily if you pick a short period of time, but it's really up to you what to set this value to.

> **NOTE** *In a production environment, you would choose a value that represented a reasonable balance between convenience and server resources. If the timeout is too short (say, 10 seconds), then your users' sessions would be timing out whenever they paused for even a few moments before moving to the next page; they'd never be able to get anything done. If the timeout is too long (say, 10 days), then your server will be tracking your users' sessions far after they have likely turned off their computers and gone to bed, which would be a waste of your server's memory. The default value of 20 minutes is actually a pretty good compromise.*

> **NOTE** *You can also adjust the session timeout on an application-by-application basis by supplying a `sessiontimeout` attribute to the `<cfapplication>` tag. Consult the ColdFusion documentation for details.*

5) Click Submit Changes to save the changes you've made.

Now play around with the search facility you created in the previous exercise. You will now find that the page's memory of the search keywords is cleared if you close and then reopen the browser. You will also find that the keywords also clear themselves if you don't visit the page (or any other pages in this application, which at this point means any of the other pages in the folder for this lesson) for a period of five minutes or more and then reload the page in your browser.

USING ARRAYS TO REMEMBER MULTIPLE SEARCHES

You've seen how ColdFusion's session variable feature can be used to remember a simple value, such as a search keyword. You can easily adapt the idea to retain a short-term memory of other types of information provided in form fields, such as the user's name, customer number, seating preference, or favorite color.

Session variables are also ideal for storing more complex pieces of information. For instance, instead of simply remembering the user's most recent search keywords, you could use the `SESSION` scope to maintain a true history of the searches they have performed. This exercise will walk you through building such a feature for your users.

Along the way, you are going to learn how to store an entirely new type of information in variables. This new type of information (or *data type*) is called an *array*. An array is similar to other types of variables in that it stores information that you can retrieve by referring to the variable by name. The big difference is that the array can store multiple pieces of information instead of only one. Conceptually, it's as if the array has a whole bunch of numbered slots in it. You can fill each slot with anything you want.

In this exercise, you will be creating an array variable called `SESSION.PriorSearchArray`. Each time the user conducts a new search with the product search form, the current search will be inserted into one of the array's slots. This will allow the page to keep track of the user's searches during the course of the session; the page can display each of the user's prior search keywords.

NOTE *The finished code for this example is a bit complicated, at least in comparison to the simple code you have seen so far in this book. You could skip the rest of this lesson for now if you don't plan on using session variables much in the near future. All that said, each step in this exercise is really pretty easy, and you will learn a lot. I say, go for it!*

1) Open the ProductSearch.cfm file in Dreamweaver, if it's not already open.

This is the file you created during the previous exercise.

2) Remove the whole `<cfif>` block at the top (including the nested `<cfif>` and `<cfelse>` logic).

You will replace this section with slightly more complicated logic, which retrieves information from the new array that represents the user's search history.

3) In place of the `<cfif>` block, add the following `<cfparam>` tag:

```
<!---This page uses a FORM.Keywords parameter --->
<cfparam name="FORM.Keywords" type="string" default="">
```

This is actually the same `<cfparam>` tag that was in the original version of the page, before you started working on this lesson.

4) After the `<cfparam>` tag, add the following code:

```
<!---Maintain a history of user's searches in this session --->
<!---Create array for history, if it doesn't exist already --->
<cfif IsDefined("SESSION.PriorSearchArray") eq False>
  <cfset SESSION.PriorSearchArray = ArrayNew(1)>
</cfif>
```

```
1  <!--- This page uses a FORM.Keywords parameter --->
2  <cfparam name="FORM.Keywords" type="string" default="">
3
4  <!--- Maintain a history of user's searches in this session --->
5  <!--- Create array for history, if it doesn't exist already --->
6  <cfif IsDefined("SESSION.PriorSearchArray") eq False>
7    <cfset SESSION.PriorSearchArray = ArrayNew(1)>
8  </cfif>
9
```

The idea here is to create the `SESSION.PriorSearchArray` variable if it doesn't already exist. The variable is created using a function you haven't seen before: `ArrayNew()`. As the name implies, `ArrayNew()` simply creates a new array (conceptually, a new set of numbered slots), so the `<cfset>` line used here creates a new array and stores it as a session variable called `SESSION.PriorSearchArray`. The rest of the page can now feel free to refer to the variable, because it is guaranteed to exist.

NOTE *Except in special conditions, you will always want to supply a value of 1 to the `ArrayNew()` function as shown here. The 1 tells ColdFusion to create a one-dimensional array. That's almost always the type of array that you want. Don't worry too much about the meaning of the 1 for now; you can look it up later in the ColdFusion documentation if you get curious about it.*

5) Further down in the page, make the following code change:

Replace this line:

```
<!---Remember keywords for remainder of user's session --->
<cfset SESSION.PriorSearchKeywords = FORM.Keywords>
```

with this line:

```
<!---Add the user's current search to their history --->
<cfset ArrayAppend(SESSION.PriorSearchArray, FORM.Keywords)>
```

```
36  <!--- Stop here if the search field is blank --->
37  <cfif FORM.Keywords eq "">
38      <cfabort>
39  </cfif>
40
41  <!--- Add the user's current search to their history --->
42  <cfset ArrayAppend(SESSION.PriorSearchArray, FORM.Keywords)>
43
44  <!--- Find matching products --->
45  <cfquery name="SearchQuery" datasource="products">
46      SELECT ProductID, ProductName
```

This code uses another array-related function that you're not familiar with yet: the `ArrayAppend()` function. The idea behind `ArrayAppend()` is simple: it tells ColdFusion to create a new "slot" in the array, inserting whatever value you specify into the slot along the way. The function takes two arguments: the first argument is the array that you're working with, and the second argument is the value to place in the new slot.

Every array starts out empty, with no slots in it at all. The first time **ArrayAppend()** is called, the first slot is created (and filled, in this case, with the user's first search keywords). The second time it is called, a second slot is added (with the user's second search), and so on. The number of slots is usually referred to as the array's *length*.

6) **Under the code for the form's submit button, add the following `<cfif>` test:**

```
<!---If there are any prior searches in session history --->
<cfif ArrayLen(SESSION.PriorSearchArray) GT 0>
  <br>Previous Searches:
</cfif>
```

Whew, this is the third step in a row that's introducing you to a new array-related function! This time, the new function is **ArrayLen()**, which returns the length of the array. If there are currently three items in the array (that is, three slots), then this function returns the number 3.

In this case, the **ArrayLen()** function is used to create a `<cfif>` block that executes only when there is at least one item in the array. If the array is still empty (that is, if the length of the array is still zero), then this `<cfif>` block will be skipped.

TIP *This is an extremely common test to perform on array variables. If you use arrays in your own pages, you will most likely use at least a few `<cfif>` blocks very much like this one.*

7) **Within the `<cfif>` block, add this code under the Previous Searches line:**

```
<!---For each item in the array of prior searches...--->
<cfloop from="1" to="#ArrayLen(SESSION.PriorSearchArray)#" index="i">
</cfloop>
```

```
31    <!--- Submit button for performing search --->
32    <input type="submit" value="Search">
33
34    <!--- If there are any prior searches in session history --->
35    <cfif ArrayLen(SESSION.PriorSearchArray) GT 0>
36      <br>Previous Searches:
37
38      <!--- For each item in the array of prior searches... --->
39      <cfloop from="1" to="#ArrayLen(SESSION.PriorSearchArray)#" index="i">
40      </cfloop>
41    </cfif>
42
43  </form>
```

The `<cfloop>` tag allows you to set up *loops* in your pages. Loops are chunks of code that you want to execute repeatedly. You can use `<cfloop>` blocks in various ways, but this is one of the most common uses of the tag.

NOTE *You may not have thought of it as such at the time, but you have already learned all about another way to create a loop. Whenever you use the `<cfoutput>` tag with a `query` attribute, you are asking ColdFusion to loop through that `<cfoutput>` block, executing the code within the block once for every record in a query recordset. The loop you are adding now just serves a different purpose: to loop over the slots in an array, rather than the records in a query.*

The idea here is this: The code inside the loop will execute repeatedly, increasing the value of the loop's *index* by one for each iteration. The first time through the loop, the index is set to 1 (because of the `from="1"` attribute). The second time through the loop, the index is set to 2, and so on. This process continues until the value specified in the `to` attribute is reached. In this case, the `to` attribute is set to the length of the user's history array. So, in plain English, this `<cfloop>` block simply means "execute this code once for each slot in the array."

TIP *If you are at all familiar with some other programming language (like Java, C++, Perl, Visual Basic, or the like), then you can compare this `<cfloop>` block with a typical `for` or `for/next` type of loop in that language.*

Within the loop, the value of the index is available as a variable with the name you specify in the `<cfloop>`'s `index` attribute. In this case, `index` is equal to `"i"`, so the code inside the loop will be able to use the variable called `i` to know which iteration of the loop is currently being executed. You'll see how this works in practice in the next step.

8) Within the `<cfloop>` block you just added, add the following:

```
<!---This is the item the user searched for in the past --->
<cfset ThisItem = SESSION.PriorSearchArray[i]>
```

This is a typical line to see within a `<cfloop>` that is looping over the contents of an array. The important thing to understand is the meaning of the square brackets at the end of the line. When used with arrays, square brackets refer to one of the slots.

You always refer to the slots by number. For instance, `SESSION.PriorSearchArray[1]` would return the value in the first slot (the first search in the user's history, if there is one). `SESSION.PriorSearchArray[2]` returns the value in the second slot, and so on.

Here, the `i` variable is used in place of the number, which means that the `ThisItem` variable will end up containing the value in the first slot the first time through the loop, the value in the second slot the second time through the loop, and so on.

9) After the `<cfset>` you just added, add the following:

```
<!---Provide a link to re-execute the prior search --->
<cfoutput>
  <a href="ProductSearch.cfm?Keywords=#ThisItem#">#ThisItem#</a>
</cfoutput>
```

This code generates a link to the ProductSearch.cfm page (the same page you are currently working on), passing the value of `ThisItem` as a URL parameter called `Keywords` In this case, `ThisItem` always contains the keywords used in one of the user's previous searches.

In other words, when the page is viewed, each of the user's previous searches will be displayed as links. Clicking one of the links will reload the page, sending the keywords from that previous search to ColdFusion as a URL parameter.

10) Wrap the `URLEncodedFormat()` function around the first use of `ThisItem` in the line you just added.

```
34  <!--- If there are any prior searches in session history --->
35  <cfif ArrayLen(SESSION.PriorSearchArray) GT 0>
36    <br>Previous Searches:
37
38    <!--- For each item in the array of prior searches... --->
39    <cfloop from="1" to="#ArrayLen(SESSION.PriorSearchArray)#" index="i">
40      <!--- This is the item the user searched for in the past --->
41      <cfset ThisItem = SESSION.PriorSearchArray[i]>
42
43      <!--- Provide a link to re-execute the prior search --->
44      <cfoutput>
45        <a href="ProductSearch.cfm?Keywords=#URLEncodedFormat(ThisItem)#">#ThisItem#</a>
46      </cfoutput>
47    </cfloop>
48  </cfif>
```

This will ensure that the link works correctly, even if the value of `ThisItem` happens to contain spaces, quotation marks, slashes, or other characters that have special meanings or are not allowed in URLs.

11) **Finally, under the `<cfparam>` at the top of the page, add the following line:**

```
<!---The Keywords may also be provided in the URL --->
<cfif IsDefined("URL.Keywords")>
  <cfset FORM.Keywords = URL.Keywords>
</cfif>
```

```
1  <!--- This page uses a FORM.Keywords parameter --->
2  <cfparam name="FORM.Keywords" type="string" default="">
3
4  <!--- The Keywords may also be provided in the URL --->
5  <cfif IsDefined("URL.Keywords")>
6    <cfset FORM.Keywords = URL.Keywords>
7  </cfif>
8
9  <!--- Maintain a history of user's searches in this session --->
10 <!--- Create array for history, if it doesn't exist already --->
11 <cfif IsDefined("SESSION.PriorSearchArray") eq False>
```

This is the part that actually makes the search history feature do something useful for the reader. If a URL parameter called `Keywords` is provided to the page, then that value is copied into the `FORM.Keywords` variable. In other words, this line tells the page to treat keywords provided in the URL just as if they were typed into the text field on the search form. The remainder of the page's logic will faithfully conduct the search and display the corresponding results. Since the link you added in the previous step supplies the user's search history entries to the `URL.Keywords` parameter, the links can now be used to re-run the searches from the user's history.

12) **Save your work and test out new search history functionality.**

Use F12 in Dreamweaver to bring up the new page in your browser, and reload the page if necessary. Run a search for some keyword, such as `Phone`. Now run a search for some other keyword, such as `Free`. The first search keyword will appear as a link under the search field. Now run a search for a third keyword, such as `Cord`. Now two links appear in the search history, one for `Phone` and one for `Free`. Clicking on one of the previous search links will re-execute that search. It's not perfect yet, but it's still pretty neat.

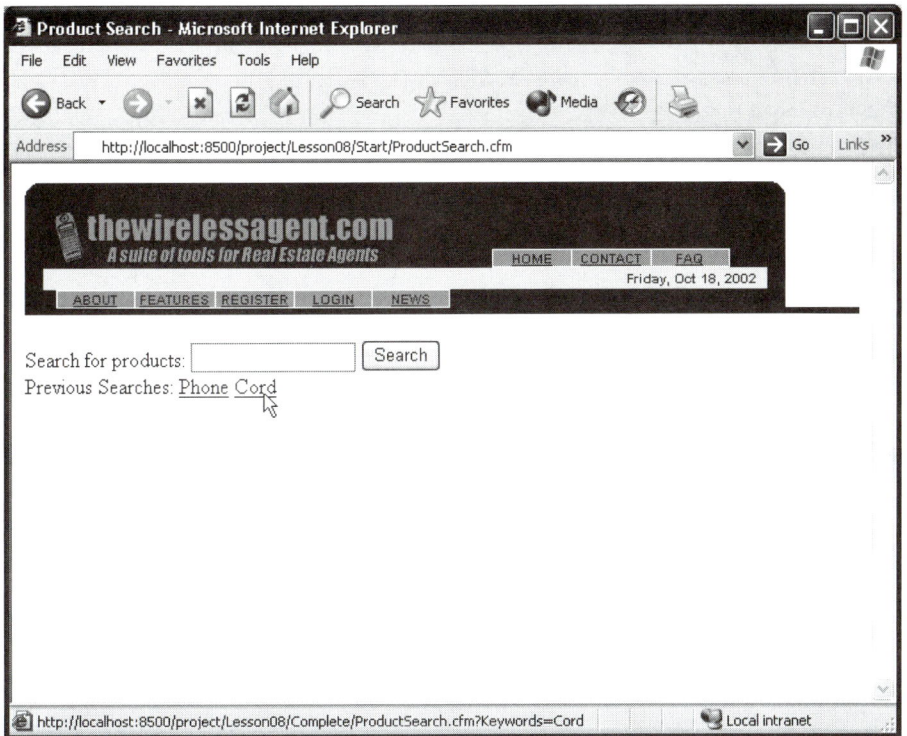

MAKING THE SEARCH HISTORY MORE INTELLIGENT

One of the problems with the search history feature at this point is that, if the user searches for the word **Phone** five times in a row, then the word Phone will show up as five separate links in the search history. It's not technically incorrect, but most users will find this confusing and unsophisticated.

Another problem is that the search history can get to be ridiculously large if the user conducts a whole lot of searches. As handy as this feature may be to your users, there is probably no need for the history to include more than the most recent five or ten search keywords.

The good news is that it's easy enough to fix both of these problems. This exercise will show you how.

1) Find the `ArrayAppend()` code that you added in Step 5 of the previous exercise.
You will be adding a bit of code to make sure that this `ArrayAppend()` line executes only when the user submits a search that isn't already in their search history.

2) Just *before* the `ArrayAppend()` code, add the following:

```
<!---Determine whether user's current search is in history --->
<cfset WasFound = False>
<cfloop from="1" to="#ArrayLen(SESSION.PriorSearchArray)#" index="i">
  <!---This is the item the user searched for in the past --->
  <cfset ThisItem = SESSION.PriorSearchArray[i]>
</cfloop>
```

First, this code sets a variable called `WasFound` to `False`. Then it sets up a `<cfloop>` that loops the contents of the `SESSION.PriorSearchArray` variable. So far, this is just like the `<cfloop>` you added in the previous exercise.

3) Within the `<cfloop>` block you just added, insert the following after the `<cfset>`:

```
<!---If we have found the current search in the history --->
<cfif ThisItem eq FORM.Keywords>
  <cfset WasFound = True>
</cfif>
```

If the item in the history array being considered by this iteration of the loop is the same as the keywords currently being searched for, that means the user is currently searching for something that they already searched for earlier in the session. If so, the `WasFound` variable is set to `True`. The end result is this: once the loop is finished executing, the `WasFound` variable will hold a value of `True` or `False`, depending on whether the user's current search is already in the search history.

4) Within the `<cfif>` block you just added, add a `<cfbreak>` tag after the `<cfset>` line.

```
62  <!--- Determine whether user's current search is in history --->
63  <cfset WasFound = False>
64  <cfloop from="1" to="#ArrayLen(SESSION.PriorSearchArray)#" index="i">
65    <!--- This is the item the user searched for in the past --->
66    <cfset ThisItem = SESSION.PriorSearchArray[i]>
67
68    <!--- If we have found the current search in the history --->
69    <cfif ThisItem eq FORM.Keywords>
70      <cfset WasFound = True>
71      <cfbreak>
72    </cfif>
73  </cfloop>
```

The `<cfbreak>` tag simply tells ColdFusion to stop executing the `<cfloop>` block, regardless of how many times it has been executed. The idea here is that once an item has been found in the search history, there is no need to continue looking through the remaining items in the array, so the loop might as well stop at this point.

NOTE *In this case, breaking out of the loop with* `<cfbreak>` *is just a way of saving ColdFusion a bit of work, and thus possibly a bit of time. Because ColdFusion is quick and efficient, though, the actual difference in performance is most likely going to be miniscule. The tag is included at this point in the lesson mainly to make sure you know it exists, in case you ever need to stop a loop for some other purpose.*

5) Now wrap a `<cfif>` block around the `ArrayAppend()` line so it looks like this:

```
<!---If the current search is not in the history --->
<cfif WasFound eq False>
  <!---Add the user's current search to their history --->
  <cfset ArrayAppend(SESSION.PriorSearchArray, FORM.Keywords)>
</cfif>
```

Now the `ArrayAppend()` line will execute only if the `WasFound` variable is `False`. In other words, the user's current search will be added to the user's history array only if it is not already in the array.

TIP *By the way, you can rephrase the* `<cfif WasFoundeqFalse>` *part to* `<cfifnotWasFound>` *if you want. They both mean the same thing.*

6) Within the `<cfif>` block you just added, add the following after the `<cfset>` line:

```
<!---If there are now more than five items, --->
<!---Remove the first item from the history --->
<cfif ArrayLen(SESSION.PriorSearchArray) gt 5>
  <cfset ArrayDeleteAt(SESSION.PriorSearchArray, 1)>
</cfif>
```

```
71     <cfbreak>
72    </cfif>
73 </cfloop>
74
75 <!--- If the current search is not in the history --->
76 <cfif WasFound eq False>
77    <!--- Add the user's current search to their history --->
78    <cfset ArrayAppend(SESSION.PriorSearchArray, FORM.Keywords)>
79
80    <!--- If there are now more than five items, --->
81    <!--- Remove the first item from the history --->
82    <cfif ArrayLen(SESSION.PriorSearchArray) gt 5>
83      <cfset ArrayDeleteAt(SESSION.PriorSearchArray, 1)>
84    </cfif>
85 </cfif>
```

This tells ColdFusion to check the number of items currently in the array (the array's length). If there are more than five items, then the first item is removed using another array-related function that you haven't seen yet: the `ArrayDeleteAt()` function. This function simply removes the value from the numbered slot you specify (in this case, 1 is always specified, so it's always the first value to get removed). All the other slots rearrange themselves automatically, so whatever was in Slot 2 is now in Slot 1, whatever was in Slot 3 is now in Slot 2, and so on.

NOTE *This is a simple but effective way to make sure that no more than five items are kept in the user's history at the same time. You can also solve the problem using slightly more complicated logic that would be somewhat more appropriate in certain cases. For instance, one problem with the current logic is that the first item will always be removed from the history, even though the first item may actually have been re-used more recently than the others. If you wish, you are encouraged to solve that little problem on your own as a learning exercise.*

7) Using the Windows Control Panel, restart the ColdFusion Application Server service.

You restart the service in the Services window of the Windows Control Panel. In most Windows 2000 and Windows XP installations, the Services window is located in the Administrative Tools portion of the Control Panel.

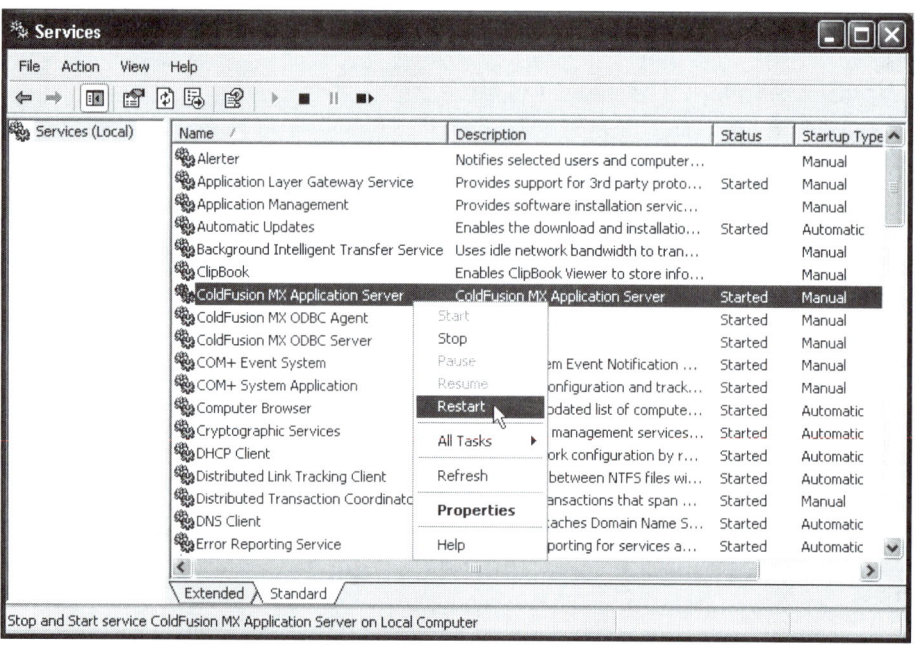

NOTE *You are restarting the service to discard all session variables from ColdFusion's memory. This is the quickest and easiest way for you to discard the session history array (or any other session variable) during development and testing. If you don't want to restart the ColdFusion server, you could skip ahead and complete the code changes in the next exercise, which provides a way for users to clear the history themselves.*

8) Save your work and test out the revised version of the page.

Perform some searches for various keywords. You will note that the session history now behaves a bit more professionally. It no longer allows duplicate searches to appear in the list of links. Additionally, the number of links never grows beyond five.

ALLOWING THE USER TO CLEAR THE SEARCH HISTORY

When providing any type of per-session history for your users—especially one that appears visually on your pages, like the search history feature you built in this lesson—you may also want to provide a way for the user to erase the history. This is particularly true if the information you are maintaining at the session level is sensitive in any way. This exercise will show you one method of allowing users to clear the session-level history maintained for them.

NOTE *Conceptually, the search history functionality you have been adding to the product search page is really not so different from what you would use for a shopping cart, wish list, or any other situation where you want a list of "somethings" to be maintained for each user. Thus, you could adapt the code in this exercise to create an "empty my shopping cart," "clear my wish list," or any other type of link that's appropriate.*

1) Still within ProductSearch.cfm, locate the `<cfif>` block under the form's submit button.

This is the block that displays the links for the items in the user's search history.

2) Add the following link to the end of the `<cfif>` block:

```
<!---Provide a link to clear the search history --->
<a href="ProductSearch.cfm?ClearHistory=Yes">[clear history]</a>
```

```
        <!--- Provide a link to re-execute the prior search --->
        <cfoutput>
            <a href="ProductSearch.cfm?Keywords=#URLEncodedFormat(ThisItem)#">#ThisItem#</a>
        </cfoutput>
    </cfloop>

    <!--- Provide a link to clear the search history --->
    <a href="ProductSearch.cfm?ClearHistory=Yes">[clear history]</a>

</cfif>

</form>
```

This simply creates a link that reloads the ProductSearch.cfm page, passing a parameter called `ClearHistory` in the URL. As shown here, the value of the parameter is always `Yes`; it doesn't matter much what the value is. The code you're about to add to the page only checks to see whether the parameter has been passed at all. If so, it takes that as a signal to clear the user's history array.

NOTE *Developers often refer to parameters such as this one (where there are really only two relevant states: existent and nonexistent) as flags.*

3) **Locate the `<cfif>` block, near the top of the page, that creates the `SESSION.PriorSearchArray` when it doesn't exist.**

As you know, that block uses the `ArrayNew()` function to create a fresh new history array for the user when the array doesn't already exist. Under normal circumstances, this block executes only once per session—on the user's first visit to the search page.

4) **After the `<cfif>` block, add the following:**

```
<!---Allow the user to clear the history via URL parameter --->
<cfif IsDefined("URL.ClearHistory")>
  <cfset ArrayClear(SESSION.PriorSearchArray)>
</cfif>
```

```
9  <!--- Maintain a history of user's searches in this session --->
10 <!--- Create array for history, if it doesn't exist already --->
11 <cfif IsDefined("SESSION.PriorSearchArray") eq False>
12   <cfset SESSION.PriorSearchArray = ArrayNew(1)>
13 </cfif>
14
15 <!--- Allow the user to clear the history via URL parameter --->
16 <cfif IsDefined("URL.ClearHistory")>
17   <cfset ArrayClear(SESSION.PriorSearchArray)>
18 </cfif>
19
20 <html>
```

This executes when the `URL.ClearHistory` variable exists—in other words, whenever the user uses the [clear history] link you added two steps back.

NOTE *Alternatively, you could use the `ArrayNew(1)` function again inside this `<cfif>` block, instead of using `ArrayNew()`. That would tell ColdFusion to create a fresh, empty array, instead of clearing the existing array. The overall effect is the same.*

5) Save your work, reload the page in your browser, and test out the new functionality.

As expected, you can now clear your session's search history at any time by clicking the link you just added to the page.

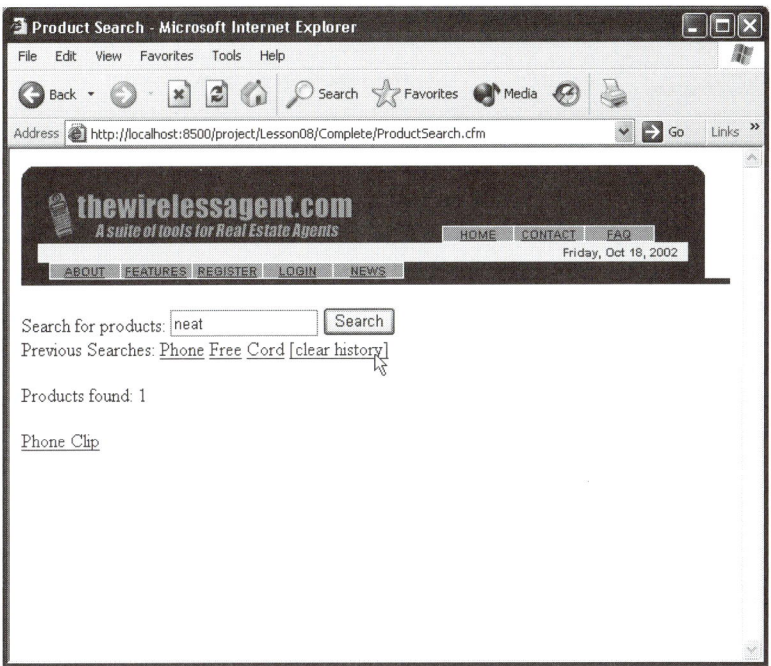

JUST FOR FUN: SWITCHING TO APPLICATION VARIABLES

This lesson has introduced you to session variables. As mentioned earlier in this lesson, ColdFusion supplies another special built-in memory scope called `APPLICATION`. Like the `SESSION` scope, variables stored in the `APPLICATION` scope are also kept in ColdFusion's memory between page requests.

There are two big differences, though. First, in the `APPLICATION` scope, variables are not kept separately for each user. Instead, they are shared amongst all users of your pages, as long as the pages are all presided over by the same Application.cfm file. Second, Application variables aren't designed to expire after a short period of time. The idea is for the variables to be maintained in ColdFusion's memory more or less indefinitely (or until the server is restarted).

There isn't space in this book for a full discussion of application variables. This shouldn't be a big problem for you, though, since they are generally only needed in relatively advanced applications. That said, you can easily change this Wireless Agent lesson's example so that it uses the `APPLICATION` scope instead of the `SESSION` scope. Let's just see what happens, just for fun, okay?

NOTE *This exercise will be more interesting if you are able to access your ColdFusion server from more than one computer. If your computer is on a local network, this will be easy enough to do—just use your machine's name or IP address instead of* `localhost` *in the URL. If not, don't worry too much about it. You'll get the idea anyway.*

1) In Dreamweaver, open the ProductSearch.cfm page that you created earlier (if it's not open already).

You will be replacing all references to the **SESSION** scope with references to the **APPLICATION** scope.

2) Use Edit > Find and Replace to open the Find and Replace Dialog.

Or you can use Ctrl+F as a shortcut for opening this dialog.

3) Specify SESSION as the text to search for, and APPLICATION as the text to replace with.

This will be a straightforward search and replace operation.

TIP *There are several other handy search-and-replace options available in this dialog. You can find out more about them by clicking the Help button.*

4) Check the Match Case check box.

Assuming you have been entering the word **SESSION** in all uppercase in the file (as shown throughout this lesson), then you should check this box to make sure you don't end up replacing the word when it is not referring specifically to the **SESSION** scope.

5) Click Replace All to perform the text replacement.

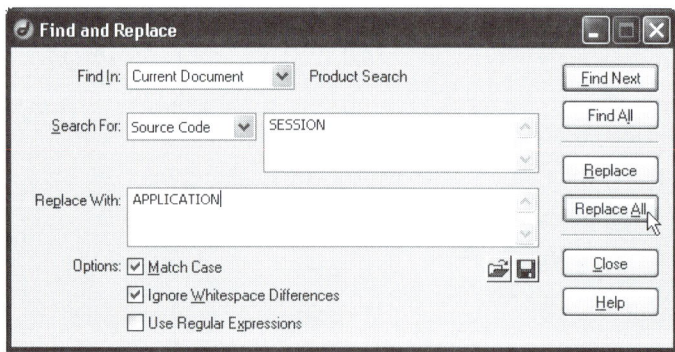

After Dreamweaver finishes the search and replace task, it will display a message to let you know how many times the word was replaced.

6) Save your work and test out the revised version of the page.

At first, it will seem as if the page now behaves the same way it did before. The search history feature still works just fine. However, if you visit your ColdFusion server using a browser on another computer and experiment with conducting searches on the two computers, you will find that the search history is shared between the two computers. If you added a third computer to the experiment, the history would be shared among all three. The point is simply that application variables are shared among all visitors to an application, rather than being kept separate for each user.

NOTE *In most cases, you can use multiple browsers on the same computer to pretend that you are using separate computers. For instance, you could open Internet Explorer, Netscape, and Opera on the same computer, and ColdFusion will most likely be fooled into thinking that they are three different computers. This is because browsers created by different vendors do not, in general, share cookies amongst each other. Mozilla and Netscape browsers may, however, depending on the versions you are using.*

WHAT YOU HAVE LEARNED

In this lesson, you have:

- Used the `SESSION` scope to track your users' actions (pages 183–192)
- Learned how to add the `<cfapplication>` tag to your Application.cfm files (pages 183–195)
- Used `ArrayNew()` to create a one-dimensional array (page 193)
- Become familiar with `ArrayAppend()`, `ArrayClear()`, and other array-related functions (pages 194–205)
- Experimented with the slightly more obscure `APPLICATION` scope (pages 205–207)

sending email

LESSON 9

So far, you have been using ColdFusion to do one thing and one thing only: build dynamic Web pages. While that is certainly ColdFusion's primary mission and greatest strength, there are lots of other things you can create using the basic CFML skills you have learned thus far. You can create dynamic Flash presentations, sophisticated Web Services for other computers to interact with, or dynamic content designed for other types of techno-tools, such as wireless phones or handheld devices.

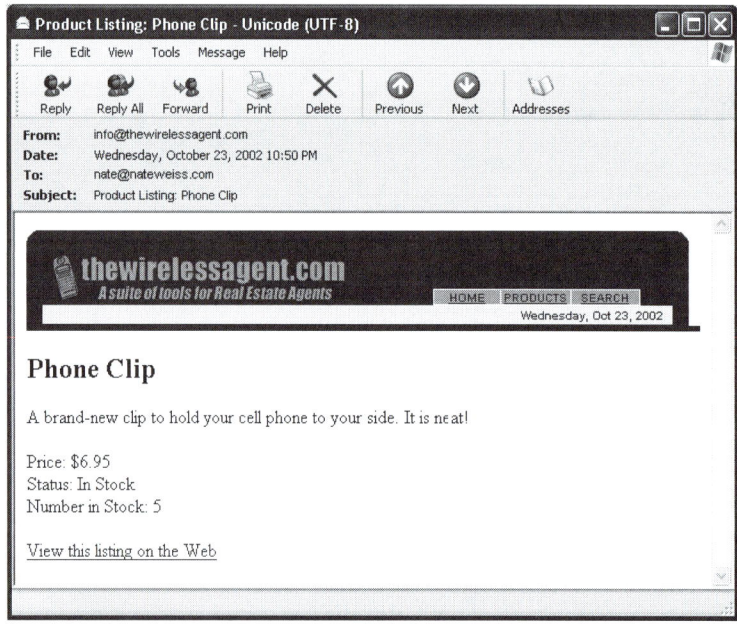

With ColdFusion, you can create rich, dynamic email messages that are packed with useful information for the recipient, and that match the look and feel of your Web pages.

This chapter will explore just one type of alternative means to deliver dynamic content: via email. You can use ColdFusion to create dynamic email messages that contain just about any type of text or information you desire. You can send an email message to one person or a hundred, and it can contain anything from static text to information retrieved on the fly from a database table.

And the best part of all is the fact that you hardly need to learn anything new to start sending email with ColdFusion. You continue using the same techniques you already know about at this point, such as using variables, running queries, and using CFML tags. To put it another way, you get to leverage the skills you have already developed during the course of this book.

WHAT YOU WILL LEARN

In this lesson you will:

- Use ColdFusion's `<cfmail>` tag to send email messages
- Send messages to an entire mailing list
- Allow recipients to unsubscribe themselves from the mailing list
- Create HTML-formatted email messages

APPROXIMATE TIME

This lesson will take approximately one hour and 30 minutes to complete.

LESSON FILES

Starting Files:

Lesson09\Start\BulkMessageAction.cfm
Lesson09\Start\BulkMessageForm.cfm
Lesson09\Start\MailingListSignup.cfm
Lesson09\Start\ProductDetail.cfm
Lesson09\Start\Unsubscribe.cfm

Completed Project:

Lesson09\Complete\BulkMessageAction.cfm
Lesson09\Complete\BulkMessageForm.cfm
Lesson09\Complete\MailingListSignup.cfm
Lesson09\Complete\ProductDetail.cfm
Lesson09\Complete\Unsubscribe.cfm

CREATING A MAILING LIST

You can use ColdFusion's email-sending abilities for many different purposes. One of the most common is to create personalized mailing lists for communicating with your company's customers, employees, or other contacts. The next few exercises will get you started with adding mailing list functionality to your own Web site. The actual mailing list will be maintained in a database table called tblMailingList, which is included in the products database that you have been working with throughout this book.

The tblMailingList table includes the following columns:

- **ListID**, which holds a unique, numeric identifier for each mailing list record
- **FirstName**, which holds the recipient's first name
- **LastName**, which holds the recipient's last name
- **EmailAddress**, which holds the recipient's Internet email address

NOTE *In a full-fledged, production-quality database, you might have additional columns to track the date that the user joined the mailing list, the number of mailings they have received, whether the record was submitted by the recipient or purchased from a third party, and so on.*

Each time a user joins the mailing list, a record will be inserted into the table. If the user chooses to unsubscribe from the list, their record will be deleted. When it comes time to send a message to the mailing list, you will simply retrieve all records from the database, sending one copy of the message to each recipient. Your first exercise is to create a signup form that people can use to join the mailing list.

1) Open the MailingListSignup.cfm page in Dreamweaver MX.

NOTE *Assuming you performed a typical installation of ColdFusion and the example files for this book, the page is located in the C:\CFusionMX\wwwroot\Project\Lesson09\Start folder.*

This page contains an HTML form that collects the user's first name, last name, and email address. To speed this exercise along, much of this page, including the form itself, has already been built for you. You will simply add the ColdFusion code that actually adds the user to the mailing list.

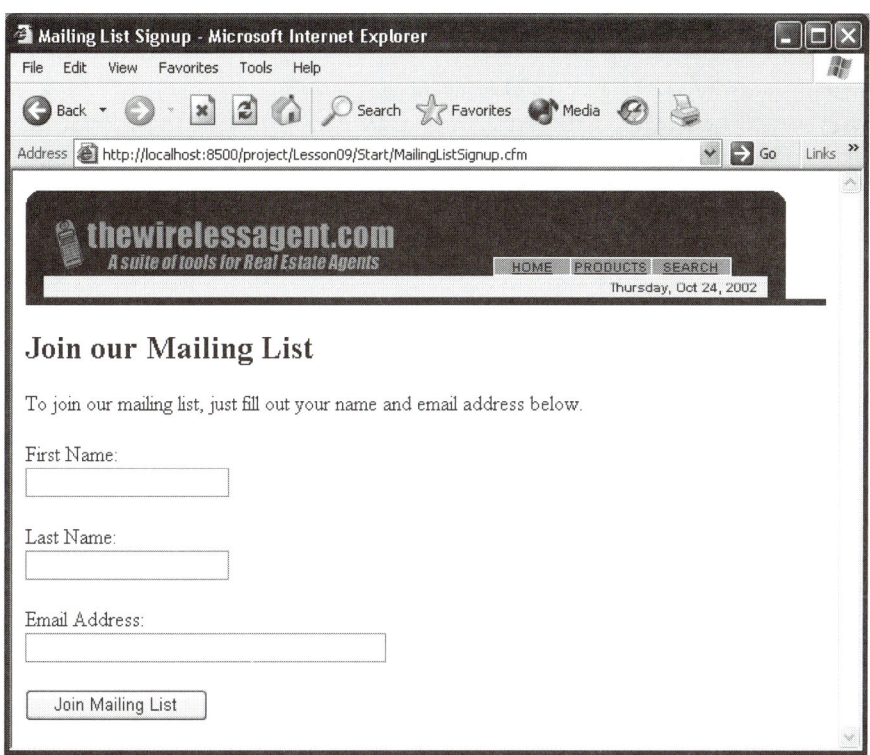

NOTE *The* `action` *attribute of this page's* `<form>` *tag is set to the page's own filename, which means that the form is self-submitting. When the user submits the form, the browser will request this page again from ColdFusion, this time including the user's form entries with the request.*

2) Under the `<cfinclude>` tag for the page header, add the following `<cfif>` block:

```
<!---If the user is submitting the signup form --->
<cfif IsDefined("FORM.EmailAddress")>
</cfif>
```

The code inside this `<cfif>` block will execute only when a form field called `EmailAddress` (which is one of the fields in the signup form) is submitted. In other words, this block executes when the user submits the signup form, but is skipped when the user first visits the page with their browser.

3) Within the `<cfif>` block you just added, add the following query:

```
<!---Quick query to see if user is already on list --->
<cfquery name="EmailQuery" datasource="products">
  SELECT * FROM tblMailingList
  WHERE EmailAddress = '#FORM.EmailAddress#'
</cfquery>
```

```
 9  <!--- Include logo and navigation header at top of page --->
10  <cfinclude template="Header.cfm">
11
12  <!--- If the user is submitting the signup form --->
13  <cfif IsDefined("FORM.EmailAddress")>
14
15    <!--- Quick query to see if user is already on list --->
16    <cfquery name="EmailQuery" datasource="products">
17      SELECT * FROM tblMailingList
18      WHERE EmailAddress = '#FORM.EmailAddress#'
19    </cfquery>
20
```

The purpose of this query is to check whether the user's email address is already on the mailing list. The idea, of course, is to try to prevent duplicate records from being inserted. If this query returns any records, then the email address being submitted is already on the mailing list. If it returns zero records, then the person is not on the list yet.

4) Under the query, add the following `<cfif>` / `<cfelse>` block:

```
<!---If the user is already on the list --->
<cfif EmailQuery.RecordCount gt 0>
<!---If the user is not on mailing list yet --->
<cfelse>
</cfif>
```

If the user is already on the list, the `<cfif>` part executes; if they are not on the list yet, the `<cfelse>` part executes. Now you'll fill those two parts in with the appropriate code.

5) **Within the `<cfif>` part of the block, add the following message:**

   ```
   <!---Show message and stop here --->
   <h2>Already on List</h2>
   <p>Thanks, but it looks like you are already
   on our mailing list. No need to join twice!</p>
   <cfabort>
   ```

   The `<cfabort>` tag is used here to so that the signup form doesn't re-appear.

6) **Within the `<cfelse>` portion you added in Step 4, add the following:**

   ```
   <!---Add user to the mailing list --->
   <cfinsert datasource="products" tablename="tblMailingList">

   <!---Show message and stop here --->
   <h2>Thank You</h2>
   <p>You have been placed on our mailing list.
   Look for lots of exciting offers via email soon.</p>
   <cfabort>
   ```

   ```
   19  </cfquery>
   20
   21  <!--- If the user is already on the list --->
   22  <cfif EmailQuery.RecordCount gt 0>
   23    <!--- Show message and stop here --->
   24    <h2>Already on List</h2>
   25    <p>Thanks, but it looks like you are already
   26    on our mailing list. No need to join twice!</p>
   27    <cfabort>
   28
   29  <!--- If the user is not on mailing list yet --->
   30  <cfelse>
   31    <!--- Add user to the mailing list --->
   32    <cfinsert datasource="products" tablename="tblMailingList">
   33
   34    <!--- Show message and stop here --->
   35    <h2>Thank You</h2>
   36    <p>You have been placed on our mailing list.
   37    Look for lots of exciting offers via email soon.</p>
   38    <cfabort>
   39
   40  </cfif>
   41 </cfif>
   ```

As you learned in Lesson 6, the `<cfinsert>` tag will add a record to whatever database table you specify, using the information submitted in a form to fill the new record's columns. This particular `<cfinsert>` tag will have the effect of adding a new mailing list entry (name and email address) to the tblMailingList table. Perfect!

7) Save your work, and then press F12 to visit the page in your browser.

The signup form appears. In a normal situation, people would navigate to this page and sign themselves up on their own. For now, you'll just add your own email address (and maybe a few lucky friends!) for testing purposes.

8) Use the form to add your own email address to the mailing list.

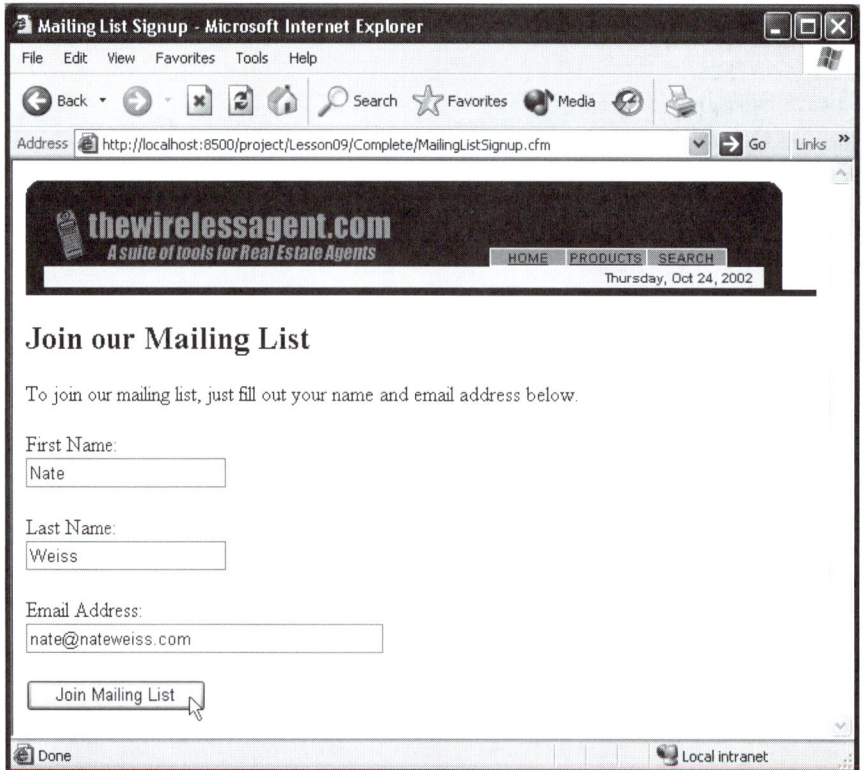

After you submit the form, the page lets you know that your name and address were added successfully to the mailing list.

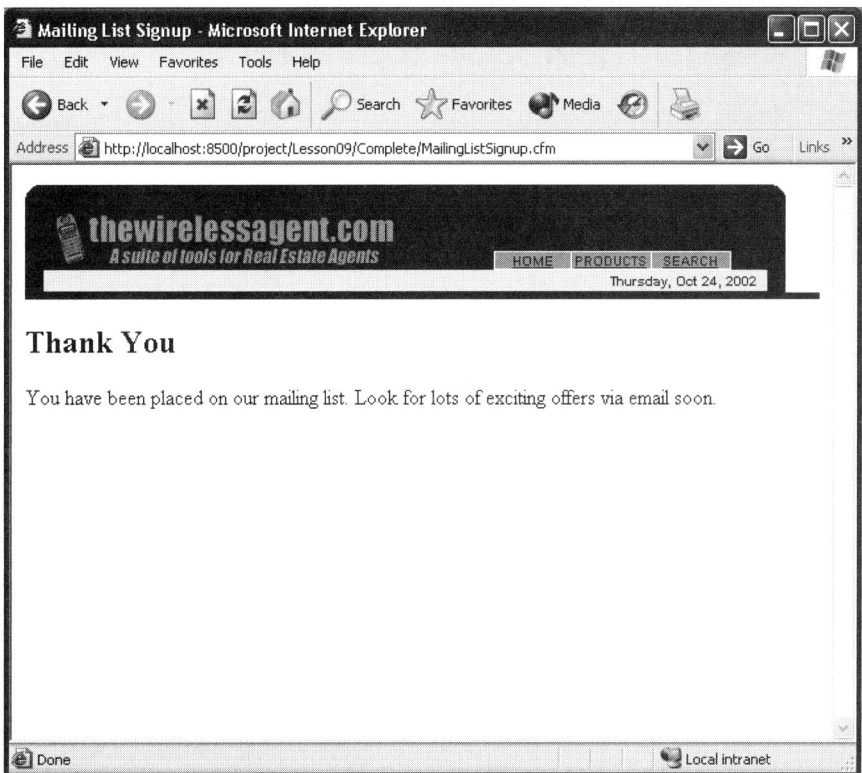

If you want, go ahead and add a few other email addresses to the list as well. Just keep in mind that ColdFusion is actually going to send emails to these addresses when you test out the message-sending page you create later on, so don't add any that you don't actually want mail sent to.

NOTE *If you try to add the same email address to the mailing list twice, you will see the message about not needing to sign up twice, which you added in Step 5.*

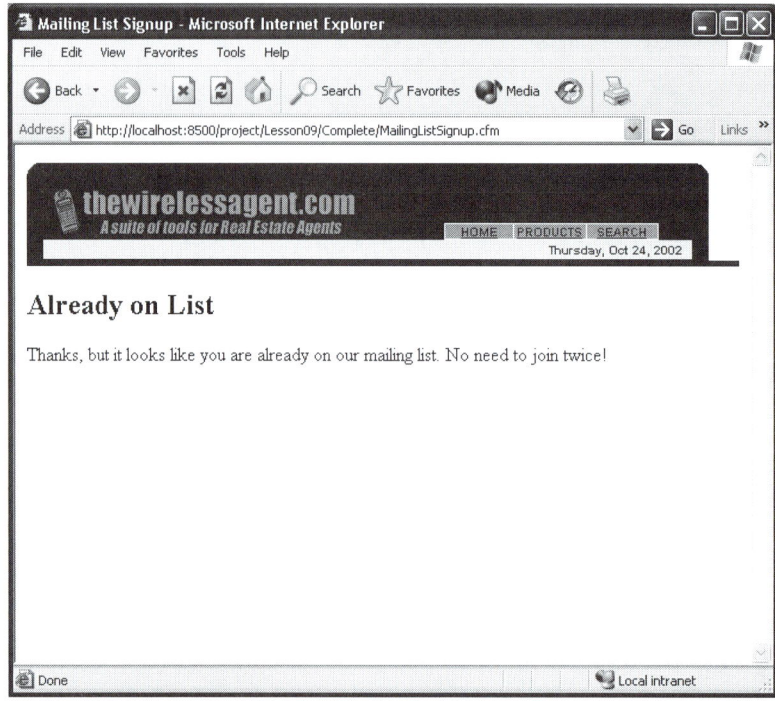

NOTE *If you wish, you can verify that the data is getting into the database properly by opening the database file in Access, or by using the View Data command on the products > Tables > tblMailingList item in Dreamweaver's Databases panel.*

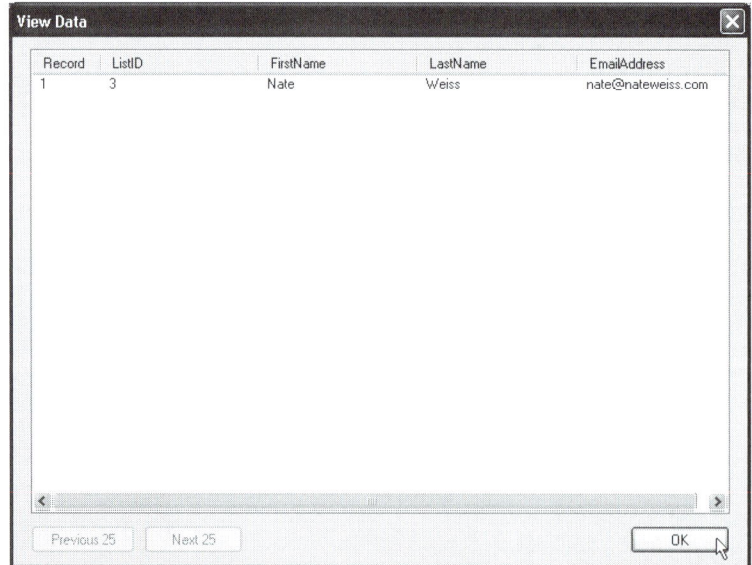

SENDING BULK EMAIL MESSAGES

Now that the mailing list is in place, you'll want to find out how to provide a means to send messages to that list. ColdFusion makes it easy to send email messages—you only need to learn a single new tag: `<cfmail>`.

The `<cfmail>` tag is extremely flexible: you can use it to send a single message to a single person, the same message to many people, or personalized messages to an entire list of people. The actual mail messages can be in either plain text or HTML format, and they can include dynamic information from forms, databases, or just about any other source. Basically, if you can display it on a ColdFusion page, you can include it in an email message.

This exercise will show you how to give authorized users the ability to compose and send a message to everyone on the Wireless Agent mailing list.

1) Open the Lesson09\Start\BulkMessageForm.cfm page in Dreamweaver.

This page contains another simple HTML form, this time with fields for the subject and body of the email message to send to the mailing list. You don't actually have to make any changes to this page—it's been created for you to save time. Just take a moment to look it over. If you bring the form up in your browser at this point, it looks like this:

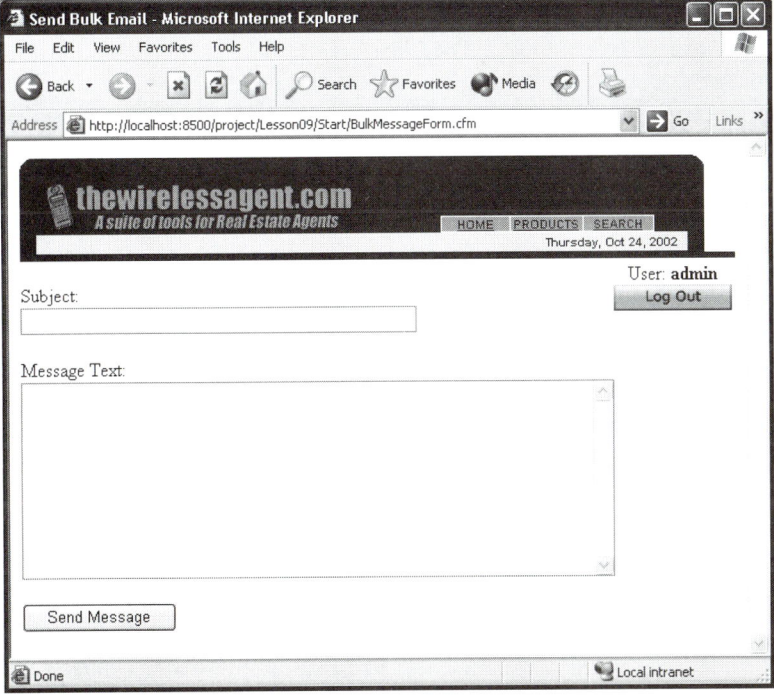

The form contains a regular text field called `EmailSubject`, and a large text area called `EmailMessage`. The form's `action` attribute is set to a page called BulkMessageAction.cfm, which you will create in the next few steps. That page will do the work of actually sending the message composed in this form.

```
15  <!--- Simple form for sending mail messages --->
16  <cfform action="BulkMessageAction.cfm" method="post">
17
18    <!--- Text entry field for email subject --->
19    <p>Subject:<br>
20    <cfinput
21      type="text"
22      name="EmailSubject"
23      size="50"
24      required="yes"
25      message="Please don't leave the Subject blank.">
26
27    <!--- Text area field for body of email itself --->
28    <p>Message Text:<br>
29    <textarea   name="EmailMessage"
30      cols="60"
31      rows="10"
32      wrap="hard"></textarea>
33
34    <!--- Submit button to actually send message --->
35    <p><input type="submit" value="Send Message">
36
37  </cfform>
```

2) Open the Lesson09\Start\BulkMessageAction.cfm page in Dreamweaver.

This is the page that gets executed when the bulk message form is submitted. The page has already been started for you. It already includes `<cfinclude>` tags to include the usual navigation header and to force the user to log in. You just need to add the code that actually sends the email messages.

3) At the very top of the page, add these `<cfparam>` lines:

```
<!---This page expects these form parameters --->
<cfparam name="FORM.EmailSubject" type="string">
<cfparam name="FORM.EmailMessage" type="string">
```

These lines simply make it clear that the page is expecting form parameters called `EmailSubject` and `EmailMessage` to be supplied. If they are not, ColdFusion will stop all execution and display an error message.

4) **Under the two `<cfinclude>` tags, add the following query:**

```
<!---Retrieve the mailing list from the database --->
<cfquery name="MailingListQuery" datasource="products">
  SELECT * FROM tblMailingList
</cfquery>
```

```
16  <!--- Include logo and navigation header at top of page --->
17  <cfinclude template="header.cfm">
18
19  <!--- Only authenticated users may access this page --->
20  <cfinclude template="ForceUserToLogin.cfm">
21
22  <!--- Retrieve the mailing list from the database --->
23  <cfquery name="MailingListQuery" datasource="products">
24    SELECT * FROM tblMailingList
25  </cfquery>
```

This query retrieves all records from the tblMailingList table. In the next step, you will add a `<cfmail>` tag that sends a message for each record retrieved by the query.

5) **After the `<cfquery>` block you just added, add the following:**

```
<!---Send the email message --->
<cfmail
  query="MailingListQuery"
  from="info@thewirelessagent.com"
  to="#MailingListQuery.EmailAddress#"
  subject="#FORM.EmailMessage#">#FORM.EmailMessage#</cfmail>
```

This is all you need to send the mail message to everyone on your mailing list! As you can see, the `<cfmail>` tag is easy to use—it practically explains itself. You supply `from`, `to`, and `subject` attributes, just like the corresponding fields when you send a message using your own email client software (like Outlook Express, Netscape, Eudora, or the like).

Then, between the opening and closing `<cfmail>` tags, you provide the actual text of the email message. That text can just be plain text, or a single variable (as shown here), or any mixture of variables, functions, and plain text. The `<cfmail>` tag processes `#` signs in the same way as the `<cfoutput>` tag, so you can create dynamic email messages using the same basic techniques that you use to create dynamic areas on a Web page. In fact, you can think of `<cfmail>` as a modified version of `<cfoutput>` that has been souped up so that it sticks the content it generates into an email message, rather than sending it to the browser. Otherwise, they are pretty similar.

The `<cfmail>` tag is also similar to `<cfoutput>` in one other respect: they both have an optional query attribute which causes the tag to "loop," doing its work once for each row of the specified query recordset. Also, with both tags you can refer to the query's columns between the opening and closing tags to include values from the current row of information from the database. In the case of the `<cfmail>` tag, you can also refer to the query's columns in the tag's `to` or `subject` attributes to customize the message further. In general, you almost always want the query to contain a column of email addresses, and to refer to that query column in the `to` attribute.

In this case, the message is always sent using `info@thewirelessagent.com` as the From address. The To address will come from the `EmailAddress` column of the `MailingListQuery` recordset, which in turn comes directly from the tblMailingList table in the database. The body of the message itself is simply set to the contents of `FORM.EmailMessage`, which is whatever the user types into the message-sending form.

NOTE *You don't have to have a query recordset to send email. The* `query` *attribute is optional—you can leave it out, which just means that the tag sends a single message (to whomever you specify in the* `to` *attribute), rather than multiple messages (one for each row of the query). You will see such a* `<cfmail>` *tag later in this lesson.*

6) **After the `<cfmail>` block you just added, add this message:**

```
<!---Success message --->
<h2>Message Submitted</h2>
<p>Your bulk email message is now being sent.</p>
```

```
27  <!--- Send the email message --->
28  <cfmail
29    query="MailingListQuery"
30    to="#MailingListQuery.EmailAddress#"
31    from="info@thewirelessagent.com"
32    subject="#FORM.EmailSubject#">#FORM.EmailMessage#</cfmail>
33
34  <!--- Success message --->
35  <h2>Message Submitted</h2>
36  <p>Your bulk email message is now being sent.</p>
37
38  </body>
39  </html>
```

This simply displays a message to the user, letting him or her know that the `<cfmail>` tag has done its work, and that the mail messages have been created.

7) Save your work, and then test the BulkMessageForm.cfm page in your browser.
Type a quick subject and message in the form and submit it. Unless you have made a small change in the ColdFusion Administrator since you installed ColdFusion, the page will now display an error message, complaining that no SMTP server has been specified for CFMAIL.

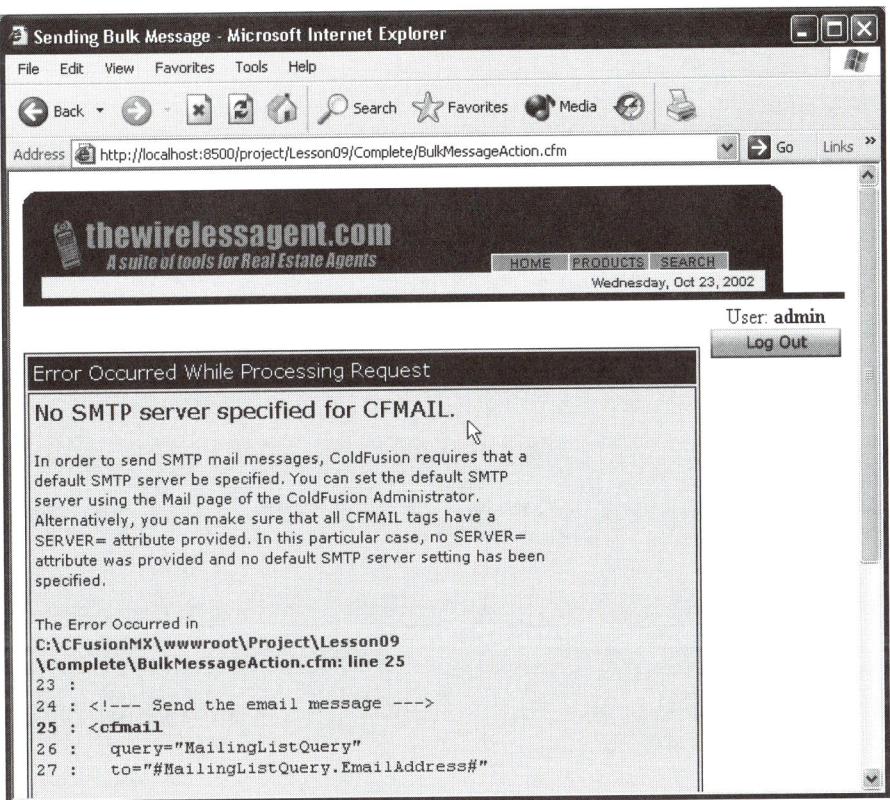

To get rid of this error message, you just need to enter your mail server's name in the Administrator. Once you do that, the mail-sending feature will be good to go.

TELLING COLDFUSION WHICH MAIL SERVER TO USE

In order for ColdFusion to be able to send email messages, it needs to know the name or IP address of a mail server to interact with. Each time one of your pages uses the `<cfmail>` tag, ColdFusion will talk to this mail server to make sure the message gets created and sent on its way. It's up to you to have a mail server ready and available for ColdFusion to interact with. In nearly all situations, there is already a mail server set up on your local network or provided by your Internet Service Provider.

NOTE *Technically, servers of this type are called Simple Mail Transport Protocol (SMTP) servers, but most people just call them mail servers.*

TIP *If you are using a mail client such as Outlook Express, Eudora, Mozilla, or Netscape to check your own mail, you can probably find the mail server's name in your account preferences within that software. Mail server names often start with* mail *or* smtp, *as in* mail.yourcompany.com *or* smtp.yourprovider.net.

1) Open the ColdFusion Administrator and enter your password.

Remember, you open the Administrator using the Programs > Macromedia ColdFusion MX > Administrator shortcut from the Windows Start Menu.

2) Click the Mail Server link in the left-hand navigation column.

This brings up the Mail Server page. The most important piece of information provided here is the mail server's name, but there are some other settings that you may wish to become familiar with. You can click the Help link at the top-right corner of the Administrator to find out more about what each setting means.

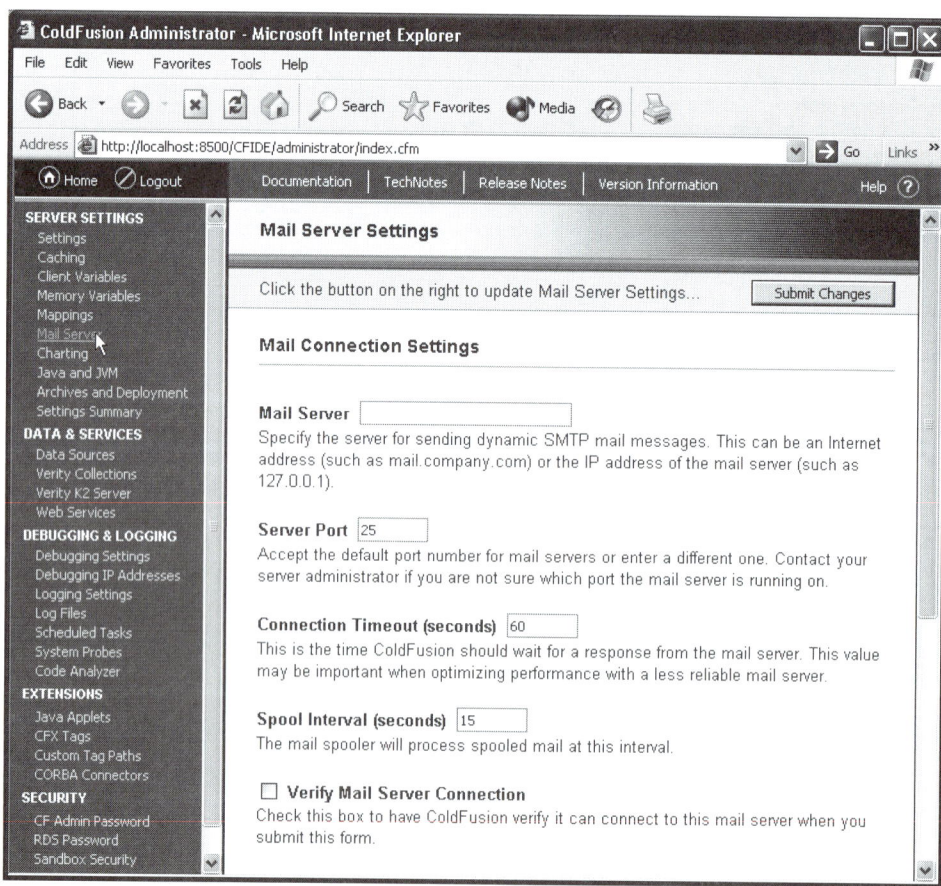

3) **Enter the name of your mail server in the Mail Server field.**

> **Mail Server** [mail.yourcompany.com]
> Specify the server for sending dynamic SMTP mail messages. This can be an Internet address (such as mail.company.com) or the IP address of the mail server (such as 127.0.0.1).

NOTE *If, for whatever reason, the mail server does not have a name registered with DNS, you can just use its IP address. A name is preferred for flexibility, but the IP address should work just fine in the short term. You'll need to speak to whoever runs your network to find out the proper name or IP address to use.*

4) **Check the Verify Mail Server Connection option.**

☑ **Verify Mail Server Connection**

This tells ColdFusion to attempt to contact the mail server you specify when you click the Submit Changes button. It's a good idea to check this box the first time you specify a given mail server, just to make sure that ColdFusion is able to find and interact with it.

5) **Click the Submit Changes button to save your changes.**

> Click the button on the right to update Mail Server Settings... [Submit Changes]

ColdFusion will now attempt to connect to the mail server you specified. If it does connect, you will see a green *Connection Verification Successful* message at the top of the page. ColdFusion should now have enough information to be able to process your `<cfmail>` tags.

6) **Return to the BulkMessageForm.cfm page and try again to send a message.**

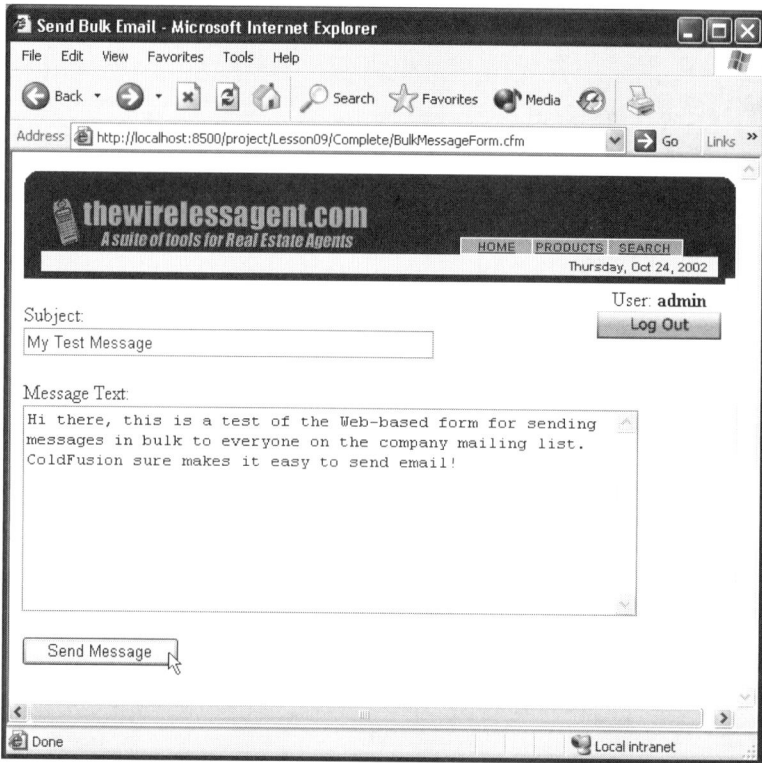

This time, the page should be able to do its job successfully. You will see a Message Submitted message, and ColdFusion will begin sending the messages out.

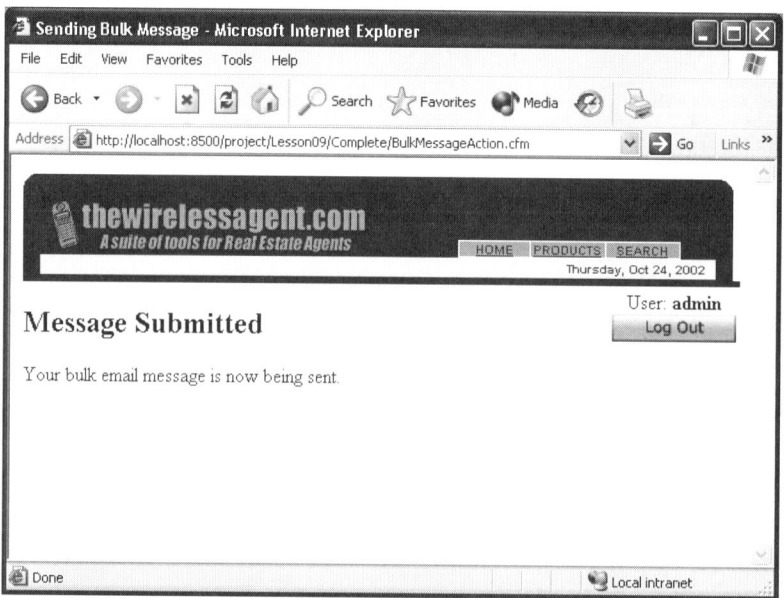

If there are only one or two records in the tblMailingList table, you (and anyone else on the mailing list) should receive the message within a few seconds. Of course, the actual amount of time may vary depending on network conditions, how busy your mail server happens to be at that moment, and various other factors.

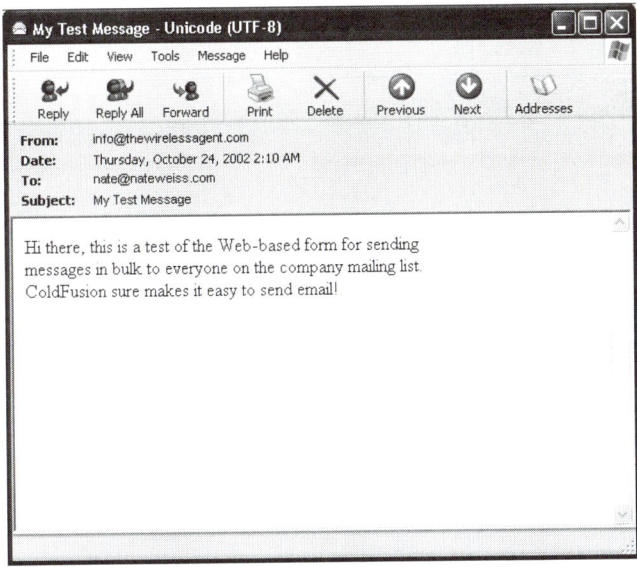

NOTE *ColdFusion doesn't necessarily send the messages out right away, especially if there are a lot of them. It queues them and sends them out in chunks so that the server can still operate efficiently, rather than being consumed by the task of sending out messages. You can control this behavior with the* `spoolenable` *attribute of the* `<cfmail>` *tag; consult the CFML Language Reference for details.*

ALLOWING USERS TO UNSUBSCRIBE

If you send email messages to people using a mailing list, you should do the courteous (and lawful) thing and provide the recipients with a reasonably easy way to remove themselves from the list. This exercise will show you how to add a short message at the bottom of each bulk email, including a link that the user can click to remove herself from the mailing list.

NOTE *This method of allowing people to unsubscribe uses a Web page to handle the actual unsubscription process. Another common method is to allow people to reply to the message with the word* unsubscribe *(or something similar) in the subject line. This reply-based "list daemon" method is not covered in this book, but you can create such a facility using the* `<cfpop>` *tag. Refer to the ColdFusion documentation for details. There is also a specific example of the reply-based method in The ColdFusion MX Web Application Construction Kit (Macromedia Press, ISBN 0321125169).*

1) **Open the BulkMessageAction.cfm page, if it's not open already.**

Remember, this is the page that actually sends messages via the `<cfmail>` tag.

2) **Add this `<cfset>` tag to the top of the page, under the `<cfparam>` tags:**

```
<!---Base URL for the Unsubscribe.cfm page --->
<cfset UnsubscribePage =
"http://localhost:8500/project/Lesson09/Complete/Unsubscribe.cfm">
```

NOTE *This `<cfset>` tag is too long to print on one line in this book, but you would normally type it on one line in your code.*

```
1  <!--- This page expects these form parameters --->
2  <cfparam name="FORM.EmailSubject" type="string">
3  <cfparam name="FORM.EmailMessage" type="string">
4
5  <!--- Base URL for the Unsubscribe.cfm page --->
6  <cfset UnsubscribePage = "http://localhost:8500/project/Lesson09/Complete/Unsubscribe.cfm">
```

This creates a variable called **UnsubscribePage**, which contains the URL for a page called Unsubscribe.cfm. You haven't created that page yet, but the basic idea is that you want to provide a link for the page at the bottom of each email message. Users will be able to click on the link in the message, which will bring them to the Unsubscribe.cfm page in their browsers.

NOTE *In a real-life situation, you would specify the actual name of your Web server in this URL, rather than using the special `localhost` name. If the ColdFusion server you are using for these examples has a proper Internet host name or static IP address, you can go ahead and put it in the `<cfset>` instead of `localhost`. Otherwise, leave the `<cfset>` alone; the unsubscribe link will still work for testing purposes as long as you are reading the email messages sent by these pages on the same computer where you've installed ColdFusion MX.*

3) **Add the following line to the beginning of the `<cfmail>` block:**

```
Dear #FirstName# #LastName#:
```

This will add the person's first and last names (from the **FirstName** and **LastName** columns of the **MailingListQuery** recordset) to the top of the message—a nice personalized touch.

4) **Add the following lines to the end of the `<cfmail>` block:**

```
----------------------------------
To remove yourself from our mailing list, please visit:
#UnsubscribePage#?ID=#ListID#&Email=#URLEncodedFormat(EmailAddress)#
```

```
27  <!--- Send the email message --->
28  <cfmail
29    query="MailingListQuery"
30    to="#MailingListQuery.EmailAddress#"
31    from="info@thewirelessagent.com"
32    subject="#FORM.EmailSubject#">Dear #FirstName# #LastName#:
33
34  #FORM.EmailMessage#
35
36  ----------------------------------
37  To remove yourself from our mailing list, please visit:
38  #UnsubscribePage#?ID=#ListID#&Email=#URLEncodedFormat(EmailAddress)#
39  </cfmail>
```

This places the URL of the unsubscribe page at the bottom of every message sent by the bulk mailing page. Two values are included as URL parameters: the ID number for the recipient's record in the database, and the recipient's email address. The unsubscribe page will use these two values as criteria to remove the recipient from the mailing list.

NOTE *Strictly speaking, either the ID number or the email address should be enough information for the unsubscribe page to identify which record to remove from the database. Therefore, you might be wondering why both items are being passed as URL parameters. The idea is to make it a little bit harder for people to mess around with the system. Because the unsubscribe page uses both values in the query that deletes the record, some mean person won't be able to remove other people's names from the mailing list using their email addresses alone. The mean person would need to know both the ID number and the email address for any given record. This is by no means bulletproof security, but should be enough to keep the page from being targeted for abuse by evil, blue meanies!*

5) **Open the Unsubscribe.cfm page in Dreamweaver.**

Most of this page has been built for you. You only need to add the part that does the actual removing from the mailing list.

6) **Add these two `<cfparam>` tags to the very top of the page:**

```
<!---This page expects these form parameters --->
<cfparam name="URL.ID" type="numeric">
<cfparam name="URL.Email" type="string">
```

These lines simply make sure that URL parameters called ID and Email are provided to the page as URL parameters, so that the unsubscribe page can do its work.

7) **Under the `<cfparam>` tags you just added, add the following query:**

```
<!---Remove the user from the list --->
<cfquery datasource="products">
  DELETE FROM tblMailingList
  WHERE ListID = #URL.ID#
  AND EmailAddress = '#URL.Email#'
</cfquery>
```

```
1  <!--- This page expects these form parameters --->
2  <cfparam name="URL.ID" type="numeric">
3  <cfparam name="URL.Email" type="string">
4
5  <!--- Remove the user from the list --->
6  <cfquery datasource="products">
7    DELETE FROM tblMailingList
8    WHERE ListID = #URL.ID#
9    AND EmailAddress = '#URL.Email#'
10 </cfquery>
11
12
13 <html>
14 <head>
```

Assuming that a record exists with the ID number and email address provided in the URL, this query permanently deletes that record from the database.

8) **Use File > Save All to save your work, and then use BulkMailingForm.cfm to send another message.**

This time, when you receive the email sent by the bulk mailing form, it will include the message about unsubscribing at the bottom, along with the link to the Unsubscribe.cfm file on the ColdFusion server.

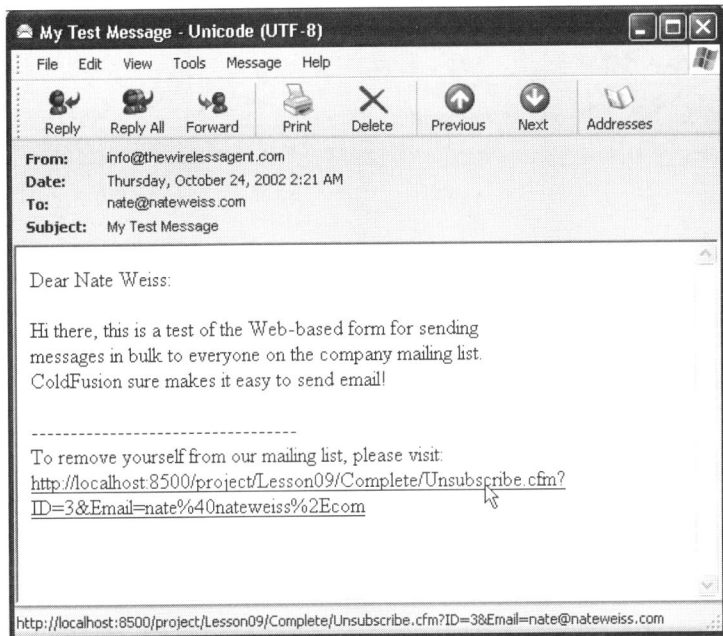

If you click on the link, your Web browser will visit the unsubscribe page, which will immediately remove you from the mailing list. When the process is complete, a message will appear, letting you know that the process is complete.

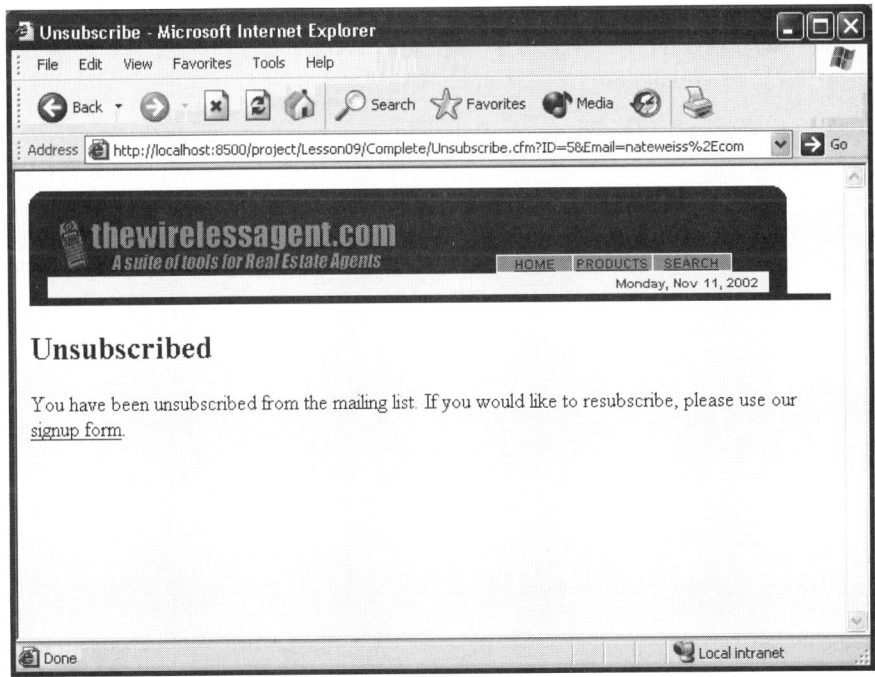

> **NOTE** *Again, because the word* localhost *is being used in the link to the unsubscribe page instead of a real host name, the link will only work if you are reading the message, clicking the link, and running these ColdFusion examples on the same computer. That should be fine for testing purposes, but to use this type of code in a real environment you would need to provide a real hostname (or IP address) in the link, instead of* localhost. *That will make the link look at lot more "normal" and familiar as well.*

SENDING DATABASE INFORMATION TO INDIVIDUAL PEOPLE

So far, you have seen how the `<cfmail>` tag can be used to send messages to groups of people, such as members of a predefined mailing list. You can also use `<cfmail>` to send single email messages, perhaps in response to something a user does on one of your Web pages. This exercise will show you how to add a feature that allows people to send product listings to themselves from a Web page. You could adapt this example so that it sent users a confirmation of an online purchase, or a confirmation of a signup process.

1) Open the Lesson09\Start\ProductDetail.cfm page in Dreamweaver.

This is the product detail page that you first created in Lesson 4, and have modified slightly and re-used throughout many of the other lessons in this book.

2) Take a look at the `<form>` tag that has been added near the bottom of the page.

```
34  <!--- Form to send product information to email address --->
35  <cfform action="ProductDetail.cfm?ProductID=#URL.ProductID#" method="post">
36
37    <!--- Instructions for the user --->
38    To send this product listing to yourself (or a friend),<br>
39    type an email address and click Send.<br>
40
41    <!--- Text input field for recipient's email address --->
42    <cfinput
43      name="EmailAddress"
44      size="15"
45      required="yes"
46      message="You must provide an email address.">
47
48    <!--- Input button to send message --->
49    <input type="submit" value="Send">
50  </cfform>
```

This code creates a very simple HTML form that collects an email address from the user. The idea is to send information about the current product via email, to the address specified on this form. If you were to view the page at this point, you would see that the form looks like this:

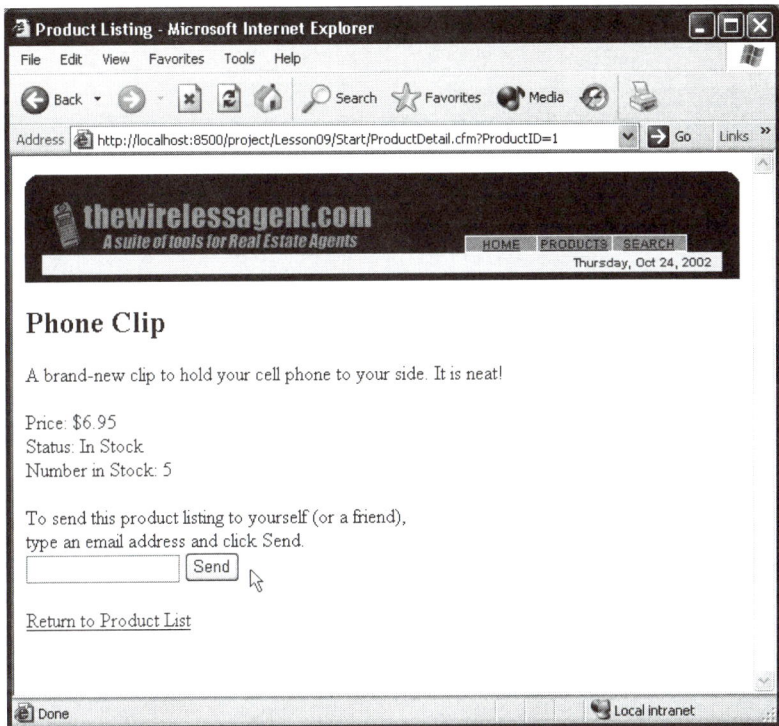

NOTE *The form is self-submitting, meaning that the* `action` *attribute of the* `<form>` *tag is the same as the filename of the page on which it appears. When the user submits the form, the browser will reload the page, this time sending the user's form entries to ColdFusion with the page request.*

3) Under the entire `<form>` block, add the following `<cfif>` test:

```
<!---If the user wants to send the product via email --->
<cfif IsDefined("FORM.EmailAddress")>
</cfif>
```

The code inside this `<cfif>` block will execute only when the user submits his email address in the send-the-product form.

4) **Within the `<cfif>` block you just added, add the following `<cfmail>` block:**

```
<!---Begin mail message --->
<cfmail
  from="info@thewirelessagent.com"
  to="#FORM.EmailAddress#"
  subject="Product Listing: #DetailQuery.ProductName#"
  type="html">
</cfmail>
```

```
53  <!--- If the user wants to send the product via email --->
54  <cfif IsDefined("FORM.EmailAddress")>
55
56    <!--- Begin mail message --->
57    <cfmail
58      from="info@thewirelessagent.com"
59      to="#FORM.EmailAddress#"
60      subject="Product Listing: #DetailQuery.ProductName#"
61      type="html">
62    </cfmail>
63
64  </cfif>
```

There are a couple of things about this `<cfmail>` tag that are different than the one you saw earlier in this lesson. First, it doesn't have a *query* attribute, so the tag is not going to loop over a query recordset—instead, it's just going to send a single message.

Second, the tag includes a `type="html"` attribute. This attribute tells ColdFusion to add a special piece of information called a *mail header* to the message, telling the mail client (Outlook Express, Eudora, or the like) that the message contains HTML-formatted text. Most mail clients are then able to interpret and display the HTML just like a Web page, including images, links, and so on.

5) **Within the body of the `<cfmail>` tag, add the following basic HTML tags:**

```
<html>
  <head>
    <title>Product Listing</title>
  </head>
  <body>
  </body>
</html>
```

These tags ought to be very familiar—they are the basic tags that appear at the top and bottom of just about any HTML page. Since the email message you are building is HTML formatted, the body of the message should contain well-formed HTML content.

6) Within the `<head>` section, after the `<title>`, add the following:

```
<base href="http://localhost:8500#CGI.SCRIPT_NAME#">
```

```
<!--- Begin mail message --->
<cfmail
    from="info@thewirelessagent.com"
    to="#FORM.EmailAddress#"
    subject="Product Listing: #DetailQuery.ProductName#"
    type="html">

    <html>
        <head>
            <title>Product Listing</title>
            <base href="http://localhost:8500#CGI.SCRIPT_NAME#">
        </head>
        <body>
        </body>
    </html>

</cfmail>
```

You may or may not have encountered the `<base>` tag in your travels through the HTML world. This tag can work in any HTML page, but it's usually used only under special circumstances where the HTML content is separated from the originating Web server. The URL that's provided in the `href` attribute becomes the URL against which any relative URLs (such as page references in links or image locations in `<img>` tags) are calculated. In other words, you are telling the rendering agent—which is normally a browser, but will be your email client in this case—to pretend that the HTML page was fetched from a Web server using the specified URL.

Because the ColdFusion `CGI.SCRIPT_NAME` variable is used to populate the `href` attribute, it will automatically contain the URL of the currently executing page (ProductDetail.cfm). Assuming a typical ColdFusion installation, that URL will be:

```
http://localhost:8500/project/Lesson09/Complete/ProductDetail.cfm
```

You can now include images and links in the body of the HTML document, and they will display and operate properly. Without the `<base>` tag, images would not be able to be found, and links would lead nowhere.

7) **Within the `<body>` block (within the `<cfmail>` block), add the following:**

```
<!---Include logo and navigation header at top of page --->
<cfinclude template="header.cfm">
```

This is the same `<cfinclude>` that you have seen throughout most of the examples in this book. It simply includes the company logo and navigation header at the top of the HTML document. It's kind of cool that you can use this same `<cfinclude>` in the body of an email, isn't it?

8) **Under the `<cfinclude>`, add code to display the product information, like so:**

```
<!---Include product information --->
<h2>#DetailQuery.ProductName#</h2>
<p>#DetailQuery.ProductDesc#</p>
<p>
  Price: #DollarFormat(DetailQuery.ProductPrice)#<br>
  Status: #DetailQuery.ProductStatus#<br>
  Number in Stock: #DetailQuery.ProductQty#<br>
</p>
```

NOTE *This is virtually the same code that appears near the top of the page. The only difference is the addition of the word `DetailQuery` before each of the query's column names. This is necessary because there is no `query` attribute in effect in this `<cfmail>` block (as there is in the `<cfoutput>` block near the top of the page), so the query must be specified directly so that ColdFusion understands what you are trying to do.*

9) **Under the code you just added, add the following link:**

```
<!---Provide link to get to product page on the Web --->
<a href="ProductDetail.cfm?ProductID=#URL.ProductID#">
View this listing on the Web</a>
```

This line adds a link to the email message, which the user can use to bring up the corresponding product page in their Web browser. From there, they might be able to get further information about the product, determine whether it is still in stock, and so on.

> **NOTE** *You really should enter this link all on one line. It's being shown here on two lines because it is too long to fit on one line in this book.*

```
92        <body>
93
94          <!--- Include logo and navigation header at top of page --->
95          <cfinclude template="header.cfm">
96
97          <!--- Include product information --->
98          <h2>#DetailQuery.ProductName#</h2>
99          <p>#DetailQuery.ProductDesc#</p>
100         <p>
101            Price: #DollarFormat(DetailQuery.ProductPrice)#<br>
102            Status: #DetailQuery.ProductStatus#<br>
103            Number in Stock: #DetailQuery.ProductQty#<br>
104         </p>
105
106         <!--- Provide link to get to product page on the Web --->
107         <a href="ProductDetail.cfm?ProductID=#URL.ProductID#">View this listing
108        </body>
109      </html>
110
111   </cfmail>
```

10) **Under the closing `</cfmail>` tag, add the following:**

```
<!---Show message indicating message was sent --->
<p><font color="red">The product listing has been sent to
<cfoutput>#FORM.EmailAddress#</cfoutput>. Thanks!</font></p>
```

```
111    </cfmail>
112
113    <!--- Show message indicating message was sent --->
114    <p><font color="red">The product listing has been sent to
115    <cfoutput>#FORM.EmailAddress#</cfoutput>. Thanks!</font></p>
116 </cfif>
```

These lines display a simple message on the Web page after the user submits the send-the-product form, informing the user that the message has been sent.

11) Save your work, and then test out the revised page with your browser.

NOTE *This page expects a `ProductID` parameter to be provided in the URL, so you will need to add it to the URL in your browser's Address field. Or, you can visit the ProductList.cfm page in your browser, and then click on one of the product links to get yourself to the page you just modified.*

You can now type your own email address into the form and press the Send button to send the product message to yourself.

Wait a few moments, then check your email with your normal mail client. When the message arrives, it should contain product information about the appropriate product, formatted very much like the information presented in the Web version of the page.

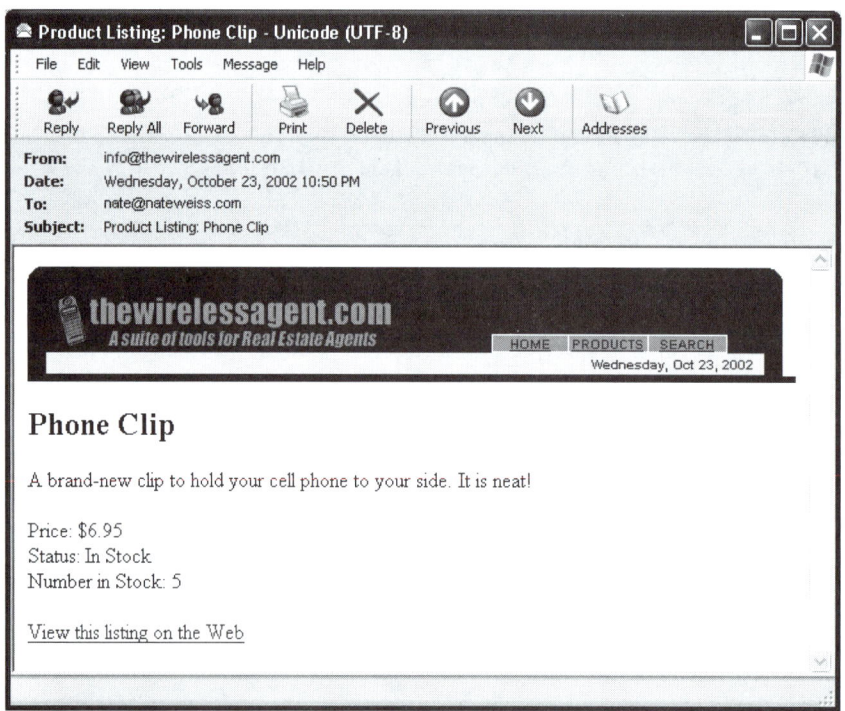

> **NOTE** Again, because `localhost` is used in this message instead of a real server host name, it is expected that you will be checking the mail using a mail client on the same computer that ColdFusion is running on. In a real live application, you would use the server's hostname (such as www.thewirelessagent.com) instead of `localhost` throughout the body of the `<cfmail>` tag.

WHAT YOU HAVE LEARNED

In this lesson, you have:

- Created a mailing list signup page (pages 210–215)
- Learned how to send email with ColdFusion's `<cfmail>` tag (pages 217–220)
- Created a form for sending messages to an entire mailing list (pages 217–221)
- Specified your mail server in the ColdFusion Administrator (pages 221–223)
- Put together a means for users to remove themselves from a mailing list (pages 225–229)
- Added a form for sending individual product listings via email (pages 230–236)
- Learned how to create HTML-formatted email messages (pages 232–235)

creating functions and tags

LESSON 10

During the course of the past nine Lessons, you have learned quite a bit about ColdFusion. You have learned how to use variables, run queries, send email, and of course generate dynamic pages that are easy to keep up to date. Along the way, you have used quite a few of ColdFusion's tags and functions to get each job done. ColdFusion also provides lots of other tags and functions that you haven't seen yet, but that you'd know how to employ if you had the need for them.

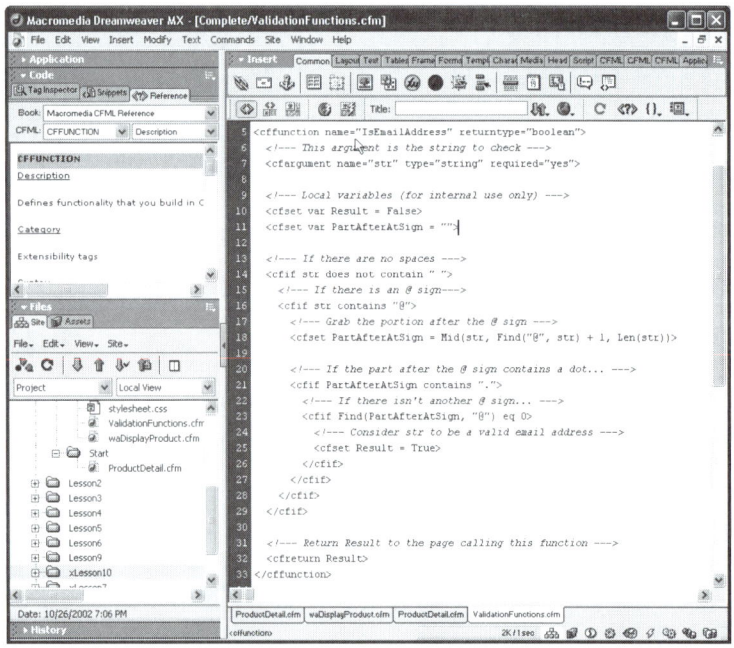

The `<cffunction>` *tag makes it easy to create new functions for use within your ColdFusion pages. And it's just as easy to create your own tags.*

Nonetheless, you will someday find yourself wishing for a particular function or tag that isn't included with the product. That is when you'll get to take advantage of one of the neatest things about ColdFusion: its extensibility. You can create functions and tags of your own, to do just about anything you wish. So, when you find yourself needing a function or tag that doesn't yet exist, you can just sit down and create it.

Sound intimidating? Don't worry—it's really quite easy to create your own functions and tags. In this final lesson, you will learn, not *everything*, but enough to be well on your way to creating the tags and functions of your dreams (you *do* dream about tags and functions, don't you?). In fact, you may find that you think about your ColdFusion pages in a whole new way after you finish this final lesson. You'll soon be working with the product on your own, and can keep the option of creating your own functions and tags in mind as you work on your first few projects.

WHAT YOU WILL LEARN

In this lesson you will:

- Learn how to create your own functions
- Learn how to create your own tags
- Use the functions and tags you create in other ColdFusion pages

APPROXIMATE TIME

This lesson will take approximately two hours to complete.

LESSON FILES

Starting Files:

Lesson10\Start\MailingListSignup.cfm
Lesson10\Start\ProductDetail.cfm

Completed Files:

Lesson10\Complete\MailingListSignup.cfm
Lesson10\Complete\ProductDetail.cfm
Lesson10\Complete\ValidationFunctions.cfm
Lesson10\Complete\waDisplayProduct.cfm

CREATING YOUR FIRST FUNCTION

ColdFusion MX introduces a set of tags for creating your own functions: `<cffunction>`, `<cfargument>`, and `<cfreturn>`. As you will see in just a moment, it is really easy to use these tags to create brand-new functions to perform whatever operations you need.

A typical function is made up of the following parts:

- The opening `<cffunction>` tag, which gives the function a name
- One or more `<cfargument>` tags to establish what values the function accepts as input
- One or more `<cfset var>` tags to establish any local variables to be used within the function
- The actual code that makes the function work, which can contain just about any CFML code
- A `<cfreturn>` tag, which returns whatever value the function wants to return
- The closing `</cffunction>` tag

This exercise will show you how these parts work together as you build a new function from scratch.

1) In Dreamweaver MX, use File > New to create a new ColdFusion document.

Remember, you choose Dynamic Page > ColdFusion within the New Document dialog to create a new ColdFusion document.

2) Erase all code in the new document so that it is completely empty.

This file will contain only the definition for a new function. Since it will not output or display any code or text to be sent to the browser, it should not contain the `<html>`, `<body>`, and other basic HTML tags found on a typical Web page. The page that uses the new function will take care of sending a complete HTML page to the browser.

3) At the top of the page, type the following set of `<cffunction>` tags:

```
<cffunction name="IsEmailAddress">
</cffunction>
```

This simply establishes that you are creating a new function called `IsEmailAddress()`. The purpose of the function is to determine whether a string is a well-formed email address. The actual code for the function—the stuff that makes it "go"—will be contained within this `<cffunction>` block.

4) Add a `returntype="boolean"` attribute to the `<cffunction>` tag.

```
1  <cffunction name="IsEmailAddress" returntype="boolean">
2  </cffunction>
3
```

It's not required that you specify a `returntype` attribute, but it's a good idea to do so when you can. This attribute makes it clear what kind of information is going to be returned by the new function. In the case of this function, the idea is for it to return a value of `True` or `False`, depending on whether the string in question meets the specified criteria for an email address. The word *boolean* is just a term for a value that is either true or false, so a `returntype` attribute of `boolean` is appropriate here.

> **NOTE** *If the function was going to return a date, you would use* `returntype="date"`. *If the function was going to return a string (such as a company name or message of some kind), you would use* `returntype="string"`. *For the complete list, look up* `<cffunction>` *in the CFML Language Reference.*

5) Within the `<cffunction>` block you just added, insert the following `<cfargument>` tag:

```
<!---This argument is the string to check --->
<cfargument name="str" type="string" required="yes">
```

```
1  <cffunction name="IsEmailAddress" returntype="boolean">
2    <!--- This argument is the string to check --->
3    <cfargument name="str" type="string" required="yes">
4
5  </cffunction>
6
```

You use the `<cfargument>` tag to establish the *arguments* that your new function will accept. Throughout this book, you have seen how arguments work with ColdFusion's built-in functions. For instance, the built-in `DateFormat()` function accepts as its first argument the date value you want to format. It also accepts a second, optional argument that specifies the mask you want the function to use to format the date. So, the information supplied to its arguments differs depending on the purpose of the function, but all arguments have one thing in common: they are the function's *input*. The function's purpose in life, then, is to take the input provided in the arguments, do something with it, and return a result.

In this case, the `IsEmailAddress()` function you are building is going to accept just one argument: the string that the function is supposed to check for validity. Since the argument has been identified as mandatory via the `required="yes"` argument, ColdFusion will display an error message if you attempt to use the function without supplying an email address to check. Because of the `type="string"` argument, ColdFusion will also display an error message for you if something other than a string (for instance, an array or a query recordset) is mistakenly supplied to the argument.

TIP *If you don't want an argument to be required, set `required="no"` and add a `default` attribute. The value you provide in `default` will be used whenever the function is called without supplying a specific value for the attribute.*

NOTE *Your functions can accept as many arguments as you wish. Just add a `<cfargument>` tag for each one. The only restriction is that the `<cfargument>` tags need to be at the very top of the `<cffunction>` block. If you try to use a `<cfargument>` tag somewhere else in the `<cffunction>` block (that is, after some line of code that is not itself a `<cfargument>` tag), ColdFusion will display an error message asking you to move it up to the top.*

6) **After the `<cfargument>` tag you just added, insert the following:**

```
<!---Local variables (for internal use only) --->
<cfset var Result = False>
```

```
1  <cffunction name="IsEmailAddress" returntype="boolean">
2    <!--- This argument is the string to check --->
3    <cfargument name="str" type="string" required="yes">
4
5    <!--- Local variables (for internal use only) --->
6    <cfset var Result = False>
7
8  </cffunction>
```

At first glance, this seems to be an ordinary `<cfset>` tag. Knowing what you do about ColdFusion, it's easy to tell what this line does: it creates a variable called `Result`, and sets the value of the variable to `False`.

So, what's that funny word `var` doing in there? Well, `var` tells ColdFusion that you want the variable to be a *local* variable—understood and known only within the body of the `<cffunction>` block. Programmers often refer to such a variable as being *local to the function*. A variable that is local to the function ceases to exist when the function has finished doing its work.

TIP *If you happen to be familiar with JavaScript, you'll note that it uses the word* `var` *in much the same way.*

Let's consider what the `var` does in this case. Say some ColdFusion page uses this function, and that page happens to have already created a variable called `Result`. Because of the `var`, the `Result` variable inside the `<cffunction>` block will not interfere with the one created by the page itself. It's as if each function has its own set of variables to play around with, and all you need to do in order to use them is to use `var` in `<cfset>` tags that appear within the function.

So, because of the `var`, a variable called `Result` has been created, and has been specified as local to the function. Furthermore, the value of `False` has been stored in the new variable. Of course, you don't have to set each local variable to `False`; you can set the value of each local variable to whatever you want. The value of `False` is just what's appropriate for this particular variable (you'll see why shortly).

NOTE *All* `<cfset>` *tags that use* `var` *must appear at the top of the* `<cffunction>` *block. They should go after any* `<cfargument>` *tags but before any of the code that makes your function work.*

NOTE *In nearly all cases, you should use the word* `var` *when using* `<cfset>` *to create a variable within a* `<cffunction>` *block. To put it another way, it is generally considered bad form to create functions that create non-local variables. Functions should be designed so that they return whatever they need to return as their official return value. Allowing a function to have "side effects" (such as creating non-local variables, which would continue to exist after the function finishes executing) is generally frowned upon.*

7) **After the `<cfset>` line you just added, add a `<cfreturn>` tag, like so:**

```
<!---Return Result to the page calling this function --->
<cfreturn Result>
```

```
1  <cffunction name="IsEmailAddress" returntype="boolean">
2    <!--- This argument is the string to check --->
3    <cfargument name="str" type="string" required="yes">
4
5    <!--- Local variables (for internal use only) --->
6    <cfset var Result = False>
7
8    <!--- Return Result to the page calling this function --->
9    <cfreturn Result>
10 </cffunction>
```

As the name implies, the `<cfreturn>` tag tells ColdFusion what value the function should return when it is actually used. In most cases, you use it to return a locally scoped variable (such as the `Result` variable used here). The value of the variable will be returned to whatever page is using the function.

TIP *Again, if you happen to be familiar with JavaScript, you'll note that the `<cfreturn>` tag is the approximate equivalent to JavaScript's `return` statement.*

NOTE *The `<cfreturn>` tag can be used only once per function. It almost always appears right at the end of the `<cffunction>` block.*

At this point, the function is complete in terms of its syntax, but it doesn't really do anything useful yet. Consider what would happen if you were to use the function as is. First, it would make sure that the `str` argument was provided, and that it was a string. Then it would create the locally scoped variable called `Result`, setting its value to False. Then it would return the value of the variable as the function's return value. No matter what value you pass to the `str` argument, the function will always return `False`.

In the next step, you will start adding the code that actually makes the function work.

NOTE *This example uses the variable name `Result` to hold the value that eventually gets returned by the function. You don't have to use the same name in your own functions, but it's a good idea to be consistent about the name when you can, just to get in the habit of keeping your code as uniform as possible.*

8) **Between the `<cfset var>` and `<cfreturn>` tags, add the following:**

   ```
   <!---If there are no spaces --->
   <cfif str does not contain " ">
   </cfif>
   ```

This `<cfif>` checks to see if the `str` argument passed to the function contains any spaces. If the argument contains a space, the entire `<cfif>` block is skipped; anything with a space in it should be rejected as a potential email address.

9) **Insert a second `<cfif>` block within the one you just added, like so:**

```
<!---If there is an @ sign--->
<cfif str contains "@">
</cfif>
```

```
8    <!--- If there are no spaces --->
9    <cfif str does not contain " ">
10     <!--- If there is an @ sign--->
11     <cfif str contains "@">
12     </cfif>
13   </cfif>
14
15   <!--- Return Result to the page calling this function --->
16   <cfreturn Result>
17 </cffunction>
```

The purpose of this `<cfif>` block is to make sure that the value passed to the `str` argument contains an @ sign. If so, code execution will continue within the `<cfif>` block.

10) **Within the second `<cfif>` block you just added, insert the following `<cfset>` tag:**

```
<!---Grab the portion after the @ sign --->
<cfset PartAfterAtSign = Mid(str, Find("@", str) + 1, Len(str))>
```

```
8    <!--- If there are no spaces --->
9    <cfif str does not contain " ">
10     <!--- If there is an @ sign--->
11     <cfif str contains "@">
12       <!--- Grab the portion after the @ sign --->
13       <cfset PartAfterAtSign = Mid(str, Find("@", str) + 1, Len(str))>
14
15     </cfif>
16   </cfif>
```

This line might look a bit confusing at first, but it's really not all that complicated when you look at each individual piece. This line uses three of ColdFusion's built-in functions to create a new variable called `PartAfterAtSign`, setting its value to the portion of `str` that comes after the @ sign.

To understand what's going on here, consider what happens if the value passed to the `str` attribute happens to be `nate@nateweiss.com` (hey, stranger things have happened). If so, the `Find("@", str)` part of the line will return `5`, since the @ sign is in the fifth position within the string. The `Len(str)` part of the line returns `18`, since there are 18 characters in `str`.

Which brings us to the `Mid()` function. This function simply returns a portion, or *substring*, of a string. It takes three arguments. The first argument is the string to return a portion of. The second argument is the character position of the beginning of the portion (where 1 means "start at the first character," 2 means "start at the second character," and so on). The third argument is the character position of the end of the portion.

So, in plain English, all these functions used together mean "give me the portion of `str` from just after the first @ sign to the end," which in turn means "give me the portion of `str` from character position 6 though 18." After this line executes, the `PartAfterAtSign` variable will be set to just what you'd expect: `nateweiss.com`.

NOTE *For more information about these functions, please consult the CFML Language Reference portion of your ColdFusion documentation. They are all discussed in the String Functions section.*

11) After the `<cfset>` you just inserted, add the following:

```
<!---If the part after the @ sign contains a dot...--->
<cfif PartAfterAtSign contains ".">
  <!---If there isn't another @ sign...--->
  <cfif Find(PartAfterAtSign, "@") eq 0>
    <!---Consider str to be a valid email address --->
    <cfset Result = True>
  </cfif>
</cfif>
```

The first of these `<cfif>` tags makes sure that the portion of the string after the @ sign contains a dot (period) character. The next `<cfif>` makes sure that it contains only that single @ sign (since an email address should contain only one). If both of these conditions are true, the `<cfset>` tag is used to set the locally scoped `Result` variable to True. In other words, if the function gets this far, it goes ahead and decides that the string in question appears to be a well-formed email address.

```
9    <!--- If there are no spaces --->
10   <cfif str does not contain " ">
11     <!--- If there is an @ sign--->
12     <cfif str contains "@">
13       <!--- Grab the portion after the @ sign --->
14       <cfset PartAfterAtSign = Mid(str, Find("@", str) + 1, Len(str))>
15
16       <!--- If the part after the @ sign contains a dot... --->
17       <cfif PartAfterAtSign contains ".">
18         <!--- If there isn't another @ sign... --->
19         <cfif Find(PartAfterAtSign, "@") eq 0>
20           <!--- Consider str to be a valid email address --->
21           <cfset Result = True>
22         </cfif>
23       </cfif>
24
25     </cfif>
26   </cfif>
```

> **NOTE** *At this point, the function is reasonably proficient at validating an email address, but far from perfect. For instance, nate@.com would be considered a valid address, even though there aren't any characters between the @ sign and the dot. If you would like the function to be more rigorous, you could add further tests based on the code you have already created.*

12) Under the `<cfset var>` line you added in Step 6, add the following:

```
<cfset var PartAfterAtSign = "">
```

```
5    <!--- Local variables (for internal use only) --->
6    <cfset var Result = False>
7    <cfset var PartAfterAtSign = "">
```

Remember, it's important to use `var` to create locally scoped versions of any variables you use within the body of a function. By adding this `<cfset var>` tag, you are telling ColdFusion to treat the `PartAfterAtSign` variable as local to the function.

You might be wondering why the value of this variable is set to an empty string (`""`). It's because, as mentioned earlier, ColdFusion MX requires you to place all `<cfset var>` tags at the top of a function (after any arguments, but before any other lines in the body of a function). In this case, the `PartAfterAtSign` variable needs to be scoped locally with `var`, but it's not possible to give the variable its final value yet, since that value is determined later on in the `<cffunction>` block. Therefore, this `<cfset var>` line just needs to create the variable with some kind of temporary, initial value. The value will be replaced with the variable's "real" value later in the function code, when the other `<cfset>` tag (the one without the `var`) is encountered.

NOTE *You can use anything you want as the variable's initial value, since it's just going to be discarded anyway. This book uses empty strings for such initial values because empty strings seem to intuitively denote "emptiness."*

NOTE *Again, without this line, ColdFusion would create a normal ColdFusion variable when it gets to the other `<cfset>` line later in the function. That variable would continue to exist in any page that calls this function, even after the function finishes doing its work. Worse, if there happened to already be a variable called `PartAfterAtSign` in the calling template, the function would overwrite its value. This sort of undesired side-effect is generally considered bad form, so you should always use `var` to scope variables locally within functions (unless you have a very specific reason not to).*

TIP *Always glance at a function when you're through with it to make sure that any variables created with `<cfset>` tags in the body of the function are scoped locally with `var` toward the top of the `<cffunction>` block.*

13) Save the new file as *ValidationFunctions.cfm*.

Make sure to save this new file in the same folder as the other files for this lesson.

You have now created a new function called `IsEmailAddress()`, which can be called just like any of ColdFusion's own built-in functions. In the next exercise, you'll see how to use the function in your own pages.

NOTE *As you have learned during this exercise, this function simply checks to see whether the email address appears to be well-formed (that is, whether it contains an @ sign, doesn't contain illegal characters, and so on). It doesn't check to see whether the email address actually exists. So, a more accurate name for the function might be `IsWellFormedEmailAddress()` instead of `IsEmailAddress()`. Sometimes you have to strike a balance between conciseness and accuracy.*

USING YOUR NEW FUNCTION

Now that the `IsEmailAddress()` function has been created, it's quite a simple matter to put it to use. You just include the file that contains the function using the `<cfinclude>` tag that you already know and love. Then you can call the function using the same syntax that you would for any other function. Let's see how it works.

1) Open the MailingListSignup.cfm page from the Lesson10\Start folder.

This is the same "signup" page you created in Lesson 9. You will now use the function you just created to make sure the email addresses provided to the page appear to be valid before they are actually inserted into the database.

2) **At the very top of the page, include the function you just created, like so:**

```
<!---Include the email validation function --->
<cfinclude template="ValidationFunctions.cfm">
```

This line simply includes the ValidationFunctions.cfm file that you created in the last exercise. When ColdFusion gets to this `<cfinclude>` tag, it will treat the `<cffunction>` block in that file as if it were part of the page you're working on now. You are thus able to use your new function anywhere after this `<cfinclude>` line.

NOTE *You can use relative paths with* `<cfinclude>` *if you want to keep your functions in a different folder from the pages in which you use them. For instance, if the* `Project` *folder for this book's examples had a subfolder called* `Functions` *(along with the subfolders for each lesson), then you could place the ValidationFunctions.cfm file in that subfolder and change the* `<cfinclude>` *line to use* `../../Functions/ValidationFunctions.cfm` *in the* `template` *attribute. Except in certain special situations, the* `../` *parts work the same way as they do when providing relative paths to image files in an HTML* `<img>` *tag.*

3) **Locate the `<cfif>` block that tests for the existence of the `FORM.EmailAddress` variable.**

If you recall from the last lesson, the code in this `<cfif>` block executes whenever a user submits the signup form for the mailing list.

4) **Just within that `<cfif>` block, add the following:**

```
<!---If the email address appears to be invalid --->
<cfif IsEmailAddress(FORM.EmailAddress) eq False>
  <h2>Invalid Email Address</h2>
  <p>Please check your email address. The
  one you provided doesn't appear to be valid.</p>
  <cfabort>
</cfif>
```

```
15  <!--- If the user is submitting the signup form --->
16  <cfif IsDefined("FORM.EmailAddress")>
17
18    <!--- If the email address appears to be invalid --->
19    <cfif IsEmailAddress(FORM.EmailAddress) eq False>
20      <h2>Invalid Email Address</h2>
21      <p>Please check your email address. The
22      one you provided doesn't appear to be valid.</p>
23      <cfabort>
24    </cfif>
25
```

5) Save your work, and then test the signup form with your browser.

If you enter a validly formed email address (which for the purposes of this example is defined as a string of characters with no spaces, containing exactly one @ sign followed by at least one dot), the form operates exactly as it did before. If, on the other hand, you enter something that is not appear to be a valid email address, the page refuses to add it to the mailing list and explains the problem to the user.

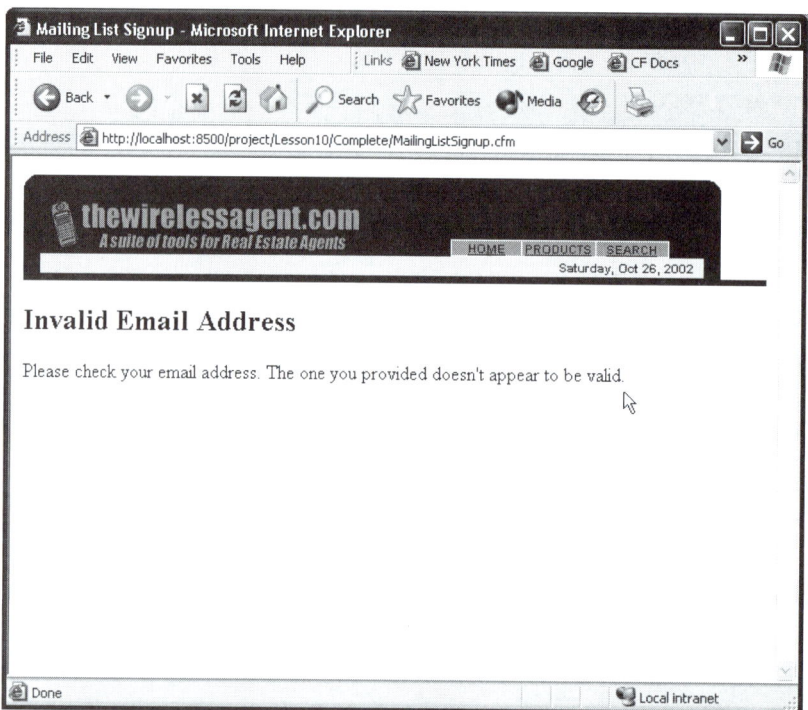

CREATING SPECIALIZED FUNCTIONS

The `IsEmailAddress()` function you created and used in the last two exercises can be thought of as a *general purpose* function, meaning that it would probably be useful in many different types of pages. It doesn't necessarily have anything to do with a specific Web site. You can also build functions that are just for a specific Web project.

Just to get your brain thinking about this idea, let's add another function to the ValidationFunctions.cfm file. This one will be called `IsOnMailingList()`, and will do the work of checking to see whether a particular email address is already on The Wireless Agent's mailing list. As you learned in Lesson 9, that determination can be made by checking for the existence of the email address in the tblMailingList table from the example database for this book. So, this new function can be thought of as a convenient way to wrap up—or encapsulate—the process of running that test against the database.

1) If it's not open already, re-open the ValidationFunctions.cfm file in Dreamweaver.

This is the same file that you created the `IsEmailAddress()` function during this lesson's first exercise.

2) After the `<cffunction>` block you created earlier, add a new one, like so:

```
<cffunction name="IsOnMailingList" returntype="boolean">
  <!---This argument is the email to check --->
  <cfargument name="Email" type="string" required="true">
</cffunction>
```

This is similar to the first `<cffunction>` block you created. The only differences are the name of the function and the name of the argument.

3) Within the new `<cffunction>` block, after the `<cfargument>`, add the following:

```
<!---Local variables (for internal use only) --->
<cfset var Result = False>
<cfset var EmailQuery = "">

<!---Return Result to the page calling this function --->
<cfreturn Result>
```

```
36  <cffunction name="IsOnMailingList" returntype="boolean">
37    <!--- This argument is the email to check --->
38    <cfargument name="Email" type="string" required="true">
39
40    <!--- Local variables (for internal use only) --->
41    <cfset var Result = False>
42    <cfset var EmailQuery = "">
43
44    <!--- Return Result to the page calling this function --->
45    <cfreturn Result>
46  </cffunction>
```

These lines are also nearly identical to the equivalent lines in the first function you created. The `Result` variable is again scoped locally using the `var` keyword, indicating that it is for the internal use of this function only. Another variable called `EmailQuery` is created, also scoped locally to the function. Then, at the bottom of the function, the value of the local `Result` variable is returned.

So, the skeleton of your second function is in place. Now you just need to add the code that makes it actually do what it's supposed to do.

4) **After the two `<cfset var>` lines you just added, type in the following query:**

```
<!---Quick query to see if user is already on list --->
<cfquery name="EmailQuery" datasource="products">
  SELECT * FROM tblMailingList
  WHERE EmailAddress = '#ARGUMENTS.Email#'
</cfquery>
```

This is essentially the same query that appears in the MailingListSignup.cfm page you created in Lesson 9. The only difference is that the reference to the `FORM.EmailAddress` variable has been replaced with `ARGUMENTS.Email`, which means the query will check the database for the presence of the email address supplied to the function's `Email` argument.

It's important to note that even though this is not a `<cfset>` tag, it still creates a variable called `EmailQuery`. Since it is good practice to make sure all variables created within a function are scoped locally to that function, the `EmailQuery` needs to be declared as local with `var`. Luckily, you had the foresight to do that in the last step!

5) **Under the `<cfquery>` you just added, insert the following:**

```
<!---Set Result to True if a record was retrieved --->
<cfif EmailQuery.RecordCount gt 0>
  <cfset Result = True>
</cfif>
```

```
36  <cffunction name="IsOnMailingList" returntype="boolean">
37    <!--- This argument is the email to check --->
38    <cfargument name="Email" type="string" required="true">
39
40    <!--- Local variables (for internal use only) --->
41    <cfset var Result = False>
42    <cfset var EmailQuery = "">
43
44    <!--- Quick query to see if user is already on list --->
45    <cfquery name="EmailQuery" datasource="products">
46      SELECT * FROM tblMailingList
47      WHERE EmailAddress = '#ARGUMENTS.Email#'
48    </cfquery>
49
50    <!--- Set Result to True if a record was retrieved --->
51    <cfif EmailQuery.RecordCount gt 0>
52      <cfset Result = True>
53    </cfif>
54
55    <!--- Return Result to the page calling this function --->
56    <cfreturn Result>
57  </cffunction>
```

This sets the value of the `Result` variable to `True` if the query is able to retrieve a record based on the email address provided to the function. So, after this `<cfif>` block, the `Result` variable will be True if the user is already on the mailing list. If not, the value will remain at its initial value of `False`. In either case, the value of the variable is returned with `<cfreturn>` in the next line of code, so whatever page is calling the function will get the `True` or `False` value, as appropriate.

6) Save your changes to ValidationFunctions.cfm.

Now both functions (the original `IsEmailAddress()` function and the new `IsOnMailingList()` function) will be available to any page that includes the ValidatationFunctions.cfm file.

7) If it's not open already, re-open the MailingListSignup.cfm page in Dreamweaver.

You will now add the new `IsOnMailingList()` function to this page, replacing the corresponding code that you created in Lesson 9.

8) Remove the `<cfquery>` tag.

The job of querying the database is now taken care of by the new `IsOnMailingList()` function, so there is no need for the page itself to include the query anymore.

9) Change the `<cfif>` block that tests the `EmailQuery.RecordCount` value to this:

```
<cfif IsOnMailingList(FORM.EmailAddress)>
```

Here's how the code looks before the change:

```
27  <!--- If the user is already on the list --->
28  <cfif EmailQuery.RecordCount gt 0>
29    <!--- Show message and stop here --->
30    <h2>Already on List</h2>
31    <p>Thanks, but it looks like you are already
32    on our mailing list. No need to join twice!</p>
33    <cfabort>
```

And here's how it looks after the change:

```
27  <!--- If the user is already on the list --->
28  <cfif IsOnMailingList(FORM.EmailAddress)>
29    <!--- Show message and stop here --->
30    <h2>Already on List</h2>
31    <p>Thanks, but it looks like you are already
32    on our mailing list. No need to join twice!</p>
33    <cfabort>
```

10) Save your work, and use F12 to test the revised signup page in your browser.

The page will continue to work exactly as it did before, even though it is now using your custom `IsOnMailingList()` function internally. If, when a user submits the form, her email address is already on the mailing list, she will not be allowed to join a second time. If her email address is not on the list yet, the page continues to the `<cfinsert>` portion of the code, which adds her to the mailing list.

So, the addition of the function hasn't changed anything for your users, but it's made your own ColdFusion code a bit cleaner, easier to read, and elegant. More importantly, you can now re-use the `IsOnMailingList()` function on any other page that might interact with the mailing list. Depending on the nature of the task, creating functions to encapsulate commonly used actions can be a real timesaver.

USING FUNCTIONS WRITTEN BY OTHER DEVELOPERS

After they create a useful function, some developers will make them available for others to download and use in their own ColdFusion pages. If you find yourself needing a function to complete a particular task, you might want to check to see if someone else has created a similar function already. Why re-invent the wheel if someone has already done the work and is willing to share it with you?

Two great places to look for functions are:

- The Common Library Function Project (www.cflib.org)
- Macromedia's own ColdFusion Developer Exchange site (http://devex.macromedia.com/developer/gallery)

NOTE *After you get some experience with writing your own functions, you might find that you want to share a few of your functions with others, to return the favor. Both of theses sites allow you to upload your own function code to share with others.*

CREATING YOUR OWN TAGS

Okay, you've seen how you can create your own functions using the `<cffunction>` tag. ColdFusion also allows you to create your own *tags*. Tags that you write yourself are called *CFML custom tags*, or just *custom tags* for short. Like functions that you write yourself, custom tags can accept input and return output. A custom tag can also include HTML content on whatever page actually uses the tag.

> **NOTE** *Custom tags can do a lot of fancy things that functions, due to their simplicity, generally cannot. You can create custom tags that are meant to be used in pairs (with opening and closing tags), which opens up the possibility of creating custom tags that behave like containers for other code. You can also create families of tags that are meant to be nested within one another. (ColdFusion's own `<cfargument>` and `<cfreturn>` tags, which are used only within the context of a `<cffunction>` block, are good examples of this kind of inter-tag relationship.) In general, this is all pretty advanced stuff that you probably won't need to delve into in the short term. You can consult the ColdFusion documentation for details whenever you start to get curious about these advanced capabilities.*

In this exercise, you will create a simple custom tag called `<CF_waDisplayProduct>`, which does the job of displaying information about a single product from the tblProducts table in the database. (The `wa` part of the custom tag's name stands for Wireless Agent.) Once the custom tag has been created, you can use it on any page that needs to display product information in a consistent, reliable manner.

1) In Dreamweaver, open the ProductDetail.cfm page from the Lesson10\Start folder.

This is the same page that you originally created in Lesson 4 and which you have seen in a number of subsequent lessons. The most recent change you made to this page was in Lesson 9, when you added the capability for a user to send product information via email, using a simple form.

2) Use File > New, then Dynamic Page > ColdFusion to create a new ColdFusion document.

This new file will contain the code for your custom tag.

3) Erase all code in the new document so that it is completely empty.

In general, you always want to start with a blank file when creating a custom tag. You don't want the file to include the `<html>`, `<body>`, and other HTML tags that Dreamweaver adds to new documents for you.

4) Cut the `<cfquery>` block from the top of ProductDetail.cfm and paste it into the new, blank document.

Just highlight the `<cfquery>` block, and choose Edit > Cut to remove it from the ProductDetail.cfm page. Then go to your new document and choose Edit > Paste to paste the `<cfquery>` block at the top.

> **TIP** *You can also use the usual Windows shortcuts for copying and pasting in Dreamweaver—Ctrl+X to cut, Ctrl+V to paste.*

5) Now cut the first `<cfoutput>` block from ProductDetail.cfm and paste it into the new document.

You should paste the `<cfoutput>` block under the `<cfquery>` code you just pasted, like so:

```
1  <!--- Retrieve information about the selected product --->
2  <cfquery name="DetailQuery" datasource="Products">
3      SELECT *
4      FROM tblProducts
5      WHERE ProductID = #ATTRIBUTES.ProductID#
6  </cfquery>
7
8  <!--- Display the product details --->
9  <cfoutput query="DetailQuery">
10     <h2>#ProductName#</h2>
11     <p>#ProductDesc#</p>
12     <p>
13       Price: #DollarFormat(ProductPrice)#<br>
14       Status: #ProductStatus#<br>
15       Number in Stock: #ProductQty#<br>
16     </p>
17 </cfoutput>
```

6) At the top of the new document, add the following `<cfparam>` tag:

```
<!---This custom tag expects a ProductID attribute --->
<cfparam name="ATTRIBUTES.ProductID" type="numeric">
```

Remember how you can use the `<cfargument>` tag to set up arguments when creating your own functions? Well, you get to do pretty much the same thing when creating custom tags. Instead of being called *arguments*, the custom tag framework calls them *attributes*, but they have about the same basic concept: both are able to supply the function or tag with whatever input it requires to do its work.

This `<cfparam>` tag tells ColdFusion that the custom tag you're creating needs to receive an attribute called `ProductID` to be able to do its work. Furthermore, the value provided to the attribute should always be a number. ColdFusion will display an error message on your behalf if a page tries to use the tag without providing a `ProductID` attribute, or specifies a value that isn't a number.

TIP *If you want an attribute to be optional, you can simply add a* `default` *attribute to the* `<cfparam>` *tag. The default value you specify there will be used whenever the custom tag doesn't see a specific value provided for the attribute.*

NOTE *Instead of using* `<cfparam>`*, you could use a* `<cfif>` *tag that tests for the existence of the attribute, as in* `<cfif IsDefined("ATTRIBUTES.ProductID") eq False>`*. Within the* `<cfif>` *block, you could specify what action you want the tag to take if it's not supplied with a* `ProductID` *attribute. You might set* `ATTRIBUTES.ProductID` *to a default value, or display an error message and halt execution with the* `<cfabort>` *tag. All that said,* `<cfparam>` *is usually more concise and easier to read, so it's better to use it when you can.*

7) **Change the variable reference in the `<cfquery>` from `URL.ProductID` to `ATTRIBUTES.ProductID`.**

```
<!--- This custom tag expects a ProductID attribute --->
<cfparam name="ATTRIBUTES.ProductID" type="numeric">

<!--- Retrieve information about the selected product --->
<cfquery name="DetailQuery" datasource="Products">
  SELECT *
  FROM tblProducts
  WHERE ProductID = #ATTRIBUTES.ProductID#
</cfquery>
```

This will cause the custom tag to query the database for the value passed to its `ProductID` attribute, rather than for a URL parameter. In other words, the code within this custom tag will no longer be dependent on any URL parameters, or any other variables external to the tag. The custom tag is thus completely independent; as long as it receives the `ProductID` attribute it is expecting, it will be able to complete the rest of its task on its own.

TIP *It's not always possible, but it's a good idea to make your custom tags be completely independent whenever you can, so try to have them rely only on attribute values, rather than URL, FORM, or other types of parameters. This makes them easier to re-use later, even in situations that you might not have thought of yet.*

8) **Use File > Save As to save the new document as waDisplayProduct.cfm.**

> **NOTE** *Make sure to save the file in the same folder as the other files you've been working on in this lesson.*

Believe it or not, that's all you need to do to create a custom tag. You just place the code for the tag in a separate file, and save the file with a name that corresponds to what you want the name of the tag to be. Since the name of the file is waDisplayProduct.cfm, it magically becomes a custom tag called `<CF_waDisplayProduct>`. If you had named the file waShowItem.cfm instead, then the custom tag would be called `<CF_waShowItem>`. The `<CF_` part always remains the same, but the rest of the tag name automatically comes from the file name.

> **TIP** *You'll notice that the filename begins with the letters* wa, *for Wireless Agent. The plan is to include the* wa *at the beginning name of all custom tag filenames that you create for the Wireless Agent site. That will help you keep from mixing up custom tags you create from this site with other custom tags. You don't have to use this kind of naming convention if you don't want to; it's just an organizational suggestion.*

The new `<CF_waDisplayProduct>` tag is complete and ready to go to work. All you need to do now is test it out by actually using it in one of your pages.

9) **Back in ProductDetail.cfm, insert the following after the `<cfinclude>` tag for the page header:**

```
<!---Insert product information here --->
<CF_waDisplayProduct
  ProductID="#URL.ProductID#">
```

```
13  <!--- Include logo and navigation header at top of page --->
14  <cfinclude template="header.cfm">
15
16  <!--- Insert product information here --->
17  <CF_waDisplayProduct
18    ProductID="#URL.ProductID#">
```

This is the spot from which you removed the `<cfoutput>` block a few moments ago. So, you have essentially replaced the `<cfoutput>` tag with the code shown above, which will accomplish the same thing.

10) Locate the second `<cfoutput>` block (within the `<cfmail>` block) and replace it with the same `<CF_waDisplayProduct>` tag.

```
60        <!--- Insert product information here --->
61        <CF_waDisplayProduct
62          ProductID="#URL.ProductID#">
63
64        <!--- Provide link to get to product page on the Web --->
65        <a href="ProductDetail.cfm?ProductID=#URL.ProductID#">View
66      </body>
67    </html>
68
69  </cfmail>
```

When you started working with this page at the beginning of this exercise, it contained two `<cfoutput>` blocks that were essentially identical. Both displayed basic product information from the `DetailQuery` recordset, using the same HTML tags to format the information.

Now, both of those blocks have been replaced with the new `<CF_waDisplayProduct>` custom tag. If you later decide to change how the information is displayed, you can do so in one place—the waDisplayProduct.cfm file. Any pages that use the custom tag will reflect the changes right away. This ensures that products are displayed consistently throughout the Wireless Agent application.

11) Save your work, and then visit the revised ProductDetail.cfm page with your browser.

> **NOTE** *This page expects a `ProductID` parameter to be provided in the URL, so you will need to add it to the URL in your browser's Address field. Or, you can visit the ProductList.cfm page in your browser, then click on one of the product links to get yourself to the page you just modified.*

Again, the page will behave just as it did before. If you visit the page with a `ProductID=1` parameter in the URL, it will display information about the product with ID number 1. If you visit it with `Product=2` in the URL, it displays information from the second product record. In addition, you can send any product listing to yourself by entering your email address into the form. Both the Web page and the email use the same code (the `<CF_waDisplayProduct>` tag) internally to show the product information.

"INSTALLING" TAGS IN THE MAGIC CUSTOMTAGS FOLDER

As you just learned, you don't have to do anything special before using a custom tag for the first time. After creating the custom tag file, you just apply it by referring to the tag in some other ColdFusion page. It almost seems *too* easy, doesn't it? Well, here's the catch: ColdFusion will only be able to find the tag if it is located in the same folder as the page on which you are trying to use it.

Here's what actually happens. When you refer to a custom tag in a page—that is, when a tag that starts with `<CF` is found in your code—ColdFusion looks for a file with the corresponding name in the same folder. If there is such a file, ColdFusion uses it as the custom tag. If there is no file with the appropriate name in the same folder, ColdFusion doesn't know what to do and displays an error message.

But what if you want to use the same custom tag in many different pages, even if those pages are in different folders? Do you have to make copies of the custom tag file, placing a copy in each folder that you intend to use the tag in? That would work just fine, but it could start to be a pain over time, especially because you'd have to remember to update all the copies every time you changed the tag.

Instead, you can just place the custom tag file in a special folder called the CustomTags folder. This special CustomTags folder is located at C:\CFusionMX\CustomTags. If you want a custom tag to be available to all ColdFusion pages on the server, simply place it in this folder, and *voilà!*—it will suddenly be available to every one of your ColdFusion pages.

NOTE *The C:\CFusionMX\CustomTags location mentioned above assumes that you performed a typical ColdFusion installation on a Windows server. If you are using a different operating system or changed the folder in which ColdFusion was installed, you will need to adjust the location accordingly.*

For further organization and control, you can even create subfolders within the CustomTags folder. As long as a custom tag file is located somewhere in it (even within subfolders, or subfolders of subfolders, and so on), ColdFusion will find it automatically. Further, you can change the location of the special CustomTags folder using the Custom Tag Paths page of the ColdFusion Administrator. You can also use this Administrator page to create additional magic folders that behave in the same way.

NOTE *If, for whatever reason, you don't have access to the special CustomTags folder or the ColdFusion Administrator, you can still use custom tags via the `<cfmodule>` or `<cfimport>` tags. Consult the ColdFusion documentation for details.*

USING CUSTOM TAGS WRITTEN BY OTHER DEVELOPERS

As with custom functions, custom tags that are particularly useful can be shared with other developers. This means that you might be able to download and use custom tags that perform certain tasks for you, rather than having to come up with the code yourself. In addition, you can let other people take advantage of your work if you come up with a tag that is particularly useful. If it's particularly great, you could probably sell your tag for a fee.

Two great places to look for and share custom tags are:

- Macromedia's ColdFusion Developer Exchange site (http://devex.macromedia.com/developer/gallery)
- The CFXtras site (http://cfxtras.com)

WHAT YOU HAVE LEARNED

In this lesson, you have:

- Created a general-purpose function called `IsEmailAddress()` (pages 240–248)
- Used the new function in a ColdFusion page, with the help of `<cfinclude>` (pages 248–250)
- Created and used a second function called `IsOnMailingList()` (pages 250–254)
- Created and used a CFML custom tag called `<CF_waDisplayProduct>` (pages 255–259)
- Learned about the CustomTags folder for storing commonly used custom tags (page 260)
- Learned how custom functions and tags can be shared with others (pages 254 and 261)

index

< > angle brackets, 135
– (dash), 50
( ) parenthesis, 53, 112
[ ] square brackets, 57, 196
* (asterisk), 82, 85
@ (at sign), 245–248, 250
= (equal sign), 48, 53, 96
 # (number sign), 48–49, 53, 85, 219
? (question mark), 158
" (quotation marks), 135
> SQL operator, 125
_ (underscore character), 52
% wildcard, 110

A

Access database, 70–74
`action` **attribute**
  mailing lists, 211, 218
  search forms, 107–108, 118, 122
  secured pages, 158–159
action pages
  combining with form pages, 118–121
  creating, 108–111
  described, 108
Active Server Pages. *See* ASP
Add Browser button, 44
Administrator
  cookies and, 18
  launching, 17
  logging into, 17–19
  memory variables, 190–192
  password, 14, 17
  tools in, 17
  user name for, 14
`AND` **condition**, 112
angle brackets < >, 135
Apache Server, 12
`APPLICATION` **scope**, 205–206
application variables, 64, 190, 205–207
Application.cfm file
  including code with, 61–63
  session variables, 183–185
applications
  drill-down, 102
  sample, 12
  timeouts, 192
  Web, 66
arguments
  `<cfargument>` tag, 240–244, 251
  functions, 56–58, 241–244
  `mask`, 57
  strings, 242, 244, 246
array variables, 192–196
`ArrayAppend()` **function**, 194–195, 199–201
`ArrayDeleteAt()` **function**, 202
`ArrayLen()` **function**, 195
`ArrayNew()` **function**, 194, 204
arrays, 192–199, 202
ASP (Active Server Pages), 21, 30
ASP documents, 30
ASP toolbars, 30
asterisk (*), 82, 85
at sign (@), 245–248, 250

attributes
  `action`. *See* `action` attribute
  `datasource`, 81
  `default`, 118, 142, 257
  `formfields`, 144
  `get`, 107
  `href`, 233
  `index`, 196
  `maxlength`, 134
  `message`, 148
  `name`. *See* `name` attribute
  `onload`, 122
  `password`, 164
  `post`, 107
  `preservedata`, 158
  `query`, 84, 220
  `required`, 148
  `returntype`, 241
  `roles`, 174–175
  `rows`, 135
  `sessionmanagement`, 185
  `sessiontimeout`, 192
  `spoolenable`, 225
  `tablename`, 144
  tag, 256–257
  `template`, 60, 249
  `type`, 157
  `value`, 119, 123, 134, 158
  `wrap`, 135

B

`<base>` **tag**, 233
bold text, 89, 130

browsers, Web. *See also* Internet Explorer; Netscape Navigator
  enabling cookies, 18
  examining ColdFusion pages in, 7–8
  logging out and, 168
  Mozilla, 44–45
  multiple, 207
  sharing cookies, 207
  specifying favorite, 44–45
  viewing files, 42–45, 49
  viewing pages, 50
  viewing source code, 7–8
bulleted lists, 86–87
Button Text field, 170
buttons
  Flash, 169–173
  Form, 133
  Log Out, 169–173
  navigational, 141
  radio, 106
  submit, 106–108, 136, 195
  text for, 170

C

Cascading Style Sheets, 30
CD-ROM drives, 22
`<cfabort>` **tag**, 120, 161–162, 179
`<cfapplication>` **tag**, 62, 183–185, 192
`<cfargument>` **tag**, 240–244, 251
`<cfbreak>` **tag**, 200–201
CFCs (ColdFusion Components), 156
`<cfelse>` **tag**, 114–115
`<CFERROR>` **tag**, 147
`<cfform>` **tag**, 148, 159
`<cffunction>` **tag**, 238, 240–244, 251
`<cfif>` **tag**, 113–117
`<cfif>` **test**, 142–144, 177
`<cfimport>` **tag**, 260
`<cfinclude>` **tag**
  Application.cfm file, 63
  custom functions, 248–249
  header.cfm file, 82
  mailing lists, 218–219
  password protection, 165–166
  search forms, 106
  `template` attribute, 60
`<cfinput>` **tag**, 148–149, 157
`<cfinsert>` **tag**, 144, 152, 214
`<cflocation>` **tag**, 138, 140
`<cflogin>` **framework**, 156
`<cflogin>` **tag**, 160, 171

`<cfloginuser>` **tag**, 160, 163–164, 169, 175
`<cflogout>` **tag**, 171
`<cfloop>` **tag**, 196, 200
.cfm extension, 7, 80
`<cfmail>` **tag**
  described, 217
  loops, 220
  sending bulk email messages, 217–221
  sending data, 230–237
  specifying mail server, 221–224
  unsubscribing users, 225–230
CFML (ColdFusion Markup Language)
  case sensitivity, 158
  comments, 50
  custom functions, 250–255
  custom tags, 255–259
  described, 6
  reference manual, 52
  viewing in browser, 7–8
  vs. HTML, 5–6
`<cfmodule>` **tag**, 260
`<cfoutput>` **tag**
  displaying date values, 56
  displaying time values, 56
  displaying variable values, 48–49
  dynamic queries, 98–100
  loops, 196
  page creation, 40–41
  `query` attribute, 84
`<cfparam>` **tag**
  action pages, 109
  custom tags, 256–257
  `default` attribute, 118
  security and, 150
  values, 97
  variables, 97
`<cfpop>` **tag**, 225
`<cfquery>` **tag**
  checking email addresses, 252–253
  database interactions, 68, 81, 84
  dynamic queries, 98–100
`<cfreturn>` **tag**, 240, 243–244
`<cfset>` **tag**
  mailing lists, 226
  session variables, 187
  `var` keyword, 243, 247
  variables, 48, 53, 60–61
`<cfset var>` **tag**, 240, 252
`<cfupdate>` **tag**, 137–138
CFXtras site, 261
CGI scope, 158

CGI variables, 158
check boxes, 106, 124–126
client-side validation, 145, 147–150
client variables, 65, 185
clients
  mail, 232
  validating form entries, 145, 147–150
code
  CFML vs. HTML, 5–6
  ColdFusion vs. SQL, 80
  executing, 62–63
  including automatically, 61–63
  indenting, 115
  SQL, 68, 80
  unindenting, 115
  viewing, 7–8, 53–55, 87
Code and Design view, 53–55
Code panel, 30
Code view, 53–55
ColdFusion Administrator
  cookies and, 18
  launching, 17
  logging into, 17–19
  memory variables, 190–192
  password, 14, 17
  tools in, 17
  user name for, 14
ColdFusion Components (CFCs), 156
ColdFusion Developer Exchange, 254, 261
ColdFusion files, 12
ColdFusion Markup Language (CFML)
  case sensitivity, 158
  comments, 50
  custom functions, 250–255
  custom tags, 255–259
  described, 6
  reference manual, 52
  viewing in browser, 7–8
  vs. HTML, 5–6
ColdFusion MX
  ColdFusion Server and, 3
  described, 1
  documentation, 12, 30
  Dreamweaver MX and, 3
  license agreement, 10
  overview, 6–8
  reference, 30
  restarting, 202–203
  sample applications, 12
  system requirements, 3

ColdFusion pages. *See also* Web pages
   action, 108–111, 118–121
   creating, 39–43
   data drill-down, 95–102
   data entry. *See* data entry pages
   data source, 71–74
   detail, 95–98
   displaying dates on, 52–53
   examining in browser, 7–8
   logging out, 168–173
   making default, 159
   passing parameters to, 96
   password protection, 165–168
   reloading, 204
   secured. *See* secured pages
   viewing in browser, 50
   viewing in Dreamweaver, 50
ColdFusion Server
   ColdFusion MX and, 3
   described, 4
   dynamic content and, 6
   installing, 8–16
   trial version, 3, 11
   validating form entries, 145–147
color, text, 89
`cols` **attribute**, 135
columns, 92, 94
commands
   `INSERT`, 82
   Replace All, 206
   Save, 50
   Save All, 166
   `SELECT`, 82
   `UPDATE`, 82
   View Source, 87
comments, 50
Common Library Function Project, 254
comparison operators, 116–117
Complete folder, 2
conditional processing, 112–116
content, 6
cookie variables, 65
cookies
   enabling, 18
   logins and, 168
   multiple browsers and, 207
   session management and, 181
   sharing, 207
Custom Tags folder, 260–261
Customer Information form, 11
customization
   error messages, 147

   functions, 250–255
   tags, 255–261

D

dash (–), 50
data
   display of, 86–90
   dynamic, 6
   emailing, 230–237
   formatting, 90–92
   outputting from queries, 84–85
   retrieving from databases, 80–84
   static, 6
data drill-down pages, 95–102
data entry pages, 128–153
   deleting database records, 139–140
   inserting database information, 141–144
   performing updates, 137–139
   product edit forms, 132–137
   product menus, 130–131
   validation rules, 145–150
data sources, 70–74
Data Sources page, 71–74
data types, 192
database fields, 69
database files, 71
Database panel, 75–80
database records
   adding, 82, 214
   deleting from database, 82, 139–140
   described, 69
   formatting, 90–92
   ID numbers, 69
   order of, 92–94, 110
   retrieving, 82, 111
   searching for. *See* search forms
   sorting, 92–94, 110
   unable to find, 113–115
   updating, 82
database servers, 70
databases, 66–103
   adding records to, 82, 214
   deleting records from, 139–140
   described, 68
   design of, 68–69
   displaying information from, 86–90
   emailing information about, 230–237
   exploring with Dreamweaver MX, 75–80
   formatting data in, 90–92

   indexes, 68
   inserting information into, 141–144
   maintenance, 68
   Microsoft Access, 70–74
   Oracle, 67–68
   overview, 68–69
   passwords, 74
   performance, 68
   queries. *See* queries
   retrieving information from, 68, 80–84
   structure, 68
   tables, 69, 92
   tuning, 68
   updating records, 137–139
Databases panel, 75–80
`datasource` **attribute**, 81
date/time values, 55–56
`Dateformat` **function**, 56–59, 241
dates
   displaying on Web pages, 52–53
   formatting, 55–59
   returning, 241
`default` **attribute**, 118, 142, 257
Default Timeout area, 191
`DELETE` **statement**, 82, 139–140
deleting items
   records, 82, 139–140
   session variables, 188–192
`DESC` **keyword**, 93–94
detail pages, 95–98
directories, 24
disks, hard, 3, 13
DNS (Domain Name Service), 223
documentation, ColdFusion MX, 12, 30
`DollarFormat()` **function**, 89–90
Domain Name Service (DNS), 223
Dreamweaver MX
   advantages, 20–21
   ColdFusion and, 3
   described, 20
   directory for, 24
   exploring databases with, 75–80
   file types, 24
   files, 24
   installing, 22–27
   launching, 26–29
   license agreement, 22–23
   overview, 29–31
   trial version, 3, 22, 27
   viewing pages in, 50
   workspace, 28
drill-down applications, 102

drives
  CD-ROM, 22
  hard, 3, 13
drop-down lists, 88, 106
dynamic content, 6
dynamic files, 44
Dynamic Page option, 39
dynamic queries, 98–102, 110

E

editing files, 36
editor window, 30
email, 208–237
  address validation, 240–248, 250
  bulk, 217–221
  links to, 234–236
  mailing lists. *See* mailing lists
  sending data via, 230–237
  specifying mail server, 221–224
`eq` **keyword**, 116
equal sign (=), 48, 53, 96
error messages. *See also* troubleshooting
  customizing, 147
  data source, 74
  incorrect values, 97
  "no records found," 113–115, 117, 120
  page execution, 109
extensions
  .cfm, 7, 80
  .swf, 170

F

fields, database, 69
fields, form
  hidden, 133, 143, 145–146
  matching multiple, 112
  required, 146
  searches and, 112, 119
  text, 107, 121–122
  text area, 135
  text entry, 106
file types, 24
files
  Application.cfm, 61–63, 183–185
  ColdFusion, 12
  database, 71
  Dreamweaver MX, 24
  dynamic, 44
  editing, 36
  header.cfm, 82
  Java, 63
  location of, 32–38, 41
  project, 32–34
  Read-only, 34, 71
  saving, 41, 50, 166
  static, 44
  viewing in Web browser, 43–45, 49
Files panel, 30, 32
Files toolbar, 38
Find and Replace dialog, 206
firewall products, 15, 150
flags, 34, 204
Flash buttons, 169–173
Flash MX, 156
Flash Remoting Service, 156
`_float` **rule**, 146–147, 149
floating-point numbers, 146
folders
  ColdFusion files, 12
  Complete, 2
  Custom Tags, 260–261
  lesson, 33
  location of, 36
  names, 34
  paths, 12, 36
  Project, 32–36
  Start, 2
  wwwroot, 32, 71
`<form>` **block**, 133
Form button, 133
form pages, 118–121
`FORM` **scope**, 109
`<form>` **tag**, 107–108
Form tag editor dialog, 133
form variables, 64. *See also* variables
formatting items
  data, 90–92
  dates, 55–59
  with HTML tables, 90–92
  lists, 86–88
  numbers, 89
  records, 90–92
  time, 55–59
`formfields` **attribute**, 144
forms
  combining with action pages, 118–121
  common elements, 106
  hidden fields, 133, 143, 145–146
  HTML. *See* HTML forms
  logging out, 168–173
  login, 156–165
  password protection, 168–173
  posting, 108
  product edit forms, 132–137
  search. *See* search forms
  self-submitting, 118, 122, 211, 231
  uses for, 104
  validating entries, 145–150
Forms tab, 133
functions, 52–56
  arguments, 56–58, 241–244
  `ArrayAppend()`, 194–195, 199–201
  `ArrayDeleteAt()`, 202
  `ArrayLen()`, 195
  `ArrayNew()`, 194, 204
  calling, 53
  Common Library Function Project, 254
  components of, 240
  creating, 239–248, 250–255
  custom, 250–255
  `Dateformat`, 56–59, 241
  described, 47
  `DollarFormat()`, 89–90
  executing, 59
  general-purpose, 250
  `GetAuthUser()`, 164, 169
  `HTMLEditFormat()`, 134–135
  `IsNumeric()`, 123, 125
  `IsUserInRole()`, 176–177
  `LSCurrencyFormat()`, 90
  `Mid()`, 246
  multiple, 56–59
  `Now()`, 52–53, 55–59
  `QueryAddRow()`, 143
  results, 52
  returning dates, 241
  returning strings, 241
  in separate files, 59–61
  sharing, 254
  specialized, 250–255
  `Timeformat`, 56–58
  `URLEncodedFormat()`, 197
  using, 52–56, 248–250
  written by other developers, 254

G

`get` **attribute**, 107
`GetAuthUser()` **function**, 164, 169
`gt` **keyword**, 116–117, 125
`gte` **keyword**, 116

H

hard disk, 3, 13
hardware requirements, 3
Help button, 44

hidden form fields, 133, 143, 145–146
history, search, 198–205, 207
`href` **attribute**, 233
HTML
  comments, 50
  reference, 30
  requirements for, 2
  sending data via email, 233
  viewing in browser, 7–8
  vs. CFML, 5–6
HTML forms, 104–127. *See also* forms
  creating basic, 106–108
  hidden fields, 133, 143, 145–146
  posting, 108
  self-submitting, 118, 122
  syntax in, 106
HTML tables, 84, 90–92
HTML tags, 30
`HTMLEditFormat()` **function**, 134–135
hyperlinks
  to data entry pages, 130–131
  to detail pages, 95–96
  to email messages, 234–236
  to insecure pages, 172
  Log Out, 169–173
  to previous searches, 197, 199
  RDS Login link, 76
  re-executing searches, 198
  record insertion, 141–142
  reloading pages, 204
  to search pages, 111
  to secured pages, 172
  to unsubscribe pages, 226, 229
  URLs as, 96

I
ID numbers
  passed in URLs, 101
  products, 96, 98, 125
  records, 69
IIS (Internet Information Services), 12
`<img>` **tag**, 84
`index` **attribute**, 196
indexes, 68, 196
Input tag editor dialog, 134
`INSERT` **command**, 82
Insert Flash Button dialog, 170
`INSERT` **statement**, 150–153

Insert toolbar, 30
Install Wizard, 8–16
installing items
  ColdFusion Server, 8–16
  Dreamweaver MX, 22–27
InstallShield Wizard, 22–26
Internet Explorer. *See also* Web browsers
  enabling cookies, 18
  specifying as primary browser, 44–45
  version, 3
  viewing source code, 7–8
Internet Information Services (IIS), 12
IP addresses, 223, 230
`is` **keyword**, 116–117
`is not` **keyword**, 116–117
`IsDefined()` **test**, 186–187
`IsNumeric()` **function**, 123, 125
`IsUserInRole()` **function**, 176–177

J
J2EE option, 191
Java, 1, 63
Java files, 63
Java Server Pages (JSP), 21, 30
JavaScript
  case-sensitivity of, 122
  search pages, 121–122
  validation and, 148, 150
JDBC specification, 56
JSP (Java Server Pages), 21, 30

K
keywords
  `DESC`, 93–94
  `eq`, 116
  `gt`, 116–117, 125
  `gte`, 116
  `is`, 116–117
  `is not`, 116–117
  `lt`, 116
  `lte`, 116
  `neq`, 116
  `OR`, 112
  `ORDER BY`, 92–94, 110
  remembering, 185–188
  search, 185–188
  `var`, 242–243, 247, 251
`Keywords` **field**, 109, 118

L
lesson folders, 33
lesson overview, 1–2
`<li>` **tag**, 87
license agreement
  ColdFusion MX, 10
  Dreamweaver MX, 22–23
`LIKE` **condition**, 112
`LIKE` **operator**, 110
Link field, 170
links
  to data entry pages, 130–131
  to detail pages, 95–96
  to email messages, 234–236
  to insecure pages, 172
  Log Out, 169–173
  to previous searches, 197, 199
  RDS Login link, 76
  re-executing searches, 198
  record insertion, 141–142
  reloading pages, 204
  to search pages, 111
  to secured pages, 172
  to unsubscribe pages, 226, 229
  URLs as, 96
Linux servers, 63
lists
  bulleted, 86–87
  drop-down, 88, 106
  formatting, 86–88
  numbered, 87
`localhost` **name**, 226, 230, 237
Log Out link, 169–173
logging out, 168–173
logins
  ColdFusion Administrator, 17–19
  cookies and, 168
  form for, 156–165
  passwords, 157–158
loops
  breaking out of, 200–201
  `<cfloop>` tag, 196, 200
  `<cfmail>` tag, 220
  `<cfoutput>` tag, 196
  described, 196
  indexes, 196
`LSCurrencyFormat()` **function**, 90
`lt` **keyword**, 116
`lte` **keyword**, 116

M

Macromedia home page, 7
Macromedia Training from the Source courses, 2
mail. *See* email
mail clients, 232
mail headers, 232
mail servers, 221–224
mailing lists
  adding users to, 210–216
  checking email addresses on, 250–254
  creating, 210–216
  sending bulk messages to, 217–221
  signup forms for, 210–216
  unsubscribing users, 225–230
`mask` **argument**, 57
`maxlength` **attribute**, 134
memory
  clearing variables from, 202–203
  session variables and, 188–192, 202–203
  system requirements, 3
`message` **attribute**, 148
messages. *See also* error messages
  "display records," 117
  "no records found," 113–115, 117, 120
Microsoft Access database, 70–74. *See also* databases
Microsoft Internet Information Services (IIS), 12
Microsoft SQL Server, 67
`Mid()` **function**, 246
Mozilla browser, 44–45
MySQL database server, 68

N

`name` **attribute**
  `<cfloginuser>` tag, 164
  `<cfquery>` tag, 81
  `<form>` tag, 107
  returning user name, 169
  session variables, 185
navigational buttons, 141
`neq` **keyword**, 116
Netscape Navigator. *See also* Web browsers
  enabling cookies, 18
  specifying as primary browser, 44–45
  viewing source code, 7–8

`Now()` **function**, 52–53, 55–59
number sign (#), 48–49, 53, 85, 219
numbered lists, 87
numbers
  floating-point, 146
  formatting, 89
  ID. *See* ID numbers
  serial, 11
  validation, 146

O

object database packages, 69
ODBC specification, 56
`onload` **attribute**, 122
operators, comparison, 116–117
`OR` **condition**, 112
`OR` **keyword**, 112
Oracle databases, 67–68
`ORDER BY` **keyword**, 92–94, 110

P

pages. *See* ColdFusion pages; Web pages
panels, 30
parameters
  passing, 96
  `ProductID`, 98, 142–143
  URL. *See* URL parameters
parenthesis ( ), 53, 112
`password` **attribute**, 164
passwords
  blank, 161–162
  ColdFusion Administrator, 14, 17
  databases, 74
  forms, 168–173
  invalid, 167
  login page, 157–158
  precautions, 14
  RDS, 76
  secured pages, 157–158, 165–168
  user, 157–158
  valid, 168
paths
  folder, 12, 36
  relative, 249
performance
  databases, 68
  variables and, 59
PHP, 21
`post` **attribute**, 107
posting forms, 108
Preferences dialog, 43–45
`preservedata` **attribute**, 158

Preview in Browser feature, 43–45
Preview Using Temporary File option, 44, 50
privileges, 174–179
problems. *See also* error messages
  incorrect database locations, 74
  installation support, 16
product display, 255–259
product edit forms, 132–137
product ID numbers, 125
product menus, 130–131
product records. *See* records
ProductDesc table, 79
`ProductID` **parameter**, 98, 142–143
ProductID table, 78
`ProductID` **value**, 97
production environments, 192
ProductName table, 79
ProductPrice table, 79
ProductQty table, 79
ProductStatus table, 79
programs. *See* applications
project files, 32–34
Project folder, 32–36

Q

queries
  database, 68, 80–84
  dynamic, 98–102, 110
  outputting results of, 84–92
  retrieving records, 111
`query` **attribute**, 84, 220
query recordsets, 84, 220
`QueryAddRow()` **function**, 143
question mark (?), 158
quotation marks ("), 135

R

radio buttons, 106
RAM. *See* memory
`_range` **rule**, 146
RDS Login link, 76
RDS password, 76
RDS (Remote Development Services), 76
Read-only files, 34, 71
receiving pages, 96
`RecordCount` **property**, 114
`RecordCount` **value**, 111
records
  adding, 82, 214
  deleting from database, 82, 139–140

described, 69
formatting, 90–92
ID numbers, 69
order of, 92–94, 110
retrieving, 82, 111
searching for. *See* search forms
sorting, 92–94, 110
unable to find, 113–115
updating, 82
recordsets
adding rows to, 143
contents of, 81
query, 84, 220
values, 111
Reference tab, 30
relative paths, 249
Remote Development Services (RDS), 76
Replace All command, 206
`required` **attribute**, 148
`_required` **rule**, 146–147
results, 52
`returntype` **attribute**, 241
roles, 174–179
`roles` **attribute**, 174–175
rows, 92, 135, 143
`rows` **attribute**, 135
rules, validation, 145–150

S

Save All command, 166
Save As field, 170
Save command, 50
saving files, 41, 50, 166
scope
`APPLICATION`, 205–206
CGI, 158
`FORM`, 109
`SESSION`, 183, 185, 192
variable, 64–65, 109, 180
search forms, 104–127
advanced searches, 122–126
combining form/action pages, 118–121
comparison operators, 116–117
creating action page for, 108–111
creating basic HTML for, 106–108
"display records" message, 117
focusing text field, 121–122
matching multiple fields, 112
"no records found" message, 113–115, 117, 120
testing, 111

search keywords, 185–188
searches
Find and Replace feature, 206
history feature, 198–205, 207
links to, 111, 197, 199
multiple, 192–199
options for, 206
re-executing, 198
for records, 104–127
remembering, 192–199
secured pages, 154–179
`<cflogin>` framework, 156
links to, 172
logging out, 168–173
login form, 156–165
password protection, 157–158, 165–168
per-user privileges, 174–179
Security Bulletin ASB99-04, 151
security issues, 150–151, 154–155
security roles, 174–179
`SELECT` **command**, 82
serial number, 11
server-side validation, 145–147
server technology, 35
servers
Apache Server, 12
ColdFusion. *See* ColdFusion Server
database, 70
IIS, 12
Linux, 63
mail, 221–224
MySQL, 68
SMTP, 221–224
SQL Server, 67
UNIX, 63
validation, 145–147
Web, 11–12
session management, 181
`SESSION` **scope**, 183, 185, 192
session tracking, 181
session variables, 180–207
clearing, 202–203
creating, 183
described, 64, 183
discarding, 188–192
enabling, 185
getting started with, 183–185
memory and, 188–192, 202–203
remembering multiple searches, 192–199
remembering search keywords, 185–188

search history, 198–205
timeouts, 191–192
vs. application variables, 205
`sessionmanagement` **attribute**, 185
`sessiontimeout` **attribute**, 192
Site Definition dialog, 34
sites. *See also* Web sites
defining URLs for, 32–38
described, 32
names, 34
selecting server technology, 35
URLs for, 36
slots, 196–197, 202
SMTP servers, 221–224
sorting records, 92–94, 110
source code
CFML vs. HTML, 5–6
ColdFusion vs. SQL, 80
executing, 62–63
including automatically, 61–63
indenting, 115
SQL, 68, 80
unindenting, 115
viewing, 7–8, 53–55, 87
`<span>` **tag**, 89
`spoolenable` **attribute**, 225
SQL code, 68, 80
SQL Server, 67
SQL (Structured Query Language)
`DELETE` statement, 82, 139–140
`INSERT` statement, 150–153
`UPDATE` statement, 137–138, 150–153
square brackets [ ], 57, 196
Start folder, 2
stateless standards, 180
statements
`DELETE`, 82, 139–140
`INSERT`, 150–153
`UPDATE`, 137–138, 150–153
static content, 6
static files, 44
`str` **argument**, 244
strings
arguments, 242, 244, 246
empty, 247–248
returning, 241
`<strong>` **tag**, 89, 130
submit buttons, 106–108, 136, 195
substrings, 246
support, ColdFusion MX, 16
.swf extension, 170
system requirements, 3

T

`tablename` attribute, 144
tables
  database, 69, 92
  HTML, 84, 90–92
  ProductDesc, 79
  ProductID, 78
  ProductName, 79
  ProductPrice, 79
  ProductQty, 79
  ProductStatus, 79
  tblLogin, 162
  tblMailingList, 210, 225, 250
  tblProducts, 78–80
Tables item, 77–80
Tag Editor dialog, 99
tags
  attributes, 256–257
  `<cfabort>`, 120, 161–162, 179
  `<cfapplication>`, 62, 183–185, 192
  `<cfargument>`, 240–244, 251
  `<cfbreak>`, 200–201
  `<cfelse>`, 114–115
  `<CFERROR>`, 147
  `<cfform>`, 148, 159
  `<cffunction>`, 238, 240–244, 251
  `<cfif>`, 113–117
  `<cfimport>`, 260
  `<cfinclude>`. See `<cfinclude>` tag
  `<cfinput>`, 148–149, 157
  `<cfinsert>`, 144, 152, 214
  `<cflocation>`, 138, 140
  `<cflogin>`, 160, 171
  `<cfloginuser>`, 160, 163–164, 169, 175
  `<cflogout>`, 171
  `<cfloop>`, 196, 200
  `<cfmail>`. See `<cfmail>` tag
  `<cfmodule>`, 260
  `<cfoutput>`. See `<cfoutput>` tag
  `<cfparam>`. See `<cfparam>` tag
  `<cfpop>`, 225
  `<cfquery>`. See `<cfquery>` tag
  `<cfreturn>`, 240, 243–244
  `<cfset>`, 226
  `<cfset var>`, 240, 252
  `<cfupdate>`, 137–138
  creating, 239, 255–259
  custom, 255–261
  HTML, 30
  `<img>`, 84
  Insert toolbar, 30
  installing in Custom Tags folder, 260–261
  `<li>`, 87
  names, 258
  sharing, 261
  `<span>`, 89
  `<strong>`, 89, 130
  `<textarea>`, 135, 150
  `<title>`, 81
  URLs and, 259
  written by other developers, 261
tblLogin table, 162
tblMailingList table, 210, 225, 250
tblProducts table, 78–80
`<td>` block, 54
`template` attribute, 60, 249
templates
  creating, 39
  default, 39
  described, 4–5
  new, 39
text
  bold, 89, 130
  button, 170
  color, 89
  wrapping words, 135
text area field, 135
text areas, 135
text editors, 22
text entry fields, 106
text fields, 107, 121–122
`<textarea>` tag, 135, 150
time
  displaying on Web pages, 52–53
  formatting, 55–59
time/date values, 55–56
`Timeformat` function, 56–58
`<title>` tag, 81
toolbars
  ASP, 30
  Files, 38
  Insert, 30
Training from the Source courses, 2
troubleshooting. See also error messages
  incorrect database locations, 74
  installation support, 16
`type` attribute, 157
typeless variables, 48

U

`<ul>` tag, 87
underscore character (_), 52
UNIX servers, 63
`UPDATE` command, 82
`UPDATE` statement, 137–138, 150–153
updates, performing, 137–139
URL parameters
  custom tags, 257
  default values, 119
  detail pages, 96–98
  passing items as, 119, 125, 133
  product ID numbers as, 125
  unsubscribe pages, 226–229
URL variables, 64, 96
`URLEncodedFormat()` function, 197
URLs
  custom tags and, 259
  defining for sites, 36
  ID numbers passed in, 101
  as links, 96
  page requests, 158–159
  viewing pages with, 50, 83
user names
  blank, 161–162
  ColdFusion Administrator, 14
  invalid, 167
  returning, 169
  valid, 168
users
  adding to mailing lists, 210–216
  passwords, 157–158
  privileges, 174–179
  unsubscribing from mailing lists, 225–230

V

validation
  client-side, 145, 147–150
  described, 145
  email addresses, 240–248, 250
  rules for, 145–150
  server-side, 145–147
`value` attribute, 119, 123, 134, 158
values
  date, 55–56
  default, 119
  error messages, 97
  incorrect, 97
  initial, 248
  `ProductID`, 97
  `RecordCount`, 111
  recordsets, 111
  time, 55–56

`var` **keyword**, 242–243, 247, 251
variable scopes, 64–65, 109, 180
variables, 48–52
    advantages, 51
    application, 64, 190, 205–207
    array, 192–196
    CGI, 158
    client, 65, 185
    cookie, 65
    creating, 48–51
    described, 46
    displaying, 49–51
    empty strings in, 247–248
    form, 64
    information stored in, 48, 51
    initial values, 248
    local, 242
    long-term, 64–65
    names, 49, 52
    non-local, 243
    ordinary, 64
    performance and, 59
    referring to, 59–61, 96
    in separate files, 59–61
    session. *See* session variables
    short-term, 64
    typeless, 48
    URL, 64, 96
    using, 48–52
    values, 48, 51, 59

View Data window, 79
View Source command, 87

W
Web applications, 66
Web browsers. *See also* Internet Explorer; Netscape Navigator
    enabling cookies, 18
    examining ColdFusion pages in, 7–8
    logging out and, 168
    Mozilla, 44–45
    multiple, 207
    sharing cookies, 207
    specifying favorite, 44–45
    viewing files, 42–45, 49
    viewing pages, 50
    viewing source code, 7–8
Web pages. *See also* ColdFusion pages
    displaying date/time on, 52–53
    Macromedia home page, 7
    unsubscribe pages, 225–230
Web servers, 11–12
Web sites. *See also* sites
    CFML reference manual, 52
    CFXtras site, 261
    ColdFusion Developer Exchange, 254, 261
    Common Library Function Project, 254
    installation support, 16
    Macromedia home page, 7
    Security Bulletin ASB99-04, 151
Welcome screen, Dreamweaver MX, 28–29
Welcome to ColdFusion MX window, 19
`WHERE` **clause**, 101, 110, 112, 140, 152
wildcard characters, 82, 85, 110
Windows-based systems, 3
Wizards
    Install, 8–16
    InstallShield, 22–26
word wrapping, 135
workspace, Dreamweaver MX, 28
`wrap` **attribute**, 135
wwwroot folder, 32, 71

X
XML packages, 69

Macromedia Tech Support: http://www.macromedia.com/support

LICENSING AGREEMENT

The information in this book is for informational use only and is subject to change without notice. Macromedia, Inc., and Macromedia Press assume no responsibility for errors or inaccuracies that may appear in this book. The software described in the book is furnished under license and may be used or copied only in accordance with terms of the license.

The software files on the CD-ROM included here are copyrighted by Macromedia, Inc. You have the non-exclusive right to use these programs and files. You may use them on one computer at a time. You may not transfer the files from one computer to another over a network. You may transfer the files onto a single hard disk so long as you can prove ownership of the original CD-ROM.

You may not reverse engineer, decompile, or disassemble the software. You may not modify or translate the software or distribute copies of the software without the written consent of Macromedia, Inc.

Opening the disc package means you accept the licensing agreement. For installation instructions, see the ReadMe file on the CD-ROM.